The
Ontario Naturalized Garden

Grow Home
Affordable Homes program
School of Architecture
McGill University
815 Sherbrooke St W
H3A 2KC
www.mcgill.ca/homes

The ONTARIO NATURALIZED GARDEN

THE COMPLETE GUIDE TO USING NATIVE PLANTS

LORRAINE JOHNSON

WHITECAP BOOKS
VANCOUVER / TORONTO

Edited by Elaine Jones
Cover design by Kurt Hafso
Interior design and typesetting by Margaret Ng
Cover illustration by Alison Watt

Printed and bound in Canada

Canadian Cataloguing in Publication Data

Johnson, Lorraine, 1960–
      The Ontario naturalized garden

      Includes bibliographical references and index.
      ISBN 1-55110-305-2

      1. Native plant gardening—Ontario. I. Title.
SB439.26.C3J63 1995   635.9'51713   C94-910959-2

CONTENTS

ILLUSTRATIONS

Large-flowered trillium, xv. Joyce Cave, courtesy of the Toronto Field Naturalists.

Purple coneflower, 1, 33, 101, 115. M. Faibish, courtesy of the Toronto Field Naturalists.

Purple coneflower, 3. Andrew Leyerle.

Map of Ontario's forest regions, 13. Reproduced with permission from *Seasons* magazine (Summer 1985), published by the Federation of Ontario Naturalists.

Solomon's seal, 15. Andrew Leyerle.

Lupine, 21. Andrew Leyerle.

Jack-in-the-pulpit with wild ginger, 35. Andrew Leyerle.

Map of the Carolinian region of southern Ontario, with a number of accessible public sites identified, 41. Reproduced with permission from *Seasons* magazine (Summer 1985), published by the Federation of Ontario Naturalists.

Dense blazing star, 49. Andrew Leyerle.

American lotus, 61. Andrew Leyerle.

Native plant design of early spring woodland garden, 69. Zile Zichmanis, courtesy of the Toronto Field Naturalists.

Lady's slipper orchid, 83. Andrew Leyerle.

Selection of rare plants found in the Rouge River Valley in Toronto, 95. Steve Varga, courtesy of the Toronto Field Naturalists.

Bergamot, 97. Mary Cumming, courtesy of the Toronto Field Naturalists.

Black-eyed Susan, 97. Joyce Cave, courtesy of the Toronto Field Naturalists.

Dense blazing star, 99. Joyce Cave, courtesy of the Toronto Field Naturalists.

Jerusalem artichoke, 99. Joyce Cave, courtesy of the Toronto Field Naturalists.

From left to right: panicled, heath and New England asters, with a fringed gentian in the lower middle, 100, 133. Dida, courtesy of the Toronto Field Naturalists.

Large-flowered bellwort with trillium and bloodroot, 101. Dida, courtesy of the Toronto Field Naturalists.

Mayapple, 105. Joyce Cave, courtesy of the Toronto Field Naturalists.

Spring beauty, 106. Diana Banville, courtesy of the Toronto Field Naturalists.

Yellow trout lily, 106. Catherine Holland, courtesy of the Toronto Field Naturalists.

Christmas fern, 107. Dida, courtesy of the Toronto Field Naturalists.

Bottle gentian, 109. Dida, courtesy of the Toronto Field Naturalists.

Cardinal flower, 110. Dida, courtesy of the Toronto Field Naturalists.

Jewelweed, 110. Mary Cumming, courtesy of the Toronto Field Naturalists.

Panic grass, 112. Steve Varga, courtesy of the Toronto Field Naturalists.

Black-eyed Susan, 117. Andrew Leyerle.

Little bluestem, cup plant, and native cacti, 125. Andrew Leyerle.

FOREWORD

The urban environment is full of examples of our attempts to impose human order on the natural world. We have constructed buildings to conform to a grid of streets, channelled streams to flow around and under our homes, paved playing fields to keep springtime mud at bay, and designed the remaining green spaces with lawns and gardens that must be maintained with fertilizers, herbicides, and pesticides. All of this has been done in an effort to establish control and predictability.

As a result, we have become disconnected from the natural world and its processes, distancing ourselves to such an extent that we are incapable of regarding ourselves as part of the natural world.

We pour chemicals on our lawns to kill the weeds without understanding that those same chemicals will end up in our drinking water. We clear land of trees without understanding that trees filter pollution from the air. We plant exotic species without understanding that they disrupt native plant communities. We pave our cities without understanding that we are destroying animal and bird habitats.

Naturalization, a concept endorsed and prac-tised by the Evergreen Foundation, is a process of ecological restoration that encourages a return of the natural environment to developed areas. This alternative approach to landscaping blends environmental concerns with an appreciation of nature's inherent beauty. Instead of fighting natural processes, naturalization embraces them.

As the 1990s progress, naturalization techniques are being adopted by a variety of urban landowners around the world. Corporations are converting their barren landscapes to forests, public parks are encouraging nature to return to open fields, schools are creating outdoor wilderness gardens, and homeowners are naturalizing their yards.

This concept of naturalization has become a long-overdue international movement and holds the promise of transforming our urban centres locally and our relationship with the natural world globally. It is an important movement, one that will have historical significance as it changes the face of our urban centres and the way we live our lives.

—*Geoff Cape, Executive Director,*
The Evergreen Foundation

ACKNOWLEDGEMENTS

Many thanks to the people who read portions of the manuscript and offered helpful comments; I am very grateful for their generous gifts of time and attention: Terry Fahey, Ross Johnson, Larry Lamb, Harvey Macklin, David Orsini, Gail Rhynard, Pierre Sassone, and Ken Towle.

Jim Hodgins, editor of *Wildflower*, read the full manuscript and was enormously helpful and thoughtful, as he has been throughout the project. I value his incisive comments and his generous assistance (*and* his wonderful garden).

Gail Rhynard, owner of Otter Valley Native Plants, wrote sections of the plant listings in Chapter 9 and was a wonderful collaborator (and a great plant source).

The Evergreen Foundation has been a great help right from the beginning of the project, and I thank them for their foreword.

Andrew Leyerle very generously provided the illustrations for the majority of chapter opening pages, and I thank him for these skillful renderings.

The Toronto Field Naturalists provided members' drawings for use throughout the book and has been a wonderful source of information. Many thanks—in particular to Helen Juhola and Joan O'Donnell.

As always, my family has provided inspiration and rock-solid support: my mother, co-conspirator in plant rescues and a seed starter par excellence; my father, partner in garden excursions and jazz; Tasha, who with her keen mind goes right to the heart of the matter, honing and clarifying, always a help, and Robert; Keith and Iz, for food, fun, and friendship; Ross, whose early comments on first drafts were immensely helpful, and Mara; Janet, who with characteristic enthusiam and generosity gave me a home for the pond and now looks after its many creatures, plant and animal; Eileen and Greg, who offered support and encouragement from Australia; and Lee and Duane, who kept me in bird seed.

To the gardeners who opened up their havens to me and answered many questions, heartfelt thanks: Jim Hodgins, Frank Kershaw, Stephen Andrews, Tom Atkinson, John Ambrose, Anna Leggatt, Larry Lamb, Victor Feodorov, Henny Markus, and Bruce Scott.

To my gardening neighbours, especially Paula for the bellwort, Jan for the mystery ferns, Linda, Dulcie, Michael, and Charles, many thanks.

Thanks also to: Ken Beck and Little Kennissis Lake, Sandy Bell, Geoff Cape, Pat Cooper, Douglas Counter, Sarah Davies, Rae Davis, Kim

Gavine, Cynthia Good, Kristina Marie Guiguet, Marjorie Harris, Daphne Hart, David Hassels, Jackie Kaiser, Reva Karstadt, Des Kennedy, Freya Kristjanson, Cecelia Lawless, Denis Lessard, Mary Ellen Leyerle, Kevin MacLaughlin, Pat Merrilees, Rod Northey, Doug Pepper, Steven Price, Tracy Read, Lori Stoltz, Lori Theoret, Judy Whalen, and the staff of the Palmerston Library.

The support of everyone at Whitecap Books is much appreciated.

INTRODUCTION

OF REVOLUTIONS THAT NEVER HAPPENED AND EVOLUTIONS THAT ARE STILL GOING STRONG

Gardening is not generally thought of as a controversial activity that nurtures dissent and argument. If anything, it's thought to offer escape from such things.

However, while researching this book, I discovered that gardening with native plants is stirring up a bit of controversy. Although some people immediately embrace the idea, there are others who react with puzzled consternation (yet want to find out more); some who are wary of the whole endeavour; and at the very end of the tolerance scale, those who dismiss the native plant movement, seeing it as a naive yearning for an Edenic and unattainable past or, worse, as a rigidly prescriptive orthodoxy. I have tried to address those concerns and challenges, yet not lose sight of the spirit of celebration and exploration that brings many people to their experiments with native plants. Of necessity, the celebration at times verges on defense, if only to acknowledge the debates and to offer responses to the critics' challenges.

As for the controversy, I think it's mainly a problem of perception rather than some intrinsic rigidity on the part of native plant enthusiasts. I didn't encounter anyone who said native plants and only native plants and anything else is suspect. No snobbery or hierarchies were in evidence. No horticultural xenophobia. Instead, I encountered native plant gardeners of all stripes, across a very broad spectrum of activity. Some made native plants their specialty, restoring highly complex ecosystems right in their own backyards. Others mixed native plants with exotics, providing an indigenous matrix to support compatible non-native species. Others plunked a few natives here and there for the simple reason that they liked them. The practices were as varied as the gardeners themselves. One native plant gardener who was carrying out a painstaking and pure restoration of native prairie and oak savanna in an abandoned farmer's field also tended non-native hibiscus and morning glories in the garden near her house. There was a man who had re-created a tiny patch of the Bruce Peninsula in the front garden, and whose backyard is almost an arboretum of exotic plant visitors knitted together with communities of native plants. A woman who runs a fine native plant nursery and whose garden is a sunny show including many non-native perennials...

Gardening with native plants is a choice like any other. These gardeners may be celebrating native plants for many reasons—aesthetic, environmental, utilitarian—but that doesn't necessarily mean that they feel the need to reject all the other reasons for gardening—such as trying out something new or experimenting with an exotic.

Native plant gardening is not some kind of unbending orthodoxy, yet another chink in the global armour of regulated activity. Rather, it's one exciting and limitless gardening option, explored by people who love native flora and want to try their hand at nurturing some in their own gardens.

You don't need to eschew all non-native plants or sign some imaginary code of honour that banishes all exotics. Your garden is a zone of personal expression, free of moral dictates. There's no need to apologize for the astilbes or defend your daffodils.

Garden with native plants for the same reasons that you garden with any plants: because you want to nurture them. Though there is much discussion in this book of the environmental issues that surround and support native plant gardening, I think the essential imperative is that of love—love for Ontario's native flora.

If you believe the gardening press, it seems that gardeners are a faddish bunch. Colours come and go in horticultural popularity contests. Styles fade in and out of, well, style. Fashions grab the attention and strain the wallet for a few short years, until we move on to the next craze. One year it's fritillaria, another it's species tulips, later on it's *Iris reticulata*. Perhaps we just like showing off our Latin.

Perhaps we're suckers for trends manufactured by excess stock at the nursery. Perhaps we're merely mimicking the fickle nature of our gardens, in which plants drift in and out of the picture, perfect one year, disappeared the next.

But the longest-running trend prediction has got to be "natural" gardening or gardening with native plants. It seems that every year one can find references to this "new" craze that is ready to take off and storm the gardening world. Don't hold your breath waiting for the revolution. I doubt there's going to be one. Instead, I think we'll see a continuation of the slow and steady *evolution* towards native plant gardening. An evolution is much more appropriate anyway. Gradual change, entrenched within the genes, inexorable, unstoppable—that's how it will take hold. As inevitable as water shortages, water restrictions, water metres of pay as you plumb, chemical panics, chemical restrictions, and all the other environmental realities of the 1990s. In other words, we'll slowly see that it makes a lot of sense.

The main stumbling block in the path of this evolution, I think, is a widespread and truly bizarre gardening bias against the common. Snobbery in disguise, one can find this bias everywhere. Black-eyed Susans aren't good enough because you can see them all over. Common as dirt, easy as pie. We want our gardens to be special, and if that means thirty bucks for a rare iris, then so be it.

Running parallel to this rejection of the common and embrace of the expensive is an equally perverse pandering to the picky. Just watch gardeners run whenever the words prolific spreader appear. You'd think that we'd *want* such fecundity in our gardens—after all, we're in the business of growing plants. But no: prolific equals easy equals common equals botanical banishment. We'd much rather coddle along a Himalayan blue poppy that really doesn't want to be here than lose control over a merrily promiscuous patch of wild ginger that won't say no. Because at the end of the day, success under difficult conditions provides a heightened sense of accomplishment. It's almost as if we want our gardens to be gladiatorial battles—with, of course, gardener as victor, triumphant hero of the ring.

Native plant gardeners, on the other hand, eschew the fight metaphor. The garden is not a battle site, but rather a partnership between gardener and nature. In fact, maybe partnership is too democratic a word—many would admit to a hierarchy, with nature on top and the gardener an industrious minion, carrying out orders, doing the work dictated by higher forces. Is it such a humiliating thing to be guided by a more knowledgeable teacher?

* * *

There seem to be two widely divergent camps when it comes to native plants. One group rejects the whole idea because wildflowers are considered to be too common, verging on weeds. (I once told an avid gardening friend about the Canadian Wildflower Society's plant sale and she summed up her lack of interest with "but don't they sell only wildflowers?" Why would you want to pay money for *those?* was the unspoken subtext.)

At the other end of the facility scale is the group of gardeners, often novices, who consider native plants almost frightening in their difficulty of cultivation. Perhaps they were weaned on tales of trilliums and orchids, and missed out on success stories like bloodroot and ferns. But somewhere they got the idea that native plants were beyond their horticultural skills and better left to forests and meadows, where nature does the work.

This situation leaves native plant enthusiasts careening between extremes: on the one hand, promoting native plants as worthy of gardening interest and on the other hand assuaging fears. Let's take the more realistic middle road: native plant gardening can be as difficult or as easy as you want to make it. A gardener who attempts a plot of many different native orchids and trilliums, starting from seed, is looking at a decades-long course in botany and much heartbreak. A gardener who decides on a free-for-all backyard of native meadow wildflowers is looking at loads of spare time for admiring the display. Many are somewhere in between.

Another strange inversion about native plant gardening is that while nothing could be further away from "exotic" gardening, native plants have taken on a bit of the sheen of the unfamiliar. It's as if we're so far removed from our floral heritage that the local has become the uncommon. Ironically, a front yard naturalized with native plants is rarer than a garden full of horticultural specimens from far-flung places. The flora of China, Japan, and the Mediterranean are more familiar in our gardens than Ontario's indigenous plants. And as Edwinna von Baeyer has documented in her history of Canadian gardening, *Rhetoric and Roses*, the emulation of foreign landscaping styles and inclusion of foreign plant species in our gardens go right back to the very beginnings of Canadian landscaping efforts. (Von Baeyer notes that wildflower gardening "was not a major component of the home landscape before 1930.")

This admiration of the "exotic" works both ways: some of Ontario's most undervalued native plants are in fact highly appreciated in the gardens of Britain and continental Europe. Almost from the beginning of European contact with the so-called New World, native North American species were sent to botanists and arboreta in Europe. In his book *Gentle Conquest*, James Reveal details such reciprocity and notes that Champlain had a botanical garden near the present site of Quebec City, from which he sent native plants to Paris. Plants that early naturalists shipped to Europe included Virginia bluebells, goldenrod, trillium, flowering dogwood, and the native sunflower. Other native plants, such as the Rose-bay rhododendron and various asters, were used by European plant breeders in the early development of hybrids, which were then sent back to North America for garden use. Like a botanical extension of the colonial attitude, native plants tended to be held in favour only after receiving the European imprimatur of approval.

*   *   *

Of course, there's more to it than botanical colonialism. Over the years, I think we've fostered a fear of native plants—and if fear is too strong a word, then at least a hesitance about using these plants in our gardens. The source? I locate it in the white trillium: I think that those well-meaning, civic-minded folks who chose the white trillium as Ontario's provincial floral emblem made a big mistake. Wildflower appreciation in general, and native plant gardening in particular, would be much further ahead in this province if their votes had instead been cast for the runner-up: our native eastern columbine.

What possible difference can an emblem make? Plenty.

Now, I love trilliums as much as the next person. In fact, throughout my life, I've held them in a kind of reverence, helped no doubt by early admonitions from teachers not to pick these floral gems and warnings never to dig them up from the wild. But maybe it's that same reverence that's the problem. Trilliums hold a kind of mystique in our shared cultural imagination. They've ceased to be flowers and instead exist as totems: symbols of the natural beauty found in our woodlands. Unfortunately, it's a beauty that's untouchable, removed, protected, to be enjoyed from afar rather than intimately experienced. You can look, says the message down the years, but don't grow.

Of course, many gardeners have had splendid luck growing these woodland beauties in their gardens, but it's with no help from the botanical quirk that guides this flower's reproductive steam. Since we're not supposed to dig them from the wild, our only guilt-free option is to either start them from seed or buy them from a reputable nursery. When was the last time you saw trilliums, guaranteed nursery propagated, for sale at the local garden centre? (Too often they're dug from the wild, or gathered from suppliers deflowering their own woodlands.) And starting trilliums from seed introduces gardeners to a long-term lesson in patience: seven years later and you might get a blossom. So our provincial floral emblem retains its guarded, difficult beauty and remains underrepresented in our gardens.

The implications for wildflower appreciation are distressing: I blame the trillium's special status for perpetuating (perhaps even creating) the myth that Ontario's native flora don't belong in our gardens and that any attempts to mimic woodland associations will be fraught with peril and failure. So we leave the trilliums in the forest and fill our plots with begonias—as if there can be no connection between the forest and the garden.

How would the situation be any different if the lovely and lowly eastern columbine were our floral emblem? Is it reading too much into our botanical heritage to say that our gardens would be more democratic places? Just compare the stately, royal carriage of the trillium to the wanton lustiness of the columbine. One withholds its treasures for seven years, the other advertises availability and spreads like mad, seeding freely and fraternally in any place where it's happy. One is hard to get, the other is hard to get rid of (though who would want to?).

If the common columbine had been the benefactor of decades of patriotic PR, as the trillium has, then perhaps people would grow it with a kind of pride and take pleasure in its cultivation, feelings now reserved for more difficult and fussier plants. Maybe our success with a native flower would spur us on to further experimentation with indigenous flora. Maybe children would not take a transgressive thrill in pillaging the contraband emblem but instead learn how easy it is to grow columbines from seed. Maybe the wonder of an awed and removed reverence would be replaced with the wonder of common success, shared in gardens throughout Ontario.

CHAPTER REFERENCES

Gentle Conquest: The Botanical Discovery of North America. James L. Reveal. Washington: Starwood Publishing, 1992.

Rhetoric and Roses: A History of Canadian Gardening. Edwinna von Baeyer. Markham: Fitzhenry and Whiteside, 1984.

Part 1

GARDENING WITH NATIVE PLANTS
THE BIG PICTURE

Chapter 1

NATIVE PLANT GARDENING
CONFESSIONS AND CONNECTIONS

The wonder of gardening is that one becomes a gardener by becoming a gardener.
—Allen Lacy, The Gardener's Eye

One should be sceptical of gardening information read in books. We don't garden in pages (though gardening often does go on in the head), we garden in dirt. Things that sound great on paper often don't work out in soil. So head into this book, and into your plot, with a healthy dose of sceptical openness. Give the ideas a try, see if they work for you, but adapt them and change them if necessary for your particular situation. Blanket advice that works for everyone isn't the point—the aim is to suggest new directions and new areas of exploration.

The path to expertise is a bit like a garden: never finished, always evolving, chameleonlike. Just when you think you've got things sorted out, the garden makes a new demand. The clump that last year completed a perfect corner, this year threatens to take over. If we accept that there is no closure—no epiphanic moment of cosmic alignment when all parts work together and then somehow stop and hold that perfection forever—then gardening will lead to pleasure. If, instead, we expect some kind of finality in the garden, we'll always be disappointed.

How many times have you toured a friend's garden only to hear all of her or his plans for tinkering and rearranging and moving the plants from here to there? Things might look absolutely fine to you, but gardening is always about "next year." So it's in this spirit of anticipation and inevitable new discoveries that this book is written: to entice rather than exhaust with complete closure, to set the wheels in motion rather than to reach a destination. That, we'll each do on our own, with information to guide us and promises of "next year" to fuel us.

Another thing about advice: don't trust it if it comes from someone who never admits to or discloses mistakes. There's something, well, unnatural, about claims of instant and widespread success. Perverse as it may sound, I think the community of gardeners is created through a bond of identification with and recognition of shared blunders. Oh,

---

When we garden with native and naturalized wildflowers, we garden not only with nature but also with history.

—*Brooklyn Botanic Garden*, Gardening With Wildflowers and Native Plants

---

I've done that too, you think to yourself when someone admits to cutting next year's flower buds off a shrub in a moment of pruning zeal. Both of you will never do it again—you've shared a minor tragedy and are now ready to move on. It's a bond forged through process and anyone who denies process in gardening is immediately suspect.

So here goes my disclosure, the condensed story of my garden, the slow but steady and ongoing evolution towards a community of native species, told mainly—and inevitably—through the lens of my many missteps. (And I wouldn't trade the mistakes for all the roses in the world.)

First of all, the place: downtown Toronto, just minutes away from one of the busiest commercial districts in the city, in a dense residential area that has somehow managed to stay a neighbourhood. The houses are relentlessly packed together on my street, and many of the gardens are ingenious assertions of individuality against crowded pressures.

When I phoned what I consider to be one of

the best native plant nurseries around (Otter Valley Native Plants) to ask advice about what to plant out front, I was not ready for the depressing evaluation of my conditions: a Norway maple, on utterly degraded clay that had more in common with concrete than soil, and glaring, drying afternoon sun beating down from the west . . . basically, a horticultural nightmare. It occurred to me that maybe my mini-environment was suffering from schizophrenia: the maple makes it want to be a small woodland, the poor soil makes it want to be a vacant lot, and the three hours of unrelenting angled glare make it want to be the Sahara. And what do I want it to be? A cool oasis of native plants, inviting to creatures, and a tentative nod or botanical reference to what was once in this area: woodland carpets of spring ephemerals leading into lush summer foliage and highlights of fall colour.

I pondered the impossibility of my habitat's contradictions for a while, then decided to do what everyone says you should do: start with the soil. My partner and I spent backbreaking days digging out the concrete clay, mindful of maple roots, saving what bulbs we could, dumping the old in preparation for the new: ten cubic yards of triple mix, delivered in one glorious, shovelable lump. What a thrill it was to dig into that friable soil without debilitating wrist reverberations. Neighbours wondered if we were not daunted by the enormity of the pile, but to me, it was like spooning whipped cream after fluffing frozen butter.

What I didn't do—and now it's too late—was even think about putting landscape cloth underneath the new soil to keep those maple feeder roots from "invading" all the goodness. I doubt I would have anyway, if I'd thought about it, since I don't begrudge that tree any search for nourishment—it's a tough old bird and I hope it lives forever, even if it turns my triple-mix into a tangled web of roots and the plants suffer for it. Make like you're in the forest, I say to those plants, where you've never heard of landscape cloth and you claim your nutrients like a fighter.

Native plants that are currently braving my compromised woodland conditions include trout lily, trillium, wild ginger, foamflower, mayapple, wild blue phlox, Solomon's seal, early meadow-rue, bellwort, Virginia bluebells, beardtongue, bloodroot, Canada anemone, monarda, Jack-in-the-pulpit, aster, goldenrod, ferns, evening primrose, wild geranium, hepatica, and more. Naturalized aliens that are being given visitation rights for a while, until the natives get more established, at which point they'll be gifts or compost, include rocket, daylilies, snow-in-summer, vinca, and chrysanthemums. I'm not sure what to do about the non-native bulbs—the tulips and scilla and daffodils and hyacinths. They bring such delight in the spring, but I suspect that as the native plants create the dominant mood and tone of the garden, such splashy exotics will seem out of place. Next year...

In another expression of botanical contradiction, my backyard couldn't be more different from the front. About all it shared was that degraded soil, better for burdock and plantain than the garden I envisioned. However, it is in full sun, allowing for another kind of experimentation: the attempt to style the backyard as a mini-reference to meadow habitat. Not a true meadow, as I haven't included many native grasses, but am using meadow forbs (non-grass herbaceous—non-woody—wildflowers). Again, there are non-natives. Some, like globe thistle, I *thought* were native when I first started out (in part because of its "wild" nature). But they work well with the native bee balm, Jerusalem artichoke, black-eyed Susan, goldenrod, gray-headed coneflower, nodding wild onion, butterfly milkweed, compass plant, ironweed, cup plant, and lupine, so they're allowed to stay for a while. As I run out of room and as my gar-

den evolves into the naturalistic landscape I'm striving for, they'll probably make way for new experiments.

When I first put in these plants, I paid little attention to their heights, so I consider myself extremely lucky that somehow they've managed to find the right balance—they, the plants, did it on their own, with no help from me.

And perhaps that's the essence of gardening with native plants, after all: allowing the evolved wisdom of these plants to express themselves. Yes, with interventions from wilful gardeners with their own likes and dislikes and ideas of beauty and occasional goof-ups, but also with a kind of faith in and love for the essential rightness of plants that are growing where they're meant to grow.

❦   ❦   ❦

Call it what you will: natural landscaping, mini-ecological gardening, wildflower gardening, natural gardening, low-maintenance landscaping or natural heritage gardening (my preferred title). The terms are less important than the changes they encompass—a movement away from the manicured look, from the fussy, high-maintenance and expensive flowerbeds towards a more unfettered, dynamic natural plant system.

—*Robert S. Dorney and Douglas H. Allen, in* The Harrowsmith Landscaping Handbook

This is a book about naturalistic gardening, but unfortunately the phrase is hopelessly inadequate if not deliberately misleading. What, for example, might the reverse be? Unnatural gardening? Well, all gardens are in some sense unnatural in that they don't just happen, they're made: once a gardener enters the picture you've got nurture not nature, or at best nurtured nature.

So what makes one garden "natural" and another "unnatural"? Is it that the "unnatural" one is ugly (hardly an absolute designation, rather a highly subjective judgement); unsuccessful (again, depends completely on who's judging the implied contest); absurd (flower shows that combine the blooming yellows of daffodils with the golds and bronzes of chrysanthemums—spring and fall flowers all jumbled together in a wrenching exercise in botanical surrealism)? We step into hazy territory by calling such gardens any more unnatural than

---

When you plant a native species, you are employing all of evolutionary history. You can't find a better reason for choosing a plant than that gained from 3 billion years of experience.

—*Carol A. Smyser*, Nature's Design

---

any other kind of garden. And just as tricky, many sins have been committed in the name of naturalness, so it's hard to see it as an absolute good.

Maybe the thing to do is to define the idea and postpone worrying about the label. Whatever the terminology, a native plant garden can range from something as grandiose as growing a prairie in your backyard to trying out a small patch of native wildflowers by the front door to gardening with native drought-tolerant meadow plants in pots on the balcony. The scale is less important, in most cases, than the intent. In this book, you'll read about an urban woodland garden, comprised almost entirely of native plants, that's about as small as city gardens come—fifteen feet by fifteen feet (less than five metres square)—and yet still manages to look stunning, perpetuate itself with little maintenance, and create urban habitat for a wide array of creatures.

The goal of native plant gardening, in its fullest expression, is to replicate functioning plant communities. (Sorry if this sounds more like Grade 11 biology than jargon-free gardening, but there's no way around this essential ecological fact of native plant gardening.) Plants are not treated as isolated specimens, plunked into arbitrary associations, but rather as pieces of an integrated whole —parts of an ecosystem. The relationships between plants, their likes and dislikes, their natural allies, needs and requirements, dictate the ways in which they're combined to create a garden.

This last point might sound very much like any kind of garden. After all, positioning plants according to their shared requirements for sun and water is a cardinal rule in all gardening. The difference is that the plant associations and relationships have a purpose beyond ease of maintenance and desire for individual plant health: after you've tamped down the soil for the final transplant, what you've set in motion is the working of an ecosystem.

While some might loathe the idea of a garden united by "concepts," native plant gardening is characterized by a few key ideas (ideas that sound dry as dust until you bring them down to earth with loppers and shovels).

• This is an ecological approach to gardening, an approach that sees the environment as a web of connections rather than as a bundle of discrete units all functioning in isolation.

• There is a commitment to fostering diversity, both plant and animal.

• It has as its goal reducing the need for high-maintenance time and labour and high inputs of water, chemicals, and fertilizers.

• There is a desire to replicate functioning, self-perpetuating ecosystems that exist in a dynamic relationship with the surrounding area.

All of the above can be illustrated through a simple, if stark, comparison. Think of a small urban garden that attempts to replicate an Ontario woodland forest floor in spring. Now think of a bed of begonias. Both are gardens that respond to conditions of shade. But how different the expression! One takes its cue from a plant community that is indigenous to the area—it is a garden full of echoes and references and a sense of place that has meaning locally. The other is a garden import that says little about where we are, here. One is a diverse community of many plants that together form a self-sustaining and self-regenerating habitat. The other eats up Saturday mornings with a regimen of weeding, watering, fertilizing, and dealing with the inevitable pests of monoculture. (And then needs to be started all over again next year.) One welcomes the seeds blown in on the wind or dropped by birds from surrounding areas. The other fights the subtle changes fortuitously brought by natural forces. One celebrates change over time. The other resists any changes except for bigger, bloomier begonias.

For the most part, the gardens we've created in Ontario cities and towns are like that bed of begonias. (Or, more likely, impatiens. According to the newsletter *The Avant Gardener*, impatiens accounted for 47 percent of all annuals sold in the U.S. in 1992, and one suspects that the situation isn't that much different in Canada. In other words, half of our plant purchases devoted to just one type of plant!) Even if the flower changes, the idea remains the same: the garden landscapes of our cities and towns are dominated by relatively few different species of plants: non-native bulbs such as tulips and daffodils in spring, given over to non-native bedding annuals such as impatiens and alyssum in the summer, or perennial beds of hostas and daylilies. (And don't get me wrong; at one time I've had all of these in my garden and right now I have half of them.)

These plants are the bread and butter of the nursery industry, the plants the beginning gar-

BENEFITS OF USING NATIVE PLANTS

- Indigenous vegetation is adapted to the area and therefore requires less maintenance.
- Plants are adapted to natural levels of rainfall and therefore don't need continual supplemental watering.
- Plants have evolved in association with local insects (for pollination, especially); pest problems tend to be minimal and rarely catastrophic.
- The genetic variations and diversity of indigenous plant populations allow them to cope better with environmental stresses such as drought and disease.
- Using native plants perpetuates local biodiversity, and thus contributes to global biodiversity.
- It restores connections and corridors with the larger landscape.
- It creates habitat (and food sources) for indigenous wildlife.
- It works with the available environmental conditions, instead of waging constant battle against those conditions; it is modelled on natural processes.
- It involves an active engagement with the local ecosystem, learning its features, cycles, and connections and associations, and thus encourages a deeper commitment to place.
- It is a triumphant gesture against homogeneity and global monoculture and a celebration of bioregional differences, so that every place does not end up looking like every other place with "the same stores in their mini-malls" (as Tyler puts it in *Generation X),* or the same plants in the garden.

dener is regaled with at the garden centre and which seem, at first, to present a bewildering and long-lasting array of choice. How quickly that sense of new-found horizons fades, only to be replaced with an exhausted exhalation of familiarity. For some, it takes only one short season of experimentation before they've outgardened the gardening

---

I want us as a culture to depart from the old tradition of evaluating land according to what can be extracted from it as commodity or abstracted from it as social asset and turn instead toward a new tradition of valuing land by the life it harbors.

—*Sara Stein*, Noah's Garden

---

centre and are combing esoteric catalogues for new seeds to try. For me, it took four years before I was itching to escape the bounds of the regular nursery and looking for a new gardening challenge. What kind of challenges would gardening with native plants offer, I asked myself. And, not surprisingly, the answer revealed itself to be very, very old.

No matter how you look at it, gardening with native plants involves making some kind of peace—or at least provisional compromise—with history. How and why native to what, where, and when are the inevitable questions and they lead one on fascinating, if controversial and unresolved, journeys.

The simplest and bluntest definition is that native plants are those that existed here prior to

European contact—they are the species that evolved without having been moved or introduced by human actions. Why pick the seemingly arbitrary point of first contact? Because that is the historical moment at which the landscape of North America experienced its most dramatic change since the last Ice Age ten thousand to twelve thousand years ago. The European settlers brought with them, both accidentally and deliberately (particularly for their agriculture), countless plants, pests, and diseases that transformed the ecology of this continent. Some of these plants were relatively well behaved and stayed in the confines of Puritan gardens. Some were agricultural crops that fed the settlers and saved them from starvation. Some botanical imports gave up the ghost in our cold winters. And some found this environment entirely to their liking and set about to reproduce and colonize, and in some instances take over, the existing vegetation. (In this admittedly stark and simplistically synoptic version of a complex history, it's tempting to see a parallel with what happened to First Nations people as well.)

If one chooses first contact as a reference point, this is not to say that the indigenous peoples of North America did not have an impact on the ecological communities of plants and animals prior to European contact. There is a rich and well-documented history of native intervention in the North American environment, which had, after all, been their home for thousands of years. Natives burned forests in order to clear land for agriculture; to remove the cover that protected their enemies; and to create conditions favourable to grazing animals, such as deer, which were then hunted for food. They developed domesticated food crops, such as many different kinds of squashes, pumpkins, and gourds, for their agriculture. As well, natives regularly burned grasslands and savannas in North America, an activity that assisted in the herding of bison for hunting. (Indeed, the persis-

Throughout this book, you will encounter the terms native, indigenous, alien, exotic, non-native, introduced, naturalized, weed, and wildflower. These are contested terms (and some of them are loaded with meaning outside the world of plants), but I have used them in the following ways.

Native

A plant that existed in a given area prior to European settlement. In the scope of this book, the area is Ontario, which is a political jurisdiction, not a biotic community, so plants listed as native are not necessarily native to the whole province. For example, twinleaf is native to Ontario's Carolinian region (and down into the U.S.) but not to Ontario's boreal forest. (See "Ontario's Ecological Zones," in this chapter, for a discussion of these differences.)

Indigenous

This is a further refinement of the idea of native: a locally adapted plant species, one that naturally grows within a close distance of your area (some people set that distance at 50 miles/80 km, others at 100 miles/160 km). While a species may be native to Ontario, the indigenous plant is one whose genetic material has adapted to a very specific location. There are some native plant gardeners who try to garden with indigenous species rather than the broader category of native plants. When they have the choice between a native plant grown 100 miles (160 km) away or the same species grown 2 miles (3 km) away, they'll choose the more locally adapted indigenous plant. The reason for this is that the indigenous plant holds a kind of genetic integrity or information that is specific to the plant's local community, and these gardeners want to preserve and perpetuate that genetic stock.

Alien, exotic, non-native, introduced

A plant that is grown outside its native range. Some alien plants arrived here accidentally; others were deliberately introduced.

Naturalized

A non-native plant that has been introduced to an area, has spread, and now grows in the wild without human cultivation. Examples of naturalized plants in Ontario include dame's rocket, Queen Anne's lace, and ox-eye daisy.

Weed

Much too complicated for a simple definition! Chapter 10 is an attempt to grapple with the term and explore its many meanings for native plant gardeners.

Wildflower

An herbaceous (non-woody) plant that has not been genetically modified by humans (as hybrids have), reproduces true from seed, and grows without cultivation.

tence of Ontario's remnant prairies and savannas may be due to the regular and ecologically necessary burning that native peoples carried out.)

These activities, while clearly having local impact, did not lead to the kind of wholesale changes of the North American landscape that occurred after European contact and, in particular,

---

*It has been said that settlers of
Southern Ontario were confronted
by a maple, beech and elm forest so
dense that a squirrel could travel
from the eastern end of Lake Ontario
to the Detroit River without
touching ground.*

—*Tim Gray and Nancy Bayly, Borealis, Fall 1993*

---

after the technological changes brought about by increasing industrialization. For one thing, the native population was too low. As William Cronon concludes in his encyclopedic *Changes in the Land: Indians, Colonists, and the Ecology of New England*, "the low Indian populations of the pre-colonial northern forests had relatively little impact on the ecosystems they inhabited." Equally important, natives moved throughout the land, so that when one area was exhausted of soil nutrients or game, for example, it was abandoned and left to regenerate. And perhaps most important of all, the nature of the natives' relationship with the land was completely different from that of the new settlers; many books have been written on the subject, but suffice it to say here that the natives had an intimate and connected understanding of the land. Thus, while native peoples were deliberately

altering the landscape, their activities did not significantly impair the long-term ecological stability of that landscape or its ability to sustain itself.

Not so for the Europeans who made their way to North America and who brought about the massive changes of industrialization. The legacy of their early encounter includes a familiar litany: denuded forests, depleted soils, weed population explosions, and plant pest introductions. All of these factors were to have an enormous transformative effect on the land. Some would argue that such changes are the unavoidable byproduct of human endeavour—that is, that we're a part of the ecosystem and so will always cause some kind of change. As William Cronon puts it: "When one asks how much an ecosystem has been changed by human influence, the inevitable next question must be: 'changed in relation to what?' " There is no unimplicated point of human reference, no outside stance from which we can evaluate a landscape that includes humans.

As Cronon again observes, it is not that a choice can be made between two landscapes: one that includes humans and one that doesn't. Rather, the choice is between two different ways of belonging to an ecosystem: "All human groups consciously change their environment to some extent . . . and the best measure of a culture's ecological stability may well be how successfully its environmental changes maintain its ability to reproduce itself."

It seems that we have chosen an alternate route: the path of environmental change that impairs and impedes the functioning of the ecosystem. These are value-laden terms and the judgements behind them need to be teased out and acknowledged, otherwise one runs the risk of romanticizing an Edenic past. Yet the ecological facts that inform this view turn more to Darwin than romanticism: prior to first contact, the landscape of North America had evolved for thousands

If gardening with native plants sounds like it requires a history or botany degree to determine what plants existed in your region prior to European contact, fear not. This is not an arcane science or a huge research project. The information is out there and easy to access—and, indeed, there are plenty of plant suggestions in this book.

For those people just starting out with native plants in Ontario, you can begin with the plant listings in Chapter 9. These are plants that are relatively easy to find in nurseries, native plant sales, and seed exchanges.

Field guides are another excellent source of information. Browse through a wildflower field guide and you'll see that they list the natural range for each species. As well, there are many other excellent resources, such as *Flowers of the Wild: Ontario and the Great Lakes Region*, that reveal the origins of Ontario's wildflowers and tell you which are native and which are introduced. Scoggan's *The Flora of Canada* is also a great source.

Naturalist groups such as the Federation of Ontario Naturalists and, in particular, the local clubs will also provide information. Many groups publish checklists of the flora native to a specific region; some have regular newsletters and magazines, which you can comb for relevant information. These people are experts in Ontario's natural heritage and they are more than willing to help spread the word and answer questions.

The Canadian Wildflower Society and their magazine, *Wildflower*, are excellent sources for native plant gardeners, and I urge you to join (membership includes a subscription to the magazine). Once you're connected with this network, you'll never be short of willing native plant enthusiasts with whom to share information, seeds, and plants.

Surprisingly, garden centres are not always the best source of information about native plants, and their catalogues rarely identify native plants. However, this is a consumer-driven movement and the more people who ask at nurseries for native plants, the more interest those nurseries will show in supplying the demand. You need to be aware, though, that increased demand may lead to increased nursery-collection of native plants from the wild. Chapter 8 offers information about how to guard against this problem, but the main thing is to let nurseries know that you do not support wild-collection and to ask about their sources for native plants.

There are a number of nurseries in Ontario that specialize in native plants (see Further Reading and Resources), and they are a good source of information. When you actually go out to spend your gardening dollars, I highly recommend that you support these nurseries devoted to native plants. We're the gardeners who keep them in business—and we all have a vested interest in their financial health and longevity.

of years with its own internal logic. Plants and animals developed mutual associations that determined the functioning of the whole system. These associations, developed in response to climate, sunlight, water, soils, and a myriad environmental factors, all worked together to create the ecology of place. They are, in fact, what define this place.

Private individuals are the stewards of more than 90% of the land in southern Ontario. In many respects, natural heritage protection begins and ends with the interest and willingness of private owners to protect their lands and waters as part of their own personal heritage.

—John L. Riley and Pat Mohr, The Natural Heritage of Southern Ontario's Settled Landscapes

---

So what happened with the arrival of North America's new settlers? The introductions of plants and animals took place not in ecological time in which changes are generally measured over thousands of years, but in an accelerated explosion of landscape alteration. To read the history of such plant and animal "invasions" is to be instructed in the terrifying logic of logarithmic fecundity.

Take the area around Massachusetts Bay in the U.S., for example. By 1672, just a short while after the first Europeans arrived, the botanist John Josselyn was able to compile a list of twenty-two European species of weeds that were common to the area. It included dandelion, chickweed, mullein, nightshade, and stinging nettle, to enu-merate just a few—and all gardeners can attest to their ubiquity today.

Not only were such opportunistic weed species advancing with the colonists' agriculture, but husbandry practices were also transforming the land. Because native grasses were not adapted to grazing by domesticated animals, they were rapidly displaced by Eurasian field plants, such as white clover, and grasses, that had adapted to the demands of grazing. Thus, a European cover began to take the place of native plants in the colonists' pastoral landscape.

❦   ❦   ❦

Just where does native plant gardening fit into all this? Is it a naive resistance to the changes wrought by a globalism that has its roots over three hundred years ago? Is it a doomed denial of inevitable change that we can no more stop than we can curb human influence on the land? I think that it's none of these things, but rather an attempt to do what Cronon calls "belonging to an ecosystem"— belonging in such a way that one's presence does not essentially impede, but rather contributes towards, the internal logic that has guided the evolution of that ecosystem over millennia. Far from banishing human influence from the land, calling for an "untouched" and unchanging nature, native plant gardening is a form of ecological restoration that encourages an active reciprocity of human involvement. Instead of denying history and trying to return to some kind of Edenic and romanticized past, native plant gardening demands a constructive participation in history, acknowledging the human role in change and offering a choice about how that change might contribute to healthy ecosystems rather than destroying them. The space that gardeners make for themselves in such an ecosystem is a place of awareness and nurturing: being aware of and attuned to plant associations that have meaning locally—that connect with the larger landscape picture—and nurturing such associations in our own small plots.

If gardening is indeed a "civilizing" thing to do, as Brian Fawcett has written in *The Compact Garden*, then I can think of few things more civilizing than the healing handshake that native plant gardening offers between culture and nature.

ONTARIO'S ECOLOGICAL ZONES

Try this exercise: redraw the map of Ontario, in your mind, based not on political boundaries but on the province's ecological zones. Think not of the major cities but rather of the landscape: more than a million square miles (2.5 million square km) of it! Think of wide bands of different regions spanning the province.

First, in the southernmost part of the province, along Lake Erie and touching the lower corner of Lake Ontario, is the Deciduous Forest Region (also known as the Carolinian Zone). Here the 170 frost-free days in the year allow for a unique deciduous forest comprised mainly of hardwoods and including such national rarities as the Kentucky coffee tree (*Gymnocladus dioicus*), cucumber tree (*Magnolia acuminata*), tulip tree (*Liriodendron tulipifera*), sycamore (*Plantanus occidentalis*), black gum (*Nyssa sylvatica*), sassafras (*Sassafras albidum*), paw paw (*Asimina triloba*), and many more.

Moving north are two transition zones, the southern Deciduous-Evergreen Forest Region and the northern Deciduous-Evergreen Forest Region, in which the southern forest mingles with more northerly species, creating the mixed-hardwood/pine forests of the Great Lakes–St. Lawrence region. Deciduous trees such as sugar maple (*Acer saccharum*), beech (*Fagus grandifolia*), yellow birch (*Betula alleghaniensis*), and basswood (*Tilia americana*) are typical in the south, while red and eastern white pine (*Pinus resinos* and *P. strobus*) dominate in the north.

Farther north is the Boreal Forest Region divided into three zones: the Southern, Central, and Northern Boreal Forest regions. In this harsh environment, black and white spruce (*Picea mariana* and *P. glauca*), jack pine (*Pinus banksiana*), tamarack (*Larix laricina*), and aspen (*Populus tremuloides*) are typical species.

And in the very far north are the Subarctic Forest Region (Taiga) and the Subarctic Tundra Region of the Hudson Bay Lowlands.

These broad bands can be further divided into countless ecological communities, each with its typical flora and fauna, species that depend on the unique combinations of geology, climate, soils, and more. To catalogue them all is the work of scientists, but suffice it to say that, according to the Ontario Natural Heritage Information Centre, the diverse habitats of Ontario support over 3,000 species of native and naturalized vascular plants, thousands of nonvascular plants (mosses, liverworts, fungi, lichens, and algae), 460 bird species, 80 mammal species, 167 butterfly and skipper species, 58 reptile and amphibian species,

FOREST REGIONS OF ONTARIO

TUNDRA

BOREAL FOREST REGION

GREAT LAKES–ST. LAWRENCE FOREST REGION

CAROLINIAN REGION

165 species of freshwater fish, 133 species of freshwater molluscs, and thousands of other species of invertebrates.

Source: *Flowers of the Wild: Ontario and the Great Lakes Region* by Zile Zichmanis and James Hodgins, and *The Flora of Canada* by H.J. Scoggan

CHAPTER REFERENCES

Changes in the Land: Indians, Colonists, and the Ecology of New England. William Cronon. New York: Hill and Wang, 1983.

The Compact Garden. Brian Fawcett. Camden East: Camden House, 1992.

The Flora of Canada. H. J. Scoggan. Ottawa: National Museums of Canada, 1978.

Flowers of the Wild: Ontario and the Great Lakes Region. Zile Zichmanis and James Hodgins. Toronto: Oxford University Press, 1982.

The Gardener's Eye. Allen Lacy. New York: Atlantic Monthly Press, 1992.

Gardening With Wildflowers and Native Plants. Claire E. Sawyers, ed. Brooklyn: Brooklyn Botanic Garden, 1990.

Generation X. Douglas Coupland. New York: St. Martin's, 1991.

The Harrowsmith Landscaping Handbook. Jennifer Bennett, ed. Camden East: Camden House, 1985.

The Natural Heritage of Southern Ontario's Settled Landscapes. John L. Riley and Pat Mohr. Aurora, Ontario: Ontario Ministry of Natural Resources, 1994.

Nature's Design: A Practical Guide to Natural Landscaping. Carol A. Smyser and editors of Rodale Press. Emmaus, Pennsylvania: Rodale, 1982.

Noah's Garden: Restoring the Ecology of Our Own Back Yards. Sara Stein. Boston: Houghton Mifflin, 1993.

Chapter 2

GARDENING AND COMMUNITY
FINDING YOUR PLACE (AND YOUR GARDEN)
IN THE BIOREGION

S ad to say, but our desires rarely match our realities—that's what makes them worth striving towards, after all. Two unrelated statistics brought this home for me. The first has to do with rural longing in city dwellers. Even though 76 percent of Canadians live in cities, six out of ten responded to a 1993 Gallup poll by saying that they would prefer to live in the country. In other words, more than half are not content with where they are.

The other has to do with lawns and a different kind of longing: for finicky fescue perfection. A 1981 survey of eight hundred lawn owners in the U.S. state of Virginia found that "80% thought their lawn was average or below and were not satisfied with its present condition" (*Redesigning the American Lawn*). That's a lot of not keeping up with the Joneses. I hate to think of the collective implications of all that dissatisfaction and self-deprecation.

Though any social scientist would skewer me for conflating U.S. and Canadian statistics, let's just call it a North American phenomenon: we're not happy in cities and yet we go about "lawning" our landscapes, citifying them, conforming to bylaws and codes, perverse reminders that we're here and not there, where we want to be. But then it turns out that these very same urban landscape expressions are yet another source of failure feelings and dissatisfaction. It sounds sort of pathetic when put that way.

I wonder if that Gallup poll explored what it is about the country that makes it such a preference for over half the population. Is it that there is a more defined sense of community? A slower pace? Cleaner air? Better bakeries? I'm convinced that it must also be the landscapes, the closer contact with a wilder nature. Sure, one would be hard-pressed to find much wilderness, as classically defined, in Canada's southern belt countryside. (And I'm not convinced that the classic definition —nature untouched by humans—is possible in much of southern Canada anyway.) But it's a question of degree and qualitative impact, and the votes—for six out of ten anyway—seem to swing towards the wilder nature of the countryside. In ecological terms, there may not be that much of a difference between a cultivated field of hay and a suburban lawn of grass, but somewhere, somehow, at the edges of those fields, a forest or a wetland manages to escape the plough, and it is those places, as much as the fields, that characterize the

---

The city that has places for foxes and owls, natural woodlands, trout lilies, marshes and fields, cultivated landscapes and formal gardens, old as well as new buildings, busy and quiet urban spaces, is a more pleasant and interesting place to live in.

—*Michael Hough*, City Form and Natural Process

---

countryside in our imaginations and nourish our longing for it.

Would we be any happier in cities, I wonder, if we somehow managed to include and cultivate a remnant of that wilderness right where we live? Is this the longing that feeds the enthusiasm for native plant gardening? I suspect that this is indeed the case, just as I'm sure that we would, in general, be happier in our cities if we could see our way to making them "wilder" places—places where it is possible to connect with nature's unbridled processes in action.

Consider just how different your city or town would look and feel if instead of vast expanses of monoculture lawns, there were diverse, individual expressions of a gardening aesthetic connected to place—that is, the indigenous landscape. The differences would permeate almost every aspect of our

urban existence. First, and most important, we would have a more informed populace—a citizenry comprised of people knowledgeable about our native flora and the conditions of our land. We would understand, not as some theoretical abstract but in a local and down-to-earth sense, the very nature of our community—the biotic processes that shape the landscape and give rise to its specific inhabitants. We would feel connected to the long history that informs the inherited nature of our community—to the native peoples who maintained it through their ancient practices, or the settlers who cleared it, or the glaciers that rolled over it, or the animals that ranged throughout it. Whatever the specifics for our particular places, they would form a continuous line of contact.

And along with this heightened awareness of our natural heritage, we would also, I think, become more informed about the many inhabitants with whom we share the land. A city or town filled with native plant gardens would help create habitat for the too-numerous creatures we have banished from the urban environment. The butterflies and insects and birds and mammals and amphibians and reptiles that we have extirpated by creating inhospitable places. The same creatures that, together, regulate the functioning of an ecosystem through the checks and balances they perform. Instead of inviting pest problems through the creation of monocultures, a diversely vegetated landscape would set in motion the dynamic functions of the ecosystem. Would so many of us harbour the irrational but pervasive fear of bats, for example, if we knew how they related to the whole web of connected species? A city of naturalistic gardens would, I think, encourage us all to relearn those connections and celebrate them in our own small places.

Clearly, such a vision of the city would not solve all the problems of endangered species and spaces, but perhaps it would start the process of valuing the natural landscape, a process that would then find its expression in protection of parks and larger restoration projects. We have to begin somewhere, and what better place to start than in our own borrowed bits of the biosphere, where we can have some degree of local control and some satisfaction in seeing immediate results?

Another significant environmental impact of a naturalized city landscape would be the reduced use of pesticides and herbicides. If you're gardening to create butterfly habitat, for example, chemicals are out. If you're maintaining a pond, no go on the chemical fixes. If you're encouraging a diversity of species in your garden, pests simply won't be as much of a problem, and hence chemical controls not as much of an issue.

Cleaner water, fewer environmental contaminants, more species diversity, more wildlife habitat, heightened awareness of the natural world and our human place in it, and a better understanding of ecological processes and how they fit together: all that and I can't think of a single down-side. This vision of a new kind of urban landscape is one to which every gardener using native plants contributes.

My sister once asked me to describe my ideal garden—to create in my head and then define in words something that would express the garden to end all gardens for me. The exercise completely stumped me. For a while, I consulted and stewed over those lists that every gardener keeps (you know, the ones like "great combinations to try some time" or "small successes I have known"), but they weren't much help. While they all suggested possibilities for pristine pockets of perfection in a garden, they hardly amounted to the grand project, the full floral fantasy my sister was looking for.

I finally realized that, for me, there was no such thing as an ideal garden. The two words together

created a contradiction impossible to contemplate, like progressive and conservative. My sister and I were starting at the wrong end of the equation: gardens don't exist in the abstract. Instead, they are nurtured in response to a very specific place. There's no point in generalizing to some Platonic ideal of "gardenness"; you've always got to

---

The aim of bioregionalism is to help our human cultural, political and social structures harmonize with natural systems. Human systems should be informed by, be aware of, be corrected by, natural systems.

—Gary Snyder, in Turtle Talk

---

return to the specifics and idiosyncrasies of the site, explore and interrogate and worry out the qualities of the place itself, and then express those unique qualities in a garden.

It is precisely this specificity of place that connects native plant gardening to another, broader movement: that of bioregionalism. It's a movement that doesn't get a lot of press, and I suspect that its adherents don't seek out the media spotlight, which may explain why so few people have heard about it. But it is slowly picking up speed and spreading its philosophy through the continent, particularly as it builds alliances with connected movements, such as that of environmentalism.

Basically, bioregionalism is a philosophy that calls for a closer relationship with nature ("bio") and a deeper understanding of locale ("region"). Its advocates see the world not in terms of political boundaries, which are contested and shifting and arbitrary, but rather in terms of natural geographic regions, which are defined by such ecological realities as flora, fauna, watersheds, landforms, and climate. They don't separate human culture from this search for home place; unlike some conservationists, they do not say "protect the wilderness out there and keep destructive humanity apart from

---

To become "dwellers in the land,"
. . . to fully and honestly come
to know the earth, the crucial and
perhaps only and all-encompassing
task is to understand the place, the
immediate, specific place, where we
live. . . . We must somehow live as
close to it as possible, be in touch
with its particular soils, its waters,
its winds, we must learn its ways, its
capacities, its limits, we must make
its rhythms our patterns, its laws our
guides, its fruits our bounty.

—*Kirkpatrick Sale*, The Ecologist,
    Vol. 14, No. 4, 1984

---

the wilderness." Instead, they are struggling to find a way, as humans, to reinhabit and restore the natural world in a meaningful, constructive, and, by this point in history, a necessarily healing way.

Their strategies for this identification with the biotic community are based on learning the landscape, truly knowing it so that connection is possible. As Peter Berg, one of the founders, puts it in the book *Turtle Talk*: "In bioregional workshops, I've said, learn these words like 'watershed' and

throw them at these scientists. Say 'Not in my watershed, you don't!' Say it like your body, or your home, or your family. Identify with that watershed, identify with that bioregion, identify with those native plants and animals!"

The appeal of bioregionalism, for me, and the reason why it presents such a departure from conventional thinking, is that it does not propose yet another hierarchy, this time with nature on top and culture a corrupted second fiddle. Natural laws may provide guidance, but human culture, too, is equally part of the equation; indeed, bioregionalism sees the finding (or recognition) of the human place as its fundamental project. And the path towards this goal is inextricably bound with developing communities that are integrated with the local, specific ecosystem.

What better way to learn our place, to find our home in the world, than to engage in the restorative work of gardening with native plants? To learn the evolved imperative of plant communities, to understand the processes that drive their continued development, to reinsert humanity and human culture into these processes, not as a controlling force but as a co-evolved partner . . . this is indeed the act of gardening the wilderness (as contradictory as this sounds), and it seems to me to be one of the most available means of reclaiming our identity, asserting our specificity, and reversing the brutal logic that fuels a homogenizing globalism.

🍁   🍁   🍁

Although I fully expected native plants would provide me with an intimate connection to place—an understanding of where it is we and they live and grow—I wasn't quite expecting my introduction to native plant gardening to provide me with an equally vivid lesson in connections with people. It was the disappearing ironweed that did it. True, this was not your average run-of-the-moist-meadow ironweed—it was a *plant with a History*. And that history had much to say about urban land use, community activism, garden generosity and communal shared knowledge . . . all that and a nice flower too.

Close to my home in Toronto, there used to be a fantastic wilderness spot known as Ecology Park. Reclaimed from asphalt, this small urban gem was the fruit of many volunteer hours and committed digging. It was the first community demonstration garden of ecologically appropriate landscaping in Canada, created to transform an old parking lot into typical Ontario flora. A half-acre (one-fifth hectare) in size and divided into many sections, there was a prairie garden, which no doubt informed countless visitors that there were prairies in Ontario too, and a young deciduous (broadleaf) forest. Open sections were a blaze of colour and mingling of textures throughout the summer and fall, when strollers would stop to sit under the sumacs, so close to Spadina and Bloor. In short, an urban oasis.

But history is no less a force in gardens than in the rest of life, and in 1993 the park's precarious tenure on this Toronto Transit Commission land came to an end. Ecology Park was to be dug up to make way for construction of a Light Rapid Transit line down Spadina. There were no mass demonstrations of outrage—after all, who would complain about increased efficiency in public transit—but there were many mournful vigils and ceremonies, and a lot more committed digging: the plants were going to be rescued, dispersed to good homes.

Shamelessly, I prowled the park during its last few weeks, mooching around for plants, asking the horticulturist what was left, offering a sunny sanctuary and some crisp bills. My booty: a cup plant and an ironweed.

I put them out back in midfall, and all during the winter I could watch the stately ironweed, seed cluster intact, from my kitchen table. You'd think

that after a long winter's gawk I could say *exactly* the square inch that harboured my ironweed . . . but in an excessive pruning moment in early spring, I cleaned up all the old stalks and a few weeks later found myself hunting around for telltale signs of new ironweed growth. Nothing. It was not helped by the fact that the location had

Language is becoming homogenized. Foods are becoming homogenized. The things people do or see are becoming homogenized too. When you characterize where you're from, you look out your window at the plants and animals, even if you don't notice them immediately. I think there's something terribly wrong with the loss of a distinct sense of being. It comes down to: Where is my home?

—Earl Campbell, *quoted in* The New York Times, November 14, 1994

expanded to a possible square yard (square metre) of intensively planted space and that ironweed looks a bit like the prolific goldenrod seedlings I was yanking out.

During a visit to *Wildflower* editor Jim Hodgins' garden, I mentioned how hopeful I was about the ironweed, how happy I was to have a fugitive remnant from Ecology Park in my backyard. It turned out that Jim not only knew the *precise* plant I was referring to, but that he had watched its progression over ten years and had been collecting the seeds for seed exchanges over the years. So now my hidden (but I hoped percolating) plant had two very pleasant personal associations, and I continued my prone hunt for the thing.

By June I was in a panic. I had been entrusted with the duty of perpetuating this plant with a History and I had somehow managed to botch it. Luckily, one of the original driving forces behind Ecology Park, Henny Markus, lives close by and I asked her to come and help me look. I milked her for all kinds of information about volunteer seedlings and took advantage of her wealth of botanical knowledge, but unfortunately the final word on our search was negative. Loads of black-eyed Susan babies but no ironweed.

By midsummer I resigned myself to the loss. I went to Otter Valley Native Plants for a replacement ironweed and the owner, Gail Rhynard, speculated that I didn't get enough of the root with my transplant. This probably explains it. But it doesn't explain the disproportionate sense of failure I felt—as if there were an inverse relationship between the disastrously short rootball and deep despair.

My failure has its roots in my sense of responsibility to Henny, to Jim, to the idea of Ecology Park and its dispersed, nurtured future in fragments throughout the city. It's as if I didn't just lose the plant but also an irretrievable connection with an urban experiment in green community space, a plant passage from countless hours of loving labour to me, where the heritage came to a full stop. Somehow I severed the bond.

But then again, maybe not. Perhaps the seed head dispersed its almost infinite potential around the garden—maybe even to neighbours—and I'll find a small seedling poking through the purple coneflower and goldenrod. Maybe then a bit of Ecology Park will return to my garden. Where, by the way, the cup plant flourishes. Phew.

Postscript: At the end of the summer, I passed by Ecology Park and noticed, along with the bulldozers and construction sheds, many tenacious local bloomers surviving the uproar. I considered a midnight raid but the Canadian Wildflower Society's ethical code of conduct got the better of my momentary transgression. With just a few phone calls, the Toronto Transit Commission agreed to a fully legal (even assisted!) plant rescue and now, happily, I feel as if my garden is even more of a mini-Ecology Park—home to some of its gray-headed coneflower, butterfly milkweed, verbena, prairie dock, asters, woodland sunflowers, and an unknown patch that I dug up as a kind of mystery grab bag. Next year . . . .

CHAPTER REFERENCES

City Form and Natural Process. Michael Hough. London: Routledge, 1989.

Redesigning the American Lawn: A Search for Environmental Harmony. F. Herbert Bormann, Diana Balmori and Gordon T. Geballe. New Haven: Yale University Press, 1993.

Turtle Talk: Voices for a Sustainable Future. Christopher and Judith Plant, eds. Gabriola B.C.: New Society Publishers, 1988.

Chapter 3

FROM INVASIVE ABUNDANCE TO THE PROBLEM OF PAUCITY

THE HABITAT CONNECTION

W e were a cheerful group of urban explorers that Saturday morning in High Park, Toronto. Organized by a local horticultural society and benefitting from the combined expertise of the park's horticulturists, we were going on a guided walk of the oak savanna, learning about the park's plant communities from people who have spent years in the field. I think of that tour as a compressed lesson in what ecologists call successional theory, because in just a few hours of time and under three acres (less than a hectare) of space, we saw two possible futures for the park.

The first possible future was the one that began the walk, and it was the vision that clearly animated and excited the whole group. We had stopped at a floppy oddity of dried straw-type stuff; it looked out of place until we learned that this clump of big bluestem, not yet greening for its summer bolt to huge heights, was an integral part of a savanna system, in particular the oak savanna of High Park. The deep roots of this plant serve as a kind of conduit, or root highway, through which

rainwater percolates down to the groundwater. Terry Fahey, a park horticulturist, talked about the difference between the big bluestem clump and turf grass, and the way in which the deep-rooted native bluestem prevents erosion by drawing water down whereas the alien turf grass actually increases the opportunity for water run-off and soil erosion. He was priming us to think systems, training us to see the whole picture in the pieces. And it was a lesson that was amply illustrated by the end of the walk.

The tone of the tour was a casual and comfortable show-and-tell. Someone would point to a plant and then the group would crowd around while Terry and his park colleague, Solomon Boye, regaled us with their store of lore and stock of connections between the specific and the general. It was just after we'd seen the glorious blue of a wild (and rare in this area) patch of lupines and while we were learning about the woodland sunflower that would later infuse the understorey with yellow, that someone pointed out a solitary plant and asked what it was. Terry and Solomon looked at the plant, then at each other, then at the plant again; their faces fell and they started a mumbled exchange of is it, it is, yes . . . it is. It was an odd moment—we were a group in paradise and here was some troubling secret. Terry said something about "remember that plant, we'll get to it later"

Without complexity, populations rise wildly or crash completely—that is, species become weeds or pests or they become extinct.

—*Sara Stein*, Noah's Garden

---

and we continued on our way, through sarsaparilla groundcover (the kids in the group savouring a stick of its licoricelike twig) and on into a sassafras grove with its eerie and airy trunks.

As we emerged from the Carolinian wonder of sassafras right in the middle of the city, we saw that mystery plant again, but this time as far from solitary as rhubarb is from sweet. There was a field of the stuff covering everything, and Terry and Solomon looked like *they'd* just had a munch on raw rhubarb; their faces were almost pained as they started to talk about this plant: the notorious dog-strangling vine. Apparently this non-native botanical intruder is one of the most threatening species of High Park's oak woodlands. It can take over whole areas of diverse plant life in a single season, but it's no superhero. Literally strangling out the native plant community, the vine turns diversity into monoculture, outcompeting instead of cohabiting. It didn't exist in the park just three short years ago; now it's an ominous and omnipresent feature. "This is what High Park might

look like in five years," said Terry disconsolately as he pulled out a symbolic clump of the stuff. Pretty soon, we were all ripping away, participating in an angry gesture of defiance against the second possible future of High Park.

There are some who would say that our gesture was futile. What can twenty people on what amounts to a Saturday stroll do to reverse the combined energy of an evolved and evolving ecosystem? And if plant communities are constantly changing, who are we—as humans—to interfere? Isn't it the height of human arrogance to try to alter and control everything in front of us? Yes—and no.

Granted, our response had more to do with a kind of spontaneous, even frenzied, mass energy (this can happen when you get a crowd of park fans together) than it did with a considered understanding of the park's ecosystem . . . but, hey, we were trusting our more experienced guides. Would it have been futile if, three years ago, someone had spotted that first little, and seemingly innocuous, clump of dog-strangling vine and decided to rip it out? In other words, if human intervention had for once made a choice on the side of good management?

Ah, says a voice that won't—and shouldn't—go away: management. What place has management, *human* (and therefore corrupted, says the voice) management, got in a natural ecosystem? Human management has delivered to us—and delivered us to, it seems—the 1990s phenomenon of environmental assessment panels and reviews, in which government bureaucrats with the help of committed scientists and lawyers make a ridiculous show of understanding, even understanding *completely*, the unknowable imbrications and complexities of an ecosystem, so that they can make supposedly informed management decisions about worthy trade-offs for unworthy dollars. No wonder the word management seems tainted.

But what's the alternative? Sitting back and watching dog-strangling vine take over the diverse vegetation that has somehow managed to survive for so long in the middle of Canada's largest city? The defenders of this sit-back, let-nature-take-its-course position are forgetting one important thing: it's impossible to talk about nature—at least in any pristine, untouched sense of the word—in the context of two hundred acres (eighty hectares) in the middle of the megatropolis. The only way the term nature can retain any meaning in this context is to talk about natural processes, and to include humans and human culture in the equation.

In this vision, what we can do is set in motion the conditions under which natural processes can charge ahead with their own logic, their own long-evolved imperative. In the case of High Park, for example, this would mean taking out the vine, an

---

INVASIVE PLANTS IN ONTARIO

A report, called *Invasive Plants of Natural Habitats in Canada*, prepared for the Canadian Wildlife Service in cooperation with the Canadian Museum of Nature, lists the following invasive alien species as problems in Ontario.

WETLAND SPECIES

- **Eurasian watermilfoil (***Myriophyllum spicatum***)** Native to Europe, Asia and northern Africa, it was probably introduced to North America in the 1940s.
- **European frog-bit (***Hydrocharis morsus-ranae***)** A Eurasian species deliberately introduced for horticultural purposes in Ottawa's Central Experimental Farm in 1932, it has now spread down Lakes Ontario and Erie to Rondeau Park and up the Ottawa River almost to Pembroke.
- **Flowering-rush (***Butomus umbellatus***)** Native to Eurasia, it displaces and outcompetes native willows and cattails.
- **Glossy buckthorn (***Rhamnus frangula***)** A European native, this small tree is one of the most invasive aliens in the Ottawa area.

- **Purple loosestrife (***Lythrum salicaria***)** Native to Eurasia, it arrived in North America in the early 1800s.
- **Reed canary grass (***Phalaris arundinacea***)** Both native to North America and introduced in the form of European cultivars as forage plants.

UPLAND SPECIES

- **Common buckthorn (***Rhamnus cathartica***)** This European native shrub or small tree is invasive mainly in southern Ontario.
- **Garlic mustard (***Alliaria petiolata***)** Native to Europe and probably introduced in Canada as a medicinal plant or a vegetable, it is primarily a problem in the forests of southern Ontario, where it displaces native ground-cover species.
- **Glossy buckthorn (***Rhamnus frangula***)** See list of wetland species.
- **Leafy spurge (***Euphorbia esula***)** A European and temperate Asia native, probably introduced to North America in contaminated ballast in the early 1800s, it is primarily a problem in southern Ontario where it decreases the diversity of native vegetation.

invasive alien species that is compromising the functioning of an ecosystem and impairing the park's natural processes.

Of course, it's at this juncture that we get into the sticky problem of judgement calls: what makes the vine any less "natural" than the native blue lupines? Who decides that the vine is impairing natural processes whereas the lupines are all a cosy, reassuring part of the picture? It may sound absurd at first, but I think we should ask the park: what does it want to be? We'll get our answer: while an ecosystem may be a lousy conversationalist (for the many of us who've yet to learn the language but are alert to its faint whispers), it's a great guide. An oak savanna wants to be just that—a diverse, functioning ecosystem, not a monoculture.

* * *

North America has experienced many high-profile incidents over the years that demonstrate the importance of biodiversity and the problems of monoculture—from the decimation of street tree elm populations via Dutch elm disease to dramatic corn crop failures—but we're continuing to court a

---

For information about purple loosestrife and to report sightings (how appropriate is the vaguely criminal inference), contact the Ontario Ministry of Natural Resource's Invading Species Hotline at 1-800-563-7711; or the Canadian Wildlife Federation's Loosestrife Sightings Hotline at 1-800-565-6305.

The Ontario Federation of Anglers and Hunters coordinates Project Purple, a community effort to educate people about this wetland weed and to assist in eradication. Contact the Federation at (705) 748-6324 for more information.

---

relearning of the lesson in habitats throughout Ontario. While dog-strangling vine may be a relatively localized example, there are countless other invasive alien species that are threatening the biodiversity, and thus health, of ecosystems across the province.

Think of all those gorgeous tracts of purple that you can see along roadsides and in wet places from late July to September: gorgeous but disastrous purple loosestrife. Like all invasive alien plant species, the problem is not simply that a botanical intruder has muscled into the landscape; it's that it has no manners whatsoever and has completely monopolized the party. Purple loosestrife takes over and displaces the original components of the community, at the expense of its native inhabitants—plant and animal. Many birds that normally nest in wetlands, such as grebes and terns, won't nest in purple loosestrife. Other animals, such as muskrat, that find their food in wetlands, won't eat it. As this quick spreader rapidly reproduces (as many as 2.7 million seeds per plant per year), it turns once thriving and complex wetlands into the ecological equivalents of monocultural lawns.

Though not an intentionally introduced species (instead, it's thought to have arrived via ship ballast or on imported animals or feed in the early 1800s), the invasion of purple loosestrife has been assisted by home gardeners and the nursery trade. Wildflower seed mixtures used to regularly contain purple loosestrife, and garden centres offer it for sale. There was a period in which nurseries were promoting a "seedless" cultivar, which unfortunately turned out to produce viable seed when the pollen from wild loosestrife fertilized it. In the absence of natural predators and with its prolific tendencies, it's no surprise that purple loosestrife is estimated to claim 469,300 acres (190,000 ha) across North America each year and is present in approximately half of Ontario's 3.04 million acres

(1.23 million ha) of wetlands, according to the Ontario Federation of Anglers and Hunters.

When dealing with such impossibly huge numbers, it's easy to see why efforts to deal with the invasion have not been successful. Chemical herbicide control is not workable because of the difficulty of restricting the effects to purple loosestrife alone, without affecting the whole aquatic ecosystem. Hand-pulling, promoted by a number of groups, may make us feel like we're doing something positive, but clearly we'd need to have the whole province involved before we actually made a dent. Instead, Ontario is going the biological predator route, by introducing three European beetles that feed exclusively on purple loosestrife. If the introduction of three non-native pests to deal with this problem seems not only ironic but potentially dangerous, about all we can do is cross our fingers, hope the scientists are right and pray for the demise of the purple plague.

One other thing we can do is to keep in mind that invasive alien species tend to colonize and have most success in areas that, for mainly human reasons, have already been degraded. Once the habitat has been disturbed and modified, it is under stress and vulnerable to invasion by opportunistic species. Thus, it makes more sense to see the invasive alien plants not as the cause of an ecological problem but as the symptom: if we make habitat health our priority, we'll have a better chance of eradicating the root cause and preventing future problems.

❦   ❦   ❦

It's important to note that most exotic or alien species that we introduce to our gardens pose no threat whatsoever to natural plant communities. However, it is the species that are capable of naturalizing that are cause for concern. According to some experts, of the approximately twenty-six hundred vascular plants that grow wild in Ontario,

roughly seven hundred are not native. Inevitably (since they've left their native checks and balances behind), some of these alien species have become invasive.

Along with the highly visible problem of invasives taking over native plant communities and outcompeting the natural vegetation, there are

From now on, it is vital that everyone who feels inclined to change or cut away or drain or spray or plant any strip or corner of the land should ask themselves three questions: what animals and plants live in it, what beauty and interest may be lost, and what extra risk changing it will add to the accumulating instability of communities.

—*Charles S. Elton*, The Ecology of Invasions by Plants and Animals

also a few less apparent but equally disturbing results. Some alien species will hybridize with native plant populations, changing the genetic make-up of indigenous species, altering the characteristics they have evolved in order to thrive in a particular location. The genetically altered plants may thus be less able to withstand local pressures and the more long-term, global climate changes due to the greenhouse effect. As well, the alien species may bring along with them certain diseases, fungi, or pests that can harm native plant populations.

Too often, we just don't know what the results

will be to an ecosystem, yet these unintentional experiments can do and have done irreparable damage.

* * *

While it might seem a bizarre leap in logic to move from the problem of overabundance in invasive alien plant species to the relative rarity of threatened plants, there is a significant connection between these two: in the case of invasive alien plants, we have so degraded the landscape that we have created the conditions required by these species to take over; in the case of rare plants, we have so degraded the landscape that the plants' habitat has disappeared, or at least been severely compromised. Thus, habitat destruction is the unifying factor for both.

In such a huge country as Canada, it's hard to imagine that we are indeed faced with the enormous problem of habitat loss. So much of our shared cultural identity is based on the idea of wilderness expanses. Yet if one enumerates the lost and threatened landscapes in this country, a different picture emerges. According to the

---

PLANT SPECIES AT RISK IN CANADA

Extirpated Blue-eyed Mary; Illinois tick trefoil.

Endangered Cucumber tree; Engelmann's quillwort; Furbish's lousewort; Gattinger's agalinis; heart-leaved plantain; hoary mountain mint; large whorled pogonia; mountain avens (Eastern population); pink coreopsis; pink milkwort; prickly pear cactus (Eastern population); Skinner's agalinis; slender bush clover; slender mouse-ear cress; small white lady's slipper; small whorled pogonia; southern maidenhair fern; spotted wintergreen; thread-leaved sundew; waterpennywort; western prairie fringed orchid; white prairie gentian; wood poppy.

Threatened American chestnut; American ginseng; American water-willow; Anticosti aster; Athabasca thrift; bird's foot violet; blue ash; bluehearts; blunt-lobed woodsia; colicroot; deerberry; giant helleborine; golden crest; golden seal; Kentucky coffee tree; mosquito fern; nodding pogonia; Pitcher's thistle; Plymouth gentian; purple twayblade; red mulberry; redroot; round-leaved greenbrier (Ontario population); sand verbena; small-flowered lipocarpha; sweet pepperbush; Tyrrell's willow; Van Brunt's Jacob's ladder; western blue flag; western spiderwort.

Vulnerable American columbo; Bathurst aster; branched bartonia; broad beech fern; dense blazing star; dwarf hackberry; false rue-anemone; few-flowered club-rush; green dragon; Gulf of St. Lawrence aster; Hill's pondweed; hop tree; Indian plantain; lilaeopsis; Long's bulrush; Macoun's meadowfoam; New Jersey rush; phantom orchid; prairie rose; prairie white-fringed orchid; Provancher's fleabane; Shumard oak; smooth goosefoot; soapweed; swamp rose mallow; Victorin's gentian; Victorin's water hemlock; western silver-leaf aster; wild hyacinth.

Source: Committee on the Status of Endangered Wildlife in Canada, 1994

World Wildlife Fund, Canada's wilderness is disappearing at a rate of .38 square mile (1 square km) *an hour.*

With approximately 25 percent of Canada's population (and more than half of Ontario's population) living in southern Ontario, this province is under particular stress from urban encroachment. The Carolinian Region (also known as the Deciduous Forest Region), for example, a region that stretches from the southernmost tip of Canada at Lake Erie and along its shore up to Grand Bend on Lake Huron and in a line across to Toronto, occupies a tiny percentage of Canada's land mass (just one-quarter of 1 percent), yet is home to an ecological community found nowhere else in this country. With disastrous consequences, over 90 percent of the original Carolinian vegetation has been destroyed. The result is that 40 percent of Canada's rare, threatened, and endangered species are Carolinian. Of the rare plant species so far identified in Ontario, approximately 40 percent are restricted to the Carolinian zone, with 65 percent occurring there. As the book *Conserving Carolinian Canada* sums it up: "More endangered species are contained here than in any other Canadian life zone."

The situation is equally dire in Canada's wetlands. Although long treated as wastelands rather than the highly productive life-support systems they are, wetlands recharge aquifers, store groundwater, break down wastes, modify water cycles, and protect land from erosion. Approximately 14 percent of Canada's total area consists of wetlands. But according to the Wildlife Habitat Canada report "Wetland Stewardship in Ontario 1990–1993," "since European settlement, three-quarters of southern Ontario's original wetland area has disappeared, and the remaining areas are threatened by continuing drainage, pollution, and development." The Federation of Ontario Naturalists estimates that a further 1 to 2 percent of Ontario's wet-

lands are lost each year—9,880 acres (4,0
Obviously, such changes cannot occur
affecting the flora and fauna that depend
lands in Ontario: over 142 species of birds, 11 of mammals, 19 of amphibians and reptiles, and over 350 of plants.

The litany could continue for forests, prairies, savannas, and on and on. The point is that such changes don't occur in isolation. Unlike invasive alien species, which don't bring along their food chains, thus making their ecological isolation the problem, habitat loss takes all the mutual associations and biotic connections down to destruction too. We lose habitat and we lose those species that depend on the habitat.

*   *   *

Bearing in mind the connection between habitat loss and rare plants, where are we in terms of protection in Canada? The groundbreaking U.N. report from the Brundtland Commission (the report that popularized the idea of sustainable development) recommended that countries set aside 12 percent of their land mass as legally protected areas. According to the World Wildlife

---

An excellent source of information about Ontario's rare plants is the Ontario Natural Heritage Information Centre. They have drawn up a draft list of 655 species that they are tracking; 543 of those species have been identified in fewer than twenty places in Ontario, 112 species at twenty to one hundred places.

To receive a copy of the rare vascular plant list or to find out how you can support the centre's work, contact the Natural Heritage Information Centre, P.O. Box 7000, Peterborough, Ontario K9J 8M5.

Fund's book *Endangered Spaces*, "Canada is well short, at 6.3 per cent (only 2.6 per cent if we excluded areas where logging, mining, or hunting are permitted)."

And we're not doing much better when it comes to protection of individual species. What we've got in Ontario is something called the Endangered Species Act, proclaimed law in 1971. Under this Act, it's illegal to "kill, injure, interfere with or take" (or attempt to do same) any species of flora or fauna listed in the regulations as threatened with extinction. It's also illegal to "destroy or interfere with" the habitat of any species listed. The Act's muscle comes in the form of a fine of up to $50,000 and/or up to two years of imprisonment. Strong-sounding stuff.

Unfortunately, only eight plants are currently listed in the regulations as threatened with extinction, and two of those are listed only in restricted locations (locations which it turns out are incorrect). In other words, out of approximately two thousand native species of flowering plants in Ontario, only eight have any legislated protection. Which would be fine if the rest, along with their habitats, were flourishing.

Not so, say the experts examining the issue. According to George W. Argus and Kathleen M. Pryer, in their 1990 book *Rare Vascular Plants in Canada*, 355 of Ontario's native vascular plants are rare. The province has the second-highest number after British Columbia, with 426. (To be designated as rare, the plant must exist in a limited area and/or in low numbers.) Nationally, their prognosis is equally startling: "There are about 3269 native species of vascular plants in the flora of Canada (Scoggan 1978–1979). We have recognized 1009 taxa, or about 25–30% of the flora, as rare in Canada." Almost one-third!

Others set a higher number. Larry Lamb, in a 1991 issue of *Wildflower*, wrote that there are approximately 450 rare, threatened, or endangered native plant species in Ontario—20 percent of all provincial flora.

Nationally, the Committee on the Status of Endangered Wildlife in Canada (COSEWIC) reviews the status of vascular plants in Canada in an ongoing project to determine which are threatened with extinction. When COSEWIC released its catalogue of species at risk in Canada in April 1994, there were 255 species listed, 84 of them plants. It's important to note that inclusion on the

BRAZIL OF THE NORTH?

According to a report called *Brazil of the North: The National and Global Crisis in Canada's Forests*, published by Canada's Future Forest Alliance of New Denver, British Columbia, there are strong parallels between the destruction of Canada's forests and the problem of global rainforest loss. The report compares the situation in Canada and Brazil, and presents the following statistics.

- In Canada, one acre (0.4 ha) of forest is clearcut or burned every 12 seconds.
- In Brazil, one acre (0.4 ha) of forest is clearcut or burned every 9 seconds.
- 45 percent of Canada is covered by forest.
- 41 percent of Brazil is covered by forest.
- Canada's size is 3.8 million square miles (9.9 million square km).
- Brazil's size is 3.2 million square miles (8.5 million square km).
- 2.6 percent of Canada's forest is officially protected.
- 9.4 percent of Brazil's forest is officially protected.

Source: *Wildflower*, Summer 1994, from *Brazil of the North*

COSEWIC list offers no protection, since there's no federal endangered species law that requires governments to protect those species or prevent the destruction of their habitat (even though the Green Plan called for the creation of a federal protection policy by the end of 1993). I guess we should consider ourselves lucky in Ontario to have even eight plants protected . . .

❦   ❦   ❦

Reading through the stack of documents on endangered species in Canada, it's easy to get the impression that everything comes down to a flat-out race between education and catastrophe. Over and over again, in reports from botanists and field biologists and scientists who have spent their professional lives trying to quantify and qualify data, one comes up against admissions of huge gaps. A 1991 Environment Canada report, for example, suggests that over 53,000 species in Canada remain to be identified and described! While plant identification is up there as a success story (with 98 percent of Canada's vascular plants positively identified), what about the insects that some plants depend on for pollination? A 1993 Environment Canada report, "Endangered Plants and Invertebrates in Canada," prepared by the Canadian Nature Federation, has this to say about insects: "In Canada, only about half of the estimated 66,610 insect species are described or formally recorded . . . and only a fraction of these have been placed in any useful biosystematic context." Or the soil bacteria and fungi with which plants live in mutual association? The same report: "With regards to soil fauna, scientists say that we do not know what we have, so we cannot estimate what we are losing, and can only speculate on the consequences of such losses," and "it is estimated that less than 5 percent of the existing fungi worldwide have been described or reported, and the situation in Canada is likely not much better."

I don't mean to dwell on this litany of losses and ignorance to discourage us all or to suggest that it's amazing we can grow anything in our gardens when, collectively, we know so little about the world of which we're a part. Rather, it's to put that staggeringly insufficient number eight in some kind of context. With years of study, with hundreds of good people working to answer questions, with lobbying and concerned groups and international agreements and conventions, with volunteers in the field counting ants and orchids . . . all this and we're still at the number eight in Ontario. Suddenly gardening becomes an urgent endeavour. And our efforts should not be limited to the growing season: we can spend the non-growing season writing letters, urging protection of what we have left.

❦   ❦   ❦

The photo was gorgeous: a sea of trilliums, bursting with white flowers, just the thing to warm gardeners' hearts after a long, cold winter. It was the caption that made me gasp: "You can transplant tril-

---

WORLD'S ENDANGERED SPECIES

According to a 1989 study by Reid and Miller, quoted in *Conserving the World's Biological Diversity*, 19,078 species of plants are threatened with extinction worldwide.

- 384 plant species are extinct post-1600.
- 3,325 plant species are endangered.
- 3,022 plant species are vulnerable.
- 6,749 plant species are rare.
- 5,598 plant species are known to be endangered, vulnerable or rare, but there is not enough information to pinpoint the category.

liums from the wild, if you can find some—just leave plenty to regenerate." Eeks. With my mind racing to the thought of hordes of Ontario gardeners illegally pillaging provincial parks (which, after all, are about the only places where such floral seas flourish), I dashed off a letter to the newspaper's editor and sat back to wonder at how a garden writer could encourage such destruction.

Depressingly, he was right about one thing: you can transplant trilliums from the wild. Not only if you can find them, but also if you don't care at all about the future of native plant communities. Because these wild plant communities are not protected in Ontario. As surprising as it sounds (particularly for those of us who grew up being told that it was illegal to dig trilliums), there is absolutely no legal protection for almost all native wildflowers growing in the wild. Sure, you can't mess with anything growing in a provincial park (unless you're a logging company, in which case, rare species or not, you can legally destroy up to half the park) but what about the rest of Ontario? Virtually unprotected.

So "if you can find some" . . . leave them for everyone to enjoy in the wild. Because it doesn't take complicated calculations to determine that a whole province of wild-plant diggers would very soon mean one more species added to the endangered list.

CHAPTER REFERENCES

Conserving Carolinian Canada. Gary M. Allen, Paul F. J. Eagles and Steven D. Price, eds. Waterloo: University of Waterloo Press, 1990.

Conserving the World's Biological Diversity. Jeffrey A. McNeely et al. Washington: International Union for Conservation of Nature and Natural Resources, 1990.

ONTARIO ENDANGERED SPECIES

PLANTS LISTED IN ONTARIO'S ENDANGERED SPECIES ACT

1. *Cypripedium candidum*, small white lady's-slipper orchid
2. *Isotria medeoloides*, small whorled pogonia
3. *Isotria verticillata*, large whorled pogonia
4. *Magnolia acuminata*, cucumber tree
5. *Opuntia humifusa*, prickly pear cactus
6. *Plantago cordata*, heart-leaved plantain
7. *Stylophorum diphyllum*, wood poppy
8. *Pycnanthemum incanum*, hoary mountain mint

"The [Ontario Endangered Species] legislation came too late, however, to save the following species. Among those now believed to be extirpated in Ontario are: trail plant (*Adenocanlon bicolor*), giant hyssop (*Agastache scrophulariaefolia*), blue-eyed mary (*Collinsia verna*), downy gentian (*Gentiana puberulenta*), yellow fringed orchis (*Habenaria ciliaris*), climbing hempweed (*Mikania scandens*), cowbane (*Oxypolis rigidior*), purple prairie clover (*Petalostemum purpureum*), fire pink (*Silene virginica*), and wood poppy (*Stylophorum diphyllum*)."

—Larry Lamb, *Wildflower*, Spring 1986

(After the above was originally published, wood poppies were rediscovered in the wild near London, Ontario.)

The Ecology of Invasions by Plants and Animals.
Charles S. Elton. New York: Wiley, 1958.

"Endangered Plants and Invertebrates in Canada."
Canadian Nature Federation. Ottawa: Canadian
Wildlife Service, Environment Canada, 1993.

Endangered Spaces: The Future for Canada's Wilderness. Monte Hummel, ed. Toronto: Key Porter,
1989.

Invasive Plants of Natural Habitats in Canada. David
J. White, Erich Haber and Cathy Keddy. Ottawa:
Canadian Wildlife Service, 1993.

*Noah's Garden: Restoring the Ecology of Our Own
Back Yards.* Sara Stein. Boston: Houghton Mifflin,
1993.

Rare Vascular Plants in Canada: Our Natural Heritage. George W. Argus and Kathleen M. Pryer.
Ottawa: Canadian Museum of Nature, 1990.

"Wetland Stewardship in Ontario 1990–1993."
Ottawa: Wildlife Habitat Canada, 1994.

Part 2

NATIVE PLANT COMMUNITIES

Chapter 4

WOODLAND HABITAT

In the past ten or fifteen years, quite a few books have been published on the subject of shade gardening. Almost all of them start from a position of assumed disenchantment, and their address to the reader takes on a tone of cheerleading and persuasion, along the lines of "don't be distraught by the hitherto disaster of shade, use it to your advantage and create a gorgeous shade garden." I assume this stance is necessitated by a gardening market dominated by advice for the "perfect" conditions of full sun. I'm not sure who first decided that full sun meant perfection, but we seem to have bought into the picture of bright, showy, sun-loving flowers for our gardens. Anything less than all-day, unimpeded solar access constitutes a "problem site."

While the sunny ideal may have been appropriate for all the treeless suburbs of the 1950s, it hardly resonates today, when tree-planting programs are in full swing throughout the province. Neighbourhood groups are lobbying for better urban tree care and replacement; conservation organizations are replanting and reforesting disturbed sites; school groups are tearing out asphalt and planting trees; municipalities are tightening up by-laws regarding tree removal, in some cases rendering the cutting down of trees, even on private property, illegal. In other words, after centuries of slash and clear, we are finally beginning to *value* trees.

For the native plant gardener, a tree-rich garden site offers one of the most exciting possibilities for beautiful landscaping: the opportunity to create woodland habitat. From the first exuberant blooms of spring, when woodland gardens are at their peak in terms of showy colour, to the soothing cooling greens of summer's lush textures, to the coloured canopy of autumn's rich blast to the dramatic patterns of winter branches—woodland gardens offer up a diverse and ever-changing plant palette for the gardener's experimentation.

Nature has evolved ingenious ways to announce forest beauty: before trees leaf out in spring, legions of native plants emerge with colourful blooms to attract pollinators. Many of these can be used in a woodland garden, creating a carpet of spring beauty. As tree leaves emerge and the shade cover increases, some spring bloomers go dormant (these are called spring ephemerals), and others take over to cover the soil with lush, green growth. Although there are relatively few brassy bloomers

---

A fast-growing forest tree absorbs up to forty-eight pounds [22 kg] of carbon dioxide a year; that adds up to ten tons per acre [0.4 ha] of trees—enough to offset the carbon dioxide produced by driving a car 21,000 miles [33,800 km].

—R. Neil Sampson, Shading Our Cities

---

in summer, native plant gardeners do have some to choose from and with careful planning your woodland garden can include summer colour. By autumn, of course, the colour interest has moved upwards, to the array of changing leaf colours in deciduous trees.

(Contrast this with the limited choices available to the conventional or exotic plant gardener in shade: impatiens, hostas, vinca, pachysandra, and not a whole lot else. No wonder shade gardening developed such a reputation for difficulty. There's not a lot more to say once you've said it with the big shady four.)

But colour is only a part of the satisfaction of woodland gardening. I can think of no other type of gardening in which textures and leaf colour and foliage shape take on such importance and provide so much in the way of interest. For a good part of

the gardening season—after the flush of spring—these are the major variables you'll be dealing with in the woodland landscape.

I have a rather arbitrary definition of urban woodland gardens, one that would perhaps startle the ecologist and alarm the purist. Chances are that many of us do not actually *live* in a forest, and thus when I talk about woodland gardens, I'm referring not so much to the presence of numerous overstorey trees but rather to the conditions of shade. I realize that this might seem strange in a book wedded to the idea of restoring natural habitats (and "shade" is in no sense a habitat designation as "woodland" is), but I'm trying to be realistic. If you've got trees, use them to provide the dominant structure for your woodland garden; if you don't have trees but you have space, plant many; but if you're in small, cramped, shady quarters with no room for trees, you can still use typical woodland plants to create a satisfying landscape that refers to, without actually re-creating, woodland habitat. I'd be out of touch with reality if I tried to claim that the one Norway maple on my small front yard is a forest, but that single tree provides all the shade I need to support the native woodland plants I've installed. It may not say much about southern Ontario's natural forests, but it has a lot to say about urban compromise and what is indeed possible in our cities. So even if you're long on shade but short on trees, this section is for you too: we'll call it woodland, even though the forest may be comprised of neighbouring apartment buildings, or monster homes, or tall fences. Urban ecology, indeed.

As with any form of naturalistic gardening, it's necessary to look at the native plant community you're trying to replicate and examine the forces that shape it. For woodland gardens, this means looking at the forest.

In the deciduous forests of southern Ontario and the more northerly mixed forests, the cycle of leaf growth and death dictates much in relation to surrounding vegetation. The bare branches of spring allow unfiltered sunlight to reach the earth and warm it, causing a flurry of growth in the woodland plants adapted to these conditions. Typically, woodlands are at their floriferous peak at this time, with trilliums, hepaticas, spring beauty, Virginia bluebells, bellwort, foamflower, trout lilies, and more—carpets of white, yellow, blue, pink, and purple. (According to John Diekelmann and Robert Schuster, in *Natural Landscaping*, 70 percent of forest plant species flower in the spring.) As the forest begins to leaf out, conditions become shadier and the floral display begins to wane. Some plants disappear above ground altogether, heading underground to store nutrients for next year's burst. Others lose their flowers and put their energy into seed and leaf production. These are just a few of the broad adaptive mechanisms woodland plants have developed to cope with the forest's shady cover.

In many ways, it is the autumn deciduous leaf drop that performs one of the most important functions in the woodland: the creation of rich, fertile, humusy soil. As the leaves fall from the trees and carpet the forest floor, they return their nutrients to the soil and help to create the friable, loose texture of woodland soils. The duff, or leaf fragments, also optimize aeration, water retention, and micro flora and fauna. (For example, leaves are preferred spider habitat, and spiders are major predators of garden "pests.")

For the woodland gardener, this is one of the most important things to remember: under natural conditions, woodland plants live in excellent soil, rich in organic matter, and every year the forest offers up more nourishment in the form of fallen leaves. For the health of your woodland plants, you'll need to re-create these conditions. If you don't have enough leaves from your own trees, you'll need to beg them from elsewhere, or supplement the soil with organic amendments such as compost. (Commercial fertilizers won't do—you need both nutrients and organic matter, and liquid

---

South of Muskoka, Haliburton, Renfrew and northern Bruce counties, about 75% of forest cover was removed during agricultural settlement. . . . About 17 counties and regional municipalities now have less than 20% forest cover, some with less than 5%.

—John L. Riley and Pat Mohr,
    The Natural Heritage of Southern Ontario's
    Settled Landscapes

---

or pellet fertilizers don't add anything in the way of that all-important organic matter.)

These are the highly general considerations in woodland habitat. There are scores of different forest communities throughout Ontario, from swampy wet forests to dry pine forests and many more. If you're interested in re-creating a locally specific and indigenous woodland community with trees specific to your area, you will need to do some research (via naturalist groups, books, native plant societies, field botanists, museums, or books).

After you've explored the forest communities of your region to learn about typical plant associations, you'll need to evaluate your own site. (See the chapter on design, Chapter 7, for more information.) There are many questions you should ask yourself and the answers will determine the kind of woodland garden you create. For example, what trees are currently on the site? Are they young or mature? Healthy or stressed? Should you be thinking about replacing old and dying trees? Would you like a denser tree cover? Is there a variety of tree species or a monoculture? Would you like to introduce more diversity into the tree community? Are the trees deciduous or evergreen, or a mix? Do the existing trees thrive in, and indeed create or maintain (through dropping leaves or needles), acidic, neutral, or alkaline conditions? How polluted is the air? (Some trees just can't cope with airborne contaminants.) Does the site receive salt from the road in winter? (Some trees can withstand this better than others.) Do the trees create a dense shade or a light and airy canopy cover? Do the trees need pruning? Is there a diversity of tree heights? Are the trees attractive to various birds, providing food source or cover? Are they attractive to you? Are there any standing stumps or snags that you can incorporate into your woodland design?

You'll need to consider the state of the soil as well. As already outlined, woodland plants require fertile, humusy soil, high in organic matter (including twigs, bark, nut shells, leaves, branches, and roots). If you're starting with sandy or clay soil, you'll need to improve the soil with additions of compost and leaf mulch—lots of it. If the soil is severely depleted and the tree cover is not too thick, you may want to consider planting a leguminous cover crop, which will be turned under, to add nitrogen and organic material to the soil before you do any woodland planting. Ken Druse, in his book *The Natural Garden*, states that a "good cover crop of legumes can provide up to 150 pounds of nitrogen per acre [68 kg per 0.4 ha], the equivalent of adding 12 1/2 tons [13.7 tonnes] of cow manure." (This is a possibility only for gardeners starting from scratch with their woodland gardens.) Even if you have good soil to begin with, you should always add organic material to your soil, once a year at least, in the form of compost or leaf mould or dead leaves.

The soil's pH is also an important consideration, as it will determine, to some degree, the species of plants you can grow. For a long time,

AESTHETIC CONSIDERATIONS REGARDING TREE CHOICES

- What size will the tree eventually reach?
- Will it interfere with overhead services and, if yes, should you choose a smaller species?
- Based on research into the tree's particular needs, what is the minimum planting distance from neighbouring trees?
- What kind of shade does it provide?
- Will the tree buffer street noises?
- What is the tree's shape: columnar (vertical, with a sence of height); fastigate (narrow, with ascending branches); rounded (provides dense shade); weeping?
- What colours are the tree's flowers, fruits, and leaves?
- What does the bark look like in winter?
- Does the tree provide fruit, nuts or nesting areas for birds and wildlife?
- Will the tree constitute a safety or security risk, especially at night?

most native plant authorities were adamant about the need for acidic soil in the woodland garden. While it is true that many native woodland plants do well in slightly acidic soil, in my own experience and in talking with native plant gardeners, I have found that the tolerance range is generally wider than those early books suggest, and that most of the plants described in the woodland plant list in Chapter 9 will do just fine in neutral soil (exceptions are noted in the list). However, there are plants that need acidic soil, and you should know your soil's pH for this reason. (See Chapter 7 for information on determining soil pH.) I would opt for a conservative approach if you determine that your soil is either highly acidic or highly alkaline: changing the pH of the soil of a large area is a daunting, ongoing activity. It's much better to work with what you have.

PLANT CHOICES

After you've evaluated your conditions thoroughly (again, see Chapter 7 for more information), you're ready to make some design decisions and plant choices. I urge you to study local woodlands to see what works in your area, as the following list is necessarily general. (For full descriptions and cultivation information about some of the plants, here marked with an asterisk, see the plant listings for shady woodlands in Chapter 9.)

WILDFLOWERS

Spring-flowering Woodland Wildflowers
bloodroot (Sanguinaria canadensis)*; Dutchman's breeches (Dicentra cucullaria)*; trout lily (Erythronium americanum)*; Canada anemone (Anemone canadensis)*; cut-leaved toothwort (Dentaria lacinata)*; trillium (Trillium grandiflorum)*; wild ginger (Asarum canadense)*; sharp-lobed hepatica (Hepatica acutiloba)*; wood poppy (Stylophorum diphyllum)*; foamflower (Tiarella cordifolia)*; spring beauty (Claytonia virginica)*; Virginia bluebells

(Mertensia virginica)*; Jack-in-the-pulpit (Arisaema triphyllum)*; baneberry (Actaea rubra)

Woodland Wildflowers That Require Acidic Soil
bluebead lily (Clintonia borealis); wintergreen (Gaultheria procumbens); Canada mayflower (Maianthemum canadense)*; starflower (Trientalis bore-

---

If you're gardening in a permanently shady site (that caused by surrounding buildings, for example), you won't have much luck with the spring ephemeral species, which require sunlight in the spring.

---

alis); wood sorrel (Oxalis montana); partridgeberry (Mitchella repens); bunchberry (Cornus canadensis); painted trillium (Trillium undulatum); round-lobed hepatica (Hepatica americana)

Woodland Groundcovers
foamflower (Tiarella cordifolia)*; wild blue phlox (Phlox divaricata)*; partridgebery (Mitchella repens); baneberry (Actaea rubra); wild ginger (Asarum canadense)*; violet (Viola canadensis)*; barren strawberry (Waldsteinia fragarioides); goldthread (Coptis groenlandica)*; wild geranium (Geranium maculatum)*

Summer-blooming Woodland Wildflowers
black snakeroot (Cimicifuga racemosa)*; wood lily (Lilium philadelphium); Canada lily (Lilium canadense)*; woodland sunflower (Helianthus divaricatus)*; bee balm (Monarda didyma)*; heart-leaved aster (Aster cordifolius); wild leek (Allium tricoccum); pale touch-me-not (Impatiens pallida); jewelweed or spotted touch-me-not (Impatiens capensis)*

Woodland Wildflowers for Foliage Interest

blue cohosh (*Caulophyllum thalictroides*)*; twinleaf (*Jeffersonia diphylla*)*; Solomon's-seal (*Polygonatum biflorum*)*; false Solomon's-seal (*Smilacina racemosa*); mayapple (*Podophyllum peltatum*)*; green dragon (*Arisaema draconitum*)*

SHRUBS

Shrubs for Sunny Sites

gray dogwood (*Cornus racemosa*); riverbank grape (*Vitis riparia*); nannyberry (*Viburnum lentago*); New Jersey tea (*Ceanothus americanus*); shadbush/serviceberry (*Amelanchier arborea*); staghorn sumac (*Rhus typhina*)

Shrubs for Sunny Wet Sites

speckled alder (*Alnus rugosa*); prickly ash (*Zanthoxylum americanum*); red osier dogwood (*Cornus stolonifera*); elderberry (*Sambucus canadensis*); large cranberry (*Vaccinium macrocarpon*); nannyberry (*Viburnum lentago*)

Shrubs for Shady Sites

nannyberry (*Viburnum lentago*); redbud (*Cercis canadensis*); alternate-leaved dogwood (*Cornus alternifolia*)

Shrubs for Shady Wet Sites

alternate-leaved dogwood (*Cornus alternifolia*); elderberry (*Sambucus canadensis*); large cranberry (*Vaccinium macrocarpon*); nannyberry (*Viburnum lentago*)

Shrubs of Ontario by James Soper and Margaret Heimburger is an excellent publication that is full of detailed information—including distribution maps—about Ontario's native shrubs.

Carolinian Shrubs

pawpaw (*Asimina triloba*); spicebush (*Lindera benzoin*); burning bush (*Euonymus atropurpureus*); flowering dogwood (*Cornus florida*); sassafras (*Sassafras albidum*); dwarf hackberry (*Celtis tenuifolia*); dwarf chestnut oak (*Quercus prinoides*); wild crabapple (*Malus coronaria*); shrubby St. John's-wort (*Hypericum prolificum*)

TREES

Trees of the Carolinian Zone (Deciduous Forest Region)

tulip (*Liriodendron tulipifera*); cucumber (*Magnolia acuminata*); Kentucky coffee tree (*Gymnocladus dioicus*); redbud (*Cercis canadensis*); pignut hickory (*Carya glabra*); hop-tree (*Ptelea trifoliata*); sycamore (*Plantanus occidentalis*); sassafras (*Sassafras albidum*); flowering dogwood (*Cornus florida*); beech (*Fagus grandifolia*); sugar maple (*Acer saccharum*); black walnut (*Juglans nigra*); shagbark hickory (*Carya ovata*); black oak (*Quercus velutina*); hornbeam or ironwood (*Carpinus caroliniana*); black maple (*Acer nigrum*); silver maple (*Acer saccharinum*); red maple (*Acer rubrum*)

Trees of the Great Lakes–St. Lawrence Forest Region

eastern white pine (*Pinus strobus*); red pine (*Pinus resinosa*); eastern hemlock (*Tsuga canadensis*); balsam fir (*Abies balsamea*); eastern white cedar (*Thuja occidentalis*); yellow birch (*Betula alleghaniensis*); American mountain ash (*Sorbus americana*); sugar maple (*Acer saccharum*); striped maple (*Acer pensylvanicum*); white ash (*Fraxinus americana*)

Trees of the Boreal Forest Region

jack pine (*Pinus banksiana*); tamarack (*Larix laricina*); white spruce (*Picea glauca*); black ash (*Fraxinus nigra*); American mountain ash (*Sorbus americana*); white elm (*Ulmus americana*); speckled alder (*Alnus rugosa*); white birch (*Betula papyrifera*); balsam poplar (*Populus balsamifera*); black willow (*Salix nigra*); balsam fir (*Abies balsamea*); trembling aspen (*Populus tremuloides*); black spruce (*Picea mariana*)

THE CAROLINIAN LIFE ZONE

It's a thin green line and it's getting thinner.
   —*Robert Preidt,* Wildflower, *Spring 1992*

If you walk through [Backus Woods, a classic Carolinian forest growing on the Norfolk Sand Plain] in warm weather, it takes on the appearance of a place much further south—it has such an incredibly thick, leafy canopy. The forest is quite mature and the canopy towers overhead. In a way, it's like walking through a cathedral because the trees are tall and straight like pillars—huge columnar tulip trees over 30 metres [98 feet] tall and straight as an arrow—and above you is this deep, even canopy.
   —*Kevin Kavanagh,* Borealis, *Fall 1993*

To hear botanists talk about it, to see photographs of it, to read descriptions or to explore first-hand the startling richness of Carolinian Canada is to bring theoretical discussions of biodiversity down to earth, where you can experience them with fully engaged senses.

We can thank the southern latitude and the moderating effects of the lower Great Lakes for the Carolinian zone: it's the warmest region in Ontario and thus the northern limit of the deciduous forest

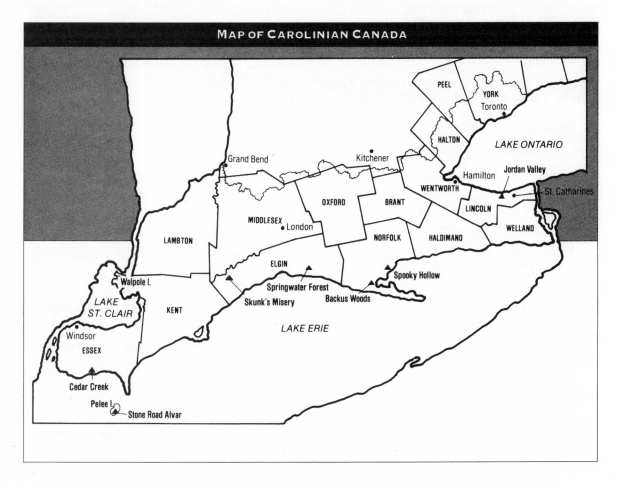

MAP OF CAROLINIAN CANADA

that stretches through the eastern U.S., from the Appalachians to the Mississippi Valley. There's an astonishing diversity of species (considering the region's size), and some estimates suggest that there may be as many as a hundred different tree species in the Carolinian zone, compared to the sixty species in the mixed forest of the Great Lakes-St. Lawrence, and the thirty-five species in the Boreal forest. As well, the region is home to over two thousand species of plants, many of them unique to the life zone and a depressingly large number of them threatened.

But conservationists have mobilized to preserve the few remnants that are left. Since 1984, the Carolinian Canada Project (launched by the World Wildlife Fund and the Nature Conservancy) has been working to support studies of the area, educate landowners about the ecological gems in their possession, and encourage conser-

vation. In a massive effort, Ontario's Natural Heritage League launched a landowner contact program, literally going door-to-door, discussing stewardship with the people who can actually make a difference: the private owners of this unique natural heritage.

Other public agencies are also involved in attempts to preserve and enhance the "thin green line" of Carolinian Canada. The Essex Region Conservation Authority, for example, recently launched a Natural Habitat Restoration Program, the goal of which is to encourage people to plant native Carolinian trees on their properties and to raise funds to plant indigenous trees (grown from locally collected seed) on public land.

In a particularly forward-looking project that combines curriculum and conservation, the University of Guelph's Arboretum has prepared a teachers' manual for naturalization of schoolyards in the Carolinian life zone: *A Life Zone Approach to School Yard Naturalization*. They also hold workshops on growing Carolinian species from seed.

If you live in the Carolinian zone, you may want to consider gardening with native Carolinian species. As Brad Cundiff has written, "It's going to take many hands and much work to stitch this system back together again" (*Borealis*, Fall 1993).

Perennial Plants of the Carolinian Zone

(Species marked with an asterisk are covered in more detail in the plant listings in Chapter 9.

CAROLINIAN LIFE ZONE

Places to see the Carolinian Life Zone and learn about its plant associations:

- Point Pelee National Park, Pelee Island (including Stone Road Alvar Nature Preserve)
- Rondeau Provincial Park
- Long Point Provincial Park
- Rock Glen Conservation Area
- Springwater Conservation Area
- Rondeau Provincial Park
- Backus Heritage Conservation Area
- Turkey Point
- Spooky Hollow
- Pinery Park
- Short Hills Provincial Park
- St. John Conservation Area
- Rockway Falls Conservation Area

For an introductory guide to the plants of Carolinian Canada, contact the Federation of Ontario Naturalists or the Canadian Wildflower Society for a copy of *Plants of Carolinian Canada* by Larry Lamb and Gail Rhynard. The text is excellent and the illustrations attractive.

Carolinian trees and shrubs are listed earlier in this chapter.)

green dragon (*Arisaema dracontium*)*; ginseng (*Panax quinquefolius*); white trout lily (*Erythronium albidum*); twinleaf (*Jeffersonia diphylla*)*; Virginia bluebells (*Mertensia virginica*)*; sessile bellwort (*Uvularia sessilifolia*); wood poppy (*Stylophorum diphyllum*)*; yellow mandarin (*Disporum lanuginosum*); spring beauty (*Claytonia caroliniana*)*; spike blazing star (*Liatris spicata*)*; prickly pear cactus (*Opuntia humifusa*); pokeweed (*Phytolacca americana*); wild lotus (*Nelumbo lutea*)*; nodding wild onion (*Allium cernuum*)*; purple milkweed (*Asclepias purpurascens*); yellow stargrass (*Hypoxis hirsuta*)

WOODLAND MAINTENANCE

For the young woodland garden, weeding and watering are the two most important maintenance chores. The soil disturbance caused by the planting preparation will encourage weed seeds to germinate and you should remove undesirables before they start to crowd out your young transplants. Life will be much easier down the road if you catch weeds before they go to seed. Once your woodland plants are established, you can expect to do less weeding.

Transplants should be kept well watered in their first growing season. After that, natural rainfall will suffice. Likewise, transplanted trees and shrubs should be well watered for their first season.

ONTARIO'S NATIVE CACTI

The first time I saw someone growing a hardy cactus in an Ontario garden, I was surprised, to say the least. Like many people, I associated them with the southern United States. But, in fact, there are four cacti native to Canada, two of which, *Opuntia humifusa* and *Opuntia fragilis*, are native to Ontario.

Growing as far west as British Columbia, *Opuntia fragilis* also grows in Ontario in the extreme northwest from Rainy Lake to Lake of the Woods, and on the Canadian Shield near Kaladar (according to *The Ontario Field Biologist*, June 1982).

Opuntia humifusa is restricted to southern Ontario, in the Carolinian zone, where wild populations can be found in Point Pelee National Park in dry, sandy, rocky areas. This fascinating plant has pads (which are actually enlarged stems) with small prickles, and it bursts into yellow bloom in the early summer. (If it's not getting enough sun, it may not flower, but it is still an interesting addition to the garden.)

Although possible to start from seed, it is much easier to propagate via pad cuttings from a gardener who's willing to share. Pads should be cut off at the joint with a sharp knife (wear gloves, but even then, expect pain); allow the cuts to dry out for a few days in full sun and form a bit of a crust at the scar. Find a sunny or part-sun location with excellent drainage. Plant in sand, with the scar end buried just an inch (a few centimetres). It should root in a week or so. I tried planting mine in the cat's favourite garden entry-point, thinking the cactus would discourage him from digging —a week later I caught him actually *sitting* on the plant, which says more about *his* bulgy anatomy than the cactus's prickles!

One phrase seems to sum up Jim Hodgins and his woodland garden in downtown Toronto: radical common sense. There's a wonderful inversion to the term, and also a subtle subversion, that suits both the person and the place, so I wasn't surprised when the phrase kept popping up while he showed me around his small backyard.

Hodgins' woodland garden is radical, first of all, because you don't see many gardens like his in the midst of a crowded urban centre. In the space of approximately fifteen square feet (less than five square metres), which he has been gardening for ten years, Hodgins has managed to restore a small piece of the original maple/beech forest community of the Toronto area. Among the many woodland natives flourishing in his calming corner are mayapple, Solomon's-seal, bellwort, trilliums, wood poppies, violets, trout lilies, yellow lady's-slipper orchids and twelve species of ferns. There are shrubs such as serviceberry, a young striped maple, leatherwood, and witch hazel, and an exuberant Virginia creeper climbing all over the fence. Moss covers the bricks, rescued from a renovation; the stump of an old cherry tree sports a carved face; and a pot with black oaks grown from acorns at Turkey Point rests by the stairs.

But the true radical nature of Hodgins' garden has little to do with its lack of conformity to the dominant neighbourhood aesthetic of clipped lawns and colourful geraniums; it has everything to do with, ironically, a different kind of conformity: step into his backyard and you have entered a small ecosystem that echoes what might have been on the site a century or two ago, maybe even as far back as the end of the last glacial age. "My garden gives me a sense of time and place," says Hodgins, "a connection that goes back eight thousand years." Now that's radical!

It's when I ask about the "why's" of such an endeavour that the common-sense part of the equation comes in. Think of all the insects and butterflies gone from Toronto, suggests Hodgins. What if we had ten thousand small gardens in Toronto restoring this kind of habitat? After just an hour in this garden, I have no doubt that the city would be a better place, not only for insects and butterflies, but for all forms of life, humans included.

Is it shameless romanticism to assume that humans benefit from this kind of ancient connection with the land? That there is some kind of inherent good in feeling rooted to place? That the radical common-sense philosophy guiding Hodgins' gardening enterprise would improve the world if multiplied thousand-fold? I think the writer Aldo Leopold had it right fifty years ago when he wrote in his book *A Sand County Almanac* that "we abuse the land because we regard it as a commodity belonging to us. When we see land as a community to which we belong, we may begin to use it with love and respect."

It's in gardens like Jim Hodgins' that this sense of community and connection get forged, not only as a working through of some philosophical ideal but as a practice and process, based in the real world of earthworms and leaf mulch.

If you're used to a "clean" garden, free of debris, you may need to reconsider your preference in a woodland garden. Think of a forest floor—full of fallen leaves, bits of stuff! This is how nutrients are recycled and soil temperature and moisture maintained, so abandon the neat and tidy compulsion. Pile on dead leaves (not thicker than 4 inches/10 cm or so, though) in the fall and let them mulch your plants and slowly decompose.

Compost and/or leaf mulch are great additions to woodland soil at any time of year. You don't need to dig these amendments in; simply top-dress around plants. If you're maintaining soil fertility with compost, leaves, or rotted manure, there's no need for any other kind of fertilizer whatsoever.

Pruning of damaged or rubbing branches of trees and shrubs should be done in very early spring.

TREES IN THE CITY

The social history of urban trees reveals much about our understanding of, and relationship with, the environment. From the new settlers' fear of forests, their clearing of trees, right up to the 1990s new-found veneration, we have enacted an ambiguous and complicated dance with their presence. (Even our recent conversion to tree appreciation has its negative aspects when, for example, invasive species like Norway maple are indiscriminately planted and then take over native forest communities.)

But our recent awakening to tree consciousness has prompted much research into trees and tree planting, particularly in the urban context, and we can use this information in our landscape efforts. First, many have learned that diversity is the key to a healthy urban forest. As many enlightened cities embark on their street greening programs, they are replacing the existing monoculture with diversified plantings. We can do the same in our gardens and urban wild areas.

Slowly, we are realizing that just sticking some Earth Day tree hand-out in the ground is not going to contribute to the long-term health of our urban forest. Instead, we are learning to take into account and mitigate against the effects of the stressful urban conditions that trees confront: not enough soil, lack of moisture, poor drainage, soil

Planting trees is a gesture into the future, it is a hand held out to other generations.

—*Mirabel Osler*, A Gentle Plea for Chaos

compaction, lack of air in the soil, insufficient nutrients, dog urine, air pollution, and salt contamination. Only when you either protect against these factors or plant species that are tolerant of them will the urban forest flourish.

PLANTING TREES

If you are planting new trees for your woodland garden or increasing the number of trees on your property, there are a few general rules about tree planting to keep in mind. In general, late fall (after the leaves have dropped) and spring are the best times to plant a tree. The idea is to do this jarring work (for the tree) when its systems are dormant or close to dormancy.

Dig a hole that is as deep as the container or root ball but at least three to five times as wide, as the tree feeder roots grow in the top few feet (metre or so) of soil. You can mix in some compost, but make sure that it is distributed throughout the hole. Loosen the soil on the sides of the hole. Position the tree so that the crown is level with the soil (though in clay soils you can raise it an inch or two/2.5 to 5 cm). If the tree is bare-rooted, the most important thing is to keep the roots from drying out. Plant it as quickly as possible. If it's in a plastic pot, water thoroughly and then remove the tree (with as little soil disturbance as possible) from the pot. If the roots are compacted and twisted around the bottom, loosen them up before

---

Where trees are ill-kept, dying, or diminishing, we often find a community that feels run down, although trees are seldom recognized as either part of the cause or a symptom of the community's woes. But the truth stands clear—trees symbolize permanence and stability. Where they thrive, a community feels good about itself. . . .

—R. Neil Sampson, in Shading Our Cities

---

planting. You don't need to remove fibre pots before planting, though you should slit the sides first. Trees that are balled-and-burlapped (b&b in the nursery trade lingo) can go straight into the ground once the burlap has been untied from the trunk and slit in a few places.

Fill in the hole with excavated soil, pressing it down firmly. Water well, and if the soil settles down too much, add more soil. Use a mulch such as wood chips or bark around the base of the tree to a depth of approximately 2 to 4 inches (5 to 10 cm). Keep well watered over the next few days and then every week in the first growing season. There's no need to fertilize newly planted trees; excessive leaf

growth might in fact hinder root development. Prune out any dead or damaged branches. Don't stake the tree unless wind is a big problem, in which case use a flexible stake or wire so that the trunk can move somewhat.

STARTING TREES FROM SEED

You should consult propagation guides (see Further Reading and Resources) for information about each species, but the general guideline is that native tree seeds should be planted in pots in the fall, to a depth of approximately three times the diameter of the seed. Cover the pot with some kind of protection, such as wire mesh, then leave outside, covered with mulch, over the winter. In the spring, remove the mulch and keep pots well-watered. For the first growing season, place the pot in a protected, partially shady spot.

TREES AND THE BIGGER PICTURE

Increasingly, citizens' groups are taking responsibility for and advocating on behalf of urban trees throughout Canada. These "tree defense" actions take many forms: from lobbying city council when development threatens a particular stand of mature trees to encouraging tree plantings on city streets. One of the most rigorous projects was carried out by a small group called Grassroots Albany, in Toronto, and their work can be used as a model for similar projects across the country. The group decided to do a tree inventory of the Annex area right in downtown Toronto to determine the composition of trees in the area, to evaluate tree health and to make recommendations regarding the future of this urban forest. They found that within the thirty-acre (more than eleven-hectare) study area there were approximately sixteen hundred trees of one hundred different species (with the maple genus comprising about one-third). They also came to a number of distressing conclusions: there is low species diversity among mature trees (with silver and Norway maples accounting for 65 percent of the trees older than thirty years); and there's a fifty-year gap between mature trees and the next generation of urban forest.

This kind of project is bioregionalism in action: intensely detailed understanding of your area so that you can best make decisions about its long-term health and stability. What better place to galvanize and focus community enthusiasm than around trees? As Donald C. Willeke puts it in *Shading Our Cities*, the planting of and caring for trees represent a symbolic dedication to the future, an act of faith, an act of renewal, "ritual confirmation of continuity."

TREES AND CLIMATE CHANGE

Of all the many benefits of trees, the one that got the most air time during the late-eighties blossoming of environmental concern in North America was the idea that trees would somehow reverse global warming. This led to all kinds of fancy equations for figuring out how many trees you would need to plant to "consume" the carbon emissions your existence is responsible for. (Each Torontonian, one study concluded, would apparently need to plant ten acres/four hectares of trees in a lifetime to take up one's personal carbon allotment!) These equations make for good guilt and action inspiration but somewhat misleading ecology. Trees take up carbon but they don't get rid of it—they store it or sequester it in their tissue. When trees are burned or decompose, that carbon is again released into circulation.

The effects of global warming on tree populations is particularly worrisome given that the rate of climate change is generally predicted to be too fast for trees to adapt to new conditions, and also because of the disconnected nature of North America's forests. As John Ambrose wrote in *Wildflower* (Winter 1990), the "islands" of forests that we have left are "disconnected and out of

genetic communication with other forests." Such genetic communication would allow for adaptations to occur within the tree population in response to the changing climate. Thus, knitting together the forest community once again by making room for trees in our cities is all the more important given the scientific consensus about global warming.

CHAPTER REFERENCES

A Gentle Plea for Chaos. Mirabel Osler. New York: Simon and Schuster, 1989.

The Natural Garden. Ken Druse. New York: Clarkson N. Potter, 1989.

The Natural Heritage of Southern Ontario's Settled Landscapes. John L. Riley and Pat Mohr. Aurora, Ontario: Ontario Ministry of Natural Resources, 1994.

Natural Landscaping. John Diekelmann and Robert Schuster. New York: McGraw Hill, 1982.

Plants of Carolinian Canada. Larry Lamb and Gail Rhynard. Don Mills: Federation of Ontario Naturalists, 1994.

A Sand County Almanac. Aldo Leopold. New York: Oxford University Press, 1966.

Shading Our Cities: A Resource Guide for Urban and Community Forests. Gary Moll and Sara Ebenreck, eds. Washington: Island Press, 1989.

Shrubs of Ontario. James H. Soper and Margaret L. Heimburger. Toronto: Royal Ontario Museum, 1982.

Chapter 5

PRAIRIE POCKETS AND
MAINTAINED MEADOWS

The history of European contact in Ontario is dominated by a narrative of deforestation. When we think of the original landscape, our imaginations are flooded with images of dense forests, filtered light forcing its way through the tall canopy, the settlers encountering trees of gigantic proportions. It may come as a surprise to hear that the landscape of southern Ontario also included significant portions of tall-grass prairie and savanna. (As is often the case, place names offer vernacular clues to the natural heritage of this region; towns such as Prairie Siding, Dover Plains, and Plainsville have dotted maps through the years, even if the objects of their original reference exist only in rare and scattered remnants.)

There are many difficulties in estimating the extent of historic prairie coverage, but some experts suggest that prairies and open grassland savannas may have originally covered at least 204 square miles (530 square km) of southwestern Ontario at the time that nineteenth-century surveys were made. Prairies and savannas were found near the lower Great Lakes, around Windsor, Chatham, Leamington, and Toronto; and also farther inland, around London, St. Thomas, Brantford, Cambridge, Rice Lake, and Peterborough. Today, only a minuscule percentage remains. Wasyl Bakowsky and John L. Riley, in their article "A Survey of the Prairies and Savannas of Southern Ontario," estimate that less than 0.5 percent (and in the Rice Lake area, just 0.1 percent) of the original prairie ecosystems persist.

One can only imagine what the vision of such tall-grass prairie subtlety might have evoked for those who first encountered it, though a few written records suggest seas of great grassy beauty. Now, we're restricted to the impressions of pockets— but what an effect they still have. I had the great pleasure of visiting several of the finer remnants on Walpole Island Indian Reserve, at the height of their display in mid-August, and it was only after experiencing the excited discovery of what was, for me, an unknown landscape that I began to appreciate the prairie heritage of this province—

and the urgent need to protect the remaining remnants and to restore the pieces wherever possible.

✦   ✦   ✦

Walpole Island First Nation is one of several islands nestled between Ontario and Michigan on the St. Clair River. As unceded native territory, it is home to approximately two thousand people of three bands: the Ojibway (keepers of the faith), the Ottawa (traders) and the Potawatomi (keepers of the fire). Together they constitute the Walpole Island First Nation—Council of the Three Fires.

Undoubtedly, it is through the well-managed stewardship of the aboriginal owners of this land that any of the original tall-grass prairie remains on Walpole. Prairies require regular burning, and the Council of the Three Fires has carried this out, ensuring that pockets of the ancient prairie have survived on Walpole.

For those who have lived their life surrounded by the disturbed and altered plant communities that make up most of southern Ontario, one of the most profound realizations on visiting the Walpole prairies is that all of the plants actually belong there as part of a functioning climax community. The familiar invaders of disturbed land—Queen Anne's lace, chicory, dandelions, and others— don't stand a chance against the incredible protective solidity of the prairie ecosystem.

If you're interested in visiting Walpole Island First Nation, call the Walpole Island Heritage Centre first to get information about the publicly accessible trails, and also for permission: (519) 627-1475. The Federation of Ontario Naturalists organizes annual tours of the Walpole prairie—spring or summer—with knowledgeable botanists as guides: (416) 444-8419.

The variety of species here is astonishing. Botanists have recorded more than eight hundred species of vascular plants on Walpole Island. Of these, approximately one hundred are rare in Ontario and nine have not been found at any other location in Canada. Rare plants on Walpole include, for example, the small white lady's-slipper orchid (*Cypripedium candidum*); yellow ladies'-tresses (*Spiranthes orchroleuca*); wild indigo (*Baptisia tinctoria*); pink milkwort (*Polygala incarnata*); and white gentian (*Gentiana alba*). Walpole is the only known Canadian location for pink milkwort and white gentian.

How many other places are there in Ontario where you can stand surrounded by vegetation and know that it has been this way for thousands of years?

However awed you may be by the sense of historical continuity expressed at Walpole, the experience of being in that prairie is also one of immediacy: the swaying stands of big bluestem growing taller than your head, the purple spikes of blazing star poking up to your neck, the white wands of culver's root punctuating the prairie grasses, the bright glow of goldenrod clusters nodding from the weight of their blooms...

The typical prairie colour palette of purple, yellow, and white is echoed in wetter parts as well: the dusty purple of Joe-pye weed beside the more exuberant purple of swamp milkweed; the electric glow of purple ironweed; the white of tiny boneset flowers; and the yellow of the giant sunflower, sometimes growing up to 7 feet (2.1 m) or more. All within the context of ribbony or rigidly erect grasses, a framework of variable green.

To walk through the prairie, to get temporarily lost in a swaying sea of grasses and forbs, is to connect with the shared heritage of the original settlers' first encounter with the indigenous people and the indigenous landscapes of southern Ontario. We can only hope that the contemporary encounter promises more in the way of respect for both than did first contact.

＊　＊　＊

I ended my weekend exploration of Walpole Island First Nation with a very hopeful glimpse at the way one person has managed to celebrate this prairie heritage. In Kitchener, Larry Lamb has re-created a tall-grass prairie ecosystem right in his backyard.

After a few days spent in the real thing, it was astounding to see how faithfully Lamb has captured the overall mood and specific details of the prairie ecosystem in his average-sized backyard. To enter his yard was to continue the prairie thread—to connect the pieces of a remnant natural system with the backyard of a typical suburb. The effect was dazzling.

From the front of the house, you have no inkling of what awaits you in the back: the front street view is of familiar suburban detached homes, with young trees, cul-de-sacs, perfectly mown lawns. But Lamb's backyard prairie offers a radically different kind of landscape. One is instantly transported away from the familiar monoculture of suburbia to the transfixing variation and subtle swaying of the tall-grass prairie.

There's no mistaking this landscape for an unintentional, neglected plot. There's too much design for that: from the pebbled paths that curl through, to the ribbons of colour that drift across sections, to the deliberate progression of heights that draws your glance to the tallest back corner. Like the best gardens, it is designed—but you also get the pleasing sensation that chance, randomness, and fortuitous change are not only allowed but encouraged.

Lamb's backyard is approximately fifty by sixty feet (fifteen by eighteen metres), partially surrounded by fence, yet one gets the impression of large distances and unending potential: after you've taken in the overall effect, the urge is for

exploration, botanizing on a small scale. And the details reward close plant scrutiny: the dried seed umbels from the spring explosion of golden alexanders stretch over the pinky white flower clusters of nodding wild onion. Peek around in the prairie grasses of big and little bluestems, side-oats grama, and Indian grass, and you might find the giant

Walpole is undoubtedly the best place to get a glimpse of what prairies at the eastern edge of their range must have looked like prior to European settlement . . . Walpole is a national treasure indeed.

—Allen Woodcliffe and Marjorie Williams, Wildflower, Spring 1992

leaves of prairie dock, about to send up its tall flowering wand. Dotted throughout, pulsing with colour, are culver's root, liatris, asters, goldenrods, ironweed, gray-headed coneflower, brown-eyed Susan, pale bergamot, giant sunflower, Virginia mountain mint, and many more prairie forbs.

Lamb estimates that he originally planted approximately three hundred species in his backyard prairie, sixty or so of which are considered rare, threatened, or endangered. His is truly an indigenous garden in that most of the plants and seeds originated within a two-hundred-mile (some three-hundred-kilometre) radius of his home. They were collected along rail lines and roadsides, along with seed from remnant prairies Lamb has visited throughout the years. Although alien weeds occasionally find their way into his garden, Lamb keeps them in check the way any gardener does, by regular pulling. But he also has an unusual (for suburban life, though not for the prairie) weed control method in his arsenal: fire. With special permission under the watchful eye of the local fire department, Lamb burns sections of his prairie, on an alternating cycle, in late April. This helps to control the non-native cool-season vegetation,

---

From a distance the prospect is glorious, especially from mid-June through to frost, when several new species commence blooming each day. The winter aspect is also splendid, with the abundance of russet grasses and… seed heads patterning newly fallen snow. I enjoy a bounty of cut flowers, wild strawberries, Saskatoon berries and teas made from pale bergamot and mountain mint. The yard has never been mowed, does not need to be watered or fertilized and weeds are becoming scarcer each year.

—*Larry Lamb,* Wildflower, *Spring 1985*

---

unadapted to the rigours of fire as the warm-season prairie species are, and stimulates the prairie plants for their late spring renewal.

Lamb's backyard prairie has been an inspiration to many and the subject of countless articles and TV programs. It is justly renowned as an example of the small-scale restoration work that is possible for those willing to invest the time and energy. On the day that I visited, it seemed ironically appropriate that the gas-guzzling roar of a lawn mower provided a background blanket of noise to impinge on our conversation and outcompete the excited insect hum. But Lamb had interesting news: in the fall, the neighbour's fence would be coming down. His neighbour had decided that it was time for the prairie to expand—to move over into her yard. And thus, another piece of Ontario has been prairied. Perhaps the news will keep spreading.

❦ ❦ ❦

Tall-grass prairie is a very specific ecosystem and one that, for whatever reasons, may not appeal to everyone. Perhaps you don't have the space in the middle of the city, or perhaps you're looking for a more managed aesthetic in your garden. Perhaps the time commitment needed to establish a prairie—a few years at least—is too long for you. Or maybe you live outside the range of the original prairie and are looking for a locally more appropriate landscape style. Whatever your reasons, as long as your site is sunny, you can still garden in a way that makes reference to the native sun-loving prairie system. You can try your hand at a meadow landscape.

First of all, some clarification about the terms. Prairies and meadows are not the same thing, even though "prairie" is a French term for meadow and they do share certain characteristics: both are sunny grasslands, mixed with forbs, without trees or shrubs (or, in the case of meadows, with few). But the main difference is that prairies are climax communities—that is, they have evolved to a stable community that perpetuates itself, maintained by fire and/or grazing—whereas meadows are transitional grassland landscapes, bordered, in their natural state, by woodlands.

Meadows are the result of some kind of disturbance that causes an opening in the forest cover, which allows sun-loving species of grasses, forbs, as well as hawthorn, aspen, sumac, pin cherry, and other species to move in and colonize the land. If left on their own, without some kind of intervention, whether in the form of grazing animals, periodic fires or mowing, meadows will quickly change over the years into woodlands, as trees and shrubs gain a foothold. This is natural succession. In some ways, then, maintaining a meadow is very much like perpetuating a state of permanent adolescence, as the gardener attempts to keep natural changes or progressions at bay. As Laura Martin puts it in her *Wildflower Meadow Book*, the meadow gardener tries "to put Mother Nature on hold at one of her most beautiful stages."

Meadows are often promoted as a low-maintenance alternative to high-energy-demanding lawns and gardens. While it's true that once they're established they perpetuate themselves with much less care, the important point is not that they may or may not be less work, but rather that they provide an entirely different aesthetic experience from the conventional garden. A meadow is less an exuberant display of showy big bloomers and is more subtle in its effects than a traditional garden.

When considering a meadow garden, prepare yourself for shifting swaths of colour and texture. Think of swaying drifts interspersed with colourful clumps, think of a predominance of graceful grasses mixed with fine forbs, think of welcoming insects such as butterflies . . . and, truthfully, think of a lot of work right at the beginning of your meadow endeavour. These are not, PR from the insta-meadow seed companies aside, no-effort landscapes. You'll need to do a lot of weeding, in the first few years especially, but the rewards are rich.

Depending on the size of your landscape, meadow gardening can take many different forms: for the purist, a true meadow includes about 50 percent native grass species (not the stumpy mown species of our lawns), with the remainder in forbs. The tall grasses serve as important mechanical sup-

port for many prairie and some meadow forbs. As well, grasses are crucial to achieving a meadow effect as they provide the overall textural mood of the landscape.

The site is maintained with annual mowing to keep out woody species. If the ground is prepared properly and weeded intensively, then this kind of

---

The prairie was almost completely destroyed before any attempt was made to understand it. In a matter of a few decades in the nineteenth century, the prairie ceased to exist as a functional ecosystem. The prairie is our [U.S.] ecological equivalent of the rain forest.

—Neil Diboll, "Social Change and the Prairie Movement"

---

meadow is relatively low maintenance in the long term. This is the meadow that most approximates, in appearance, the tall-grass prairie.

However, many Ontario gardeners also have the option of creating habitats that refer to, without fully re-creating, a true meadow: gardening with meadow species rather than creating meadow habitat. In this meadowlike landscape, gardeners can use a good number of typical meadow species, but they may plant them in larger clumps, which has an effect quite unlike the random, more subtle effect of meadows, and they may opt for a smaller percentage (that is, less than 50 percent) of grass species.

Whichever you choose—prairie, meadow, or meadowlike garden—depends on the amount of space you have, your aesthetic preferences and the kind of habitat you want to re-create. In my tiny backyard, for example, it would be next to impossible to make a meadow or tall-grass prairie—if I did manage, it would look too much like a landscape in bondage, straining at the confines of fences and deck (and who's ever heard of two com-

---

One virtue that all meadow gardeners share—or learn to share—is patience. Whatever the ads may suggest, you cannot just scatter seed and jump back to avoid the sprouts.

—William Bryant Logan, Wildflower, *Spring 1986*

---

post bins in a meadow?). But I continue to add typical meadow and prairie species, treating them in a more traditional garden manner, and they seem to entice the bees and butterflies that buzz the place all summer.

If, however, you want to create a meadow or prairie from scratch, you've got an exciting and rewarding task ahead (a euphemism for work). You'll need a sunny spot, obviously—at least five hours a day. Unlike woodland gardens, the soil doesn't need to be high in organic matter and nutrients; average soil fertility is fine. But you do need good drainage.

SITE PREPARATION

Since invasive alien weeds are the enemy of prairies and meadows, you need to start with as "clean" a soil bed as possible. Unfortunately, the soil cultivation that you do in your sunny spot will provide the perfect environment for many weeds, so the trick is to spend at least one season of inten-

sive weeding and repeated cultivation before you plant your prairie and meadow species. Starting in early spring or late fall, either till (if you have a larger plot) or hand-pull (if smaller) all weeds. After a few weeks, the soil's dormant seed bank will kick in and many more weeds will germinate. Again, pull them or plough them before they go to seed, and repeat this procedure throughout the growing season.

If you're gardening in a small area, you have an easier option of using a large piece of black plastic to shade out weeds. In the spring, completely cover the area with the plastic and leave it on for the growing season. The heat generated under the sheet will kill many weeds and seeds (and, unfortunately, many beneficial soil organisms, so it's a trade-off).

Many meadow books suggest using herbicides to kill off the weeds. While certainly much easier than the methods above, the ease doesn't justify the environmental cost, to my mind, though there's much debate about this point. There is much research on the subject of the environmental costs of chemical use in the garden and elsewhere; take a look at some of these reports or contact an environmental group before going the chemical route. Meadow gardening is a long-term commitment, so it's appropriate that the initial stage should require not a quick and easy chemical fix but a commitment to slow and steady soil preparation; this approach will help build the right attitude for the longer haul ahead!

SEEDS OR TRANSPLANTS

There are many factors involved in the decision of whether to use seeds or to transplant seedlings into your meadow or prairie. Seeds, obviously, are cheaper. If you're dealing with a large site, they may be the most realistic option. It's much easier to find a greater variety of plant species in seed than in seedlings from a nursery. As well, some prairie grasses don't always transplant well, so they may be best started from seed right in place.

Seedlings, on the other hand, will be established more quickly (sometimes flowering in the first season, compared to the usual two- or three-year wait with seeds) and will most likely outcompete weeds with more success. If you're really ambitious, you might want to raise all the seedlings for your meadow from seed yourself—a large undertaking but possibly the one that provides the most rewarding sense of accomplishment. A compromise that will hold impatience at bay but also maintain the pocketbook might be to use a combination of seeds and seedlings.

If you decide to use seeds, they can be broadcast either in late fall or spring, after the soil has been prepared as above. Fall seeding has the advantage of most closely mimicking the natural processes—the seeds will go through the necessary period of cold dormancy. (Seeds broadcast in fall might be vulnerable to some degree of predation, but it's unlikely that this will be a big problem.) Spring seeding, on the other hand, allows for a closer check on weed competition, since many cool-season weeds (as opposed to warm-season prairie plants) will germinate about a month before your meadow or prairie plants, thus allowing you to weed out undesirables.

You'll need to stratify seeds (see "The Life of a Seed" in Chapter 8) first, though, if planting in the spring: place one part seed to three or four parts moist sand in the refrigerator (at approximately 38°F/3°C) for six to eight weeks.

When broadcasting seeds, the easiest way to ensure even coverage is to mix one part seed with three parts sand. Then tamp down firmly, sprinkle with a thin layer of soil, and water. If you are seeding in spring, you may have to continue weekly watering until the plants are well established.

If you're using seedlings, they can be planted either in spring or fall, when they are somewhat dormant. The most important thing is that transplants need to be kept well watered. Even if you plant them in fall, make sure they get a good soaking.

PLANT CHOICES

The plant listings in Chapter 9 provide detailed descriptions and cultivation information for some of the sunny meadow and prairie species (those marked with an asterisk here), but the following list gives an idea of the range of plants you might want to consider and their period of bloom.

GRASSES

big bluestem (*Andropogon gerardii*)*; little bluestem (*Andropogon scoparius*)*; Indian grass (*Sorghastrum nutans*)*; June grass (*Koeleria cristata*); sideoats grama (*Bouteloua curtipendula*)*; needle grass (*Stipa spartea*); switch grass (*Panicum virgatum*)*; prairie dropseed (*Sporobolus heterolepis*)

WILDFLOWERS

Early-summer-flowering Wildflowers
blue-eyed grass (*Sisyrinchium montanum*)*; golden alexanders (*Zizia aurea*); spiderwort (*Tradescantia virginiana*—may become invasive)*; prairie smoke (*Geum triflorum*)*; Canada anemone (*Anemone canadensis*—also invasive)*

Summer-flowering Wildflowers
showy tick trefoil (*Desmodium canadense*); purple coneflower (*Echinacea purpurea*)*; evening prim-

If you're starting your meadow or prairie from seed, you can count on approximately 10 pounds (4.5 kg) of seed (5 pounds/ 2.2 kg each of grasses and forbs) per acre (0.4 ha), or 4 to 5 ounces (113 to 141 g) per 1,000 square feet (92 square m), or 1 ounce (28 g) per 100 square feet (9.2 square m).

rose (*Oenothera biennis*)*; culver's root (*Veronicastrum virginicum*)*; butterfly milkweed (*Asclepias tuberosa*)*; blazing star (*Liatris spicata*)*; compass plant (*Silphium laciniatum*)*; gray-headed coneflower (*Ratibida pinnata*)*; nodding wild onion (*Allium cernuum*)*; black-eyed Susan (*Rudbeckia hirta*)*; prairie dock (*Silphium terebinthinaceum*);

"Yes, you can recreate a natural prairie ecosystem," the biologist explained to the enthused group of listeners. "You'll somehow have to gain access to at least 150 different plant species. You should get a glacier or two, the occasional buffalo stampede, some wildfire, drought and a few other factors we have no clue about today. Then you'll need a minimum of 10,000 years to let the system fine-tune itself."

—from Native Prairie Plants *by Ducks Unlimited (referring to western Canada)*

---

bergamot (*Monarda fistulosa*)*; cup plant (*Silphium perfoliatum*)*; ironweed (*Vernonia altissima*)*; blue vervain (*Verbena hastata*); false dragonhead (*Physostegia virginiana*)*; lance-leaved coreopsis (*Coreopsis lanceolata*)*; wild lupine (*Lupinus perennis*)*

Fall-flowering Wildflowers
bottle gentian (*Gentiana andrewsii*)*; New England aster (*Aster novae-angliae*)*; Canada goldenrod (*Solidago canadensis*)*; smooth aster (*Aster laevis*); gray goldenrod (*Solidago nemoralis*)

WET MEADOW PLANTS
Joe-pye weed (*Eupatorium purpureum*); milkweed (*Asclepias* spp.)*; gentian (*Gentiana* spp.)*; wild garlic (*Allium canadense*); New England aster (*Aster novae-angliae*)*; cardinal flower (*Lobelia cardinalis*)*; ironweed (*Vernonia altissima*)*; blue flag (*Iris versicolor*)*; black snakeroot (*Cimicifuga racemosa*)*; culver's root (*Veronicastrum virginicum*)*; Canada lily (*Lilium canadense*)*; panic grass (*Panicum virgatum*)*

MAINTENANCE
Keep in mind that prairie or meadow gardens in nature are adapted to—in fact require—catastrophe at rather regular intervals. If you're like me and even deadheading gives you a chill, you'll need to overcome your fear of drastic measures in the garden—because prairies and meadows benefit from dramatic alteration every now and then. What could be more reassuring to the gardener thick of boot or klutzy with the mower?

The adaptation of prairie plants to catastrophe is not too surprising when you consider that these landscapes evolved under the harsh conditions of wind, drought, high heat alternated with freezing cold, the grazing and trampling of animals, and periodic ignition by lightning fires and fires set by native peoples. In other words, they're tough. And natural meadows owe their existence to some kind of drama in the forest—whether fire, disease, or flooding—that opens a clearing.

In Ontario, such landscapes will evolve themselves right out of existence (and into woodlands in approximately five to ten years) if we don't in some way maintain the drama that keeps them going—either by mowing prairie or meadow gardens, or by burning them.

MOWING
In the first growing season, you should plan to mow all the growth to a height of approximately 4 to 6

inches (10 to 15 cm) at least once. (If your mower can't be adjusted to this height, then you'll need to use something like a scythe.) Mowing won't harm the desired species—they're busy working on establishing strong root growth in the first year and don't mind the shearing. What mowing will do is reduce competition from the annual weeds that make their way into your disturbed land.

After the first year, you should continue to mow once a year, either in spring or fall. Spring mowing will mean that birds and small animals have the benefit of seeds and standing growth throughout the winter, but it may affect spring-flowering plants. Fall mowing should be done after at least one hard frost.

BURNING

I include this for interest—not as a recommendation—because, obviously, fire is a major concern for safety officials. In cities, it's out of the question for most of us (Larry Lamb's prairie garden being a notable exception); in the country, you'll need to contact local officials before even considering a prairie or meadow burn. In the absence of bison, the tall-grass prairies of Ontario were maintained by natural fires set by lightning and by deliberate fires set by aboriginal people. Far from obliterating the landscape's grasses and forbs, burning serves many useful purposes: it kills off the non-native species unadapted to fire, keeps out many woody species, recycles nutrients back to the soil, burns off thatch accumulation that may stop seed germination, and blackens the earth so it can absorb the solar radiation necessary for warm-season prairie species.

If you're interested in learning more about burning a prairie, Wayne Pauly has written an informative pamphlet called "How To Manage Small Prairie Fires," which is available from Prairie Nursery Wildflowers (P.O. Box 306, Westfield, Wisconsin 53964) for a small fee.

WEEDING

Weeding is a necessity, especially during the early life of your meadow or prairie. Not only should you be removing alien weeds *before* they go to seed, but you'll also need to keep an eye out for the woody plants that will populate your site. If you're dealing with a large area and hand-pulling annual weeds is a problem in the first few years, you can high-mow or scythe the meadow during the summer before the weeds go to seed—you'll forfeit some attractive above-ground growth, but this won't harm the plants.

MEADOWS, PRAIRIES, AND NEIGHBOURS

If there's one thing that ignites the fury of local officials and threatens the security of neighbour-hoods, it is the appearance of neglect. By definition, gardening involves intentionality, but if your neighbours don't know that your meadow or prairie is the way it is because you've gardened that way on purpose, they may get fussed. And even worse than neighbourhood dissention is official intervention: your prairie or meadow might be against the law in your area.

So if you're contemplating this type of garden in the city or suburbs, you should first familiarize

Although maintaining soil fertility through the addition of organic matter (often in the form of compost or leaf mulch) is an ongoing necessity in the woodland garden, you do not need to fertilize or otherwise supplement the soil of your prairie or meadow garden. Fertilizer will cause prairie plants to get leggy and will also encourage non-native weeds. Prairie and meadow gardens should not be mulched. Good drainage is the most important factor.

yourself with local lawn bylaws. Such regulation might include height restrictions or they may be limited to lists of contraband species. Whatever the case, you should know the law because chances are you'll be called upon to defend your plot.

One of the best ways to prevent complaints from neighbours is to let them know what you're doing. Reassure them that you're not neglecting your yard or just "letting it go"; tell them of your interest in native plants and of the need to restore habitat. Perhaps circulate the information via a flyer. Connect your garden to the larger environmental issues and to history.

If your neighbours think your garden is unsightly, I doubt you'll be able to *talk* about the beauty you see in your landscape with much success—aesthetics tend to be non-negotiable. But, who knows, maybe your growing example will do all the convincing for you. I've seen countless naturalized gardens that, far from creating neighbourhood problems, have actually sparked more interest in the native plant movement. (Sharing surplus seeds and plants with neighbours helps in this regard!) You may have to put up with a grudging, live-and-let-live attitude for a while, but let the word spread at its own pace.

Another option is to put up a small sign—a great invitation to passersby to stop and talk with you about your gardening efforts. I've read about a meadow gardener in Buffalo, New York, for example, who put up a sign that says "This yard is not an example of sloth."

WILDFLOWERS IN A CAN: THE MAJOR MEADOW MYTH

Think of all the things in your life that come in a can. Would you ever ever choose the tinned version over the fresh? Soggy string beans over the fresh green snap from the garden? Niblet kernels of pale corn over a crunchy cob? Canned foods offer convenience but they tend to compromise the full sensory experience, homogenizing and mechanizing what was once a varied, textured, and nuanced pleasure.

The same applies to meadows. The canned versions started to make their appearance about ten years ago. Specialty shops offered quaint packaged perversions variously known as meadow-in-a-can, instant meadow, and so on. These flowers in a tin held great appeal as stocking stuffers, gifts for hosts, presents for someone who had everything except a meadow. Their pretty packaging promised eye-popping colour and dazzling, shimmering swaths of sun-loving flowers. All with the twitch of an arm.

But do such shake-a-gardens deliver? Unfortunately, no. If the package lists the contents, you'll notice that insta-meadows rarely include grasses in the mix—a mystifying omission considering that grasses are an integral if not dominant part of the meadow landscape. What they do include, however, is non-native (to eastern North America) annuals, lots of them. While they may provide exuberant blooms in the first year, very often they

---

PRAIRIES AND OAK SAVANNAS

- Sarnia Clearwater Nature Trail
- Rondeau Provincial Park
- Ojibway Prairie Provincial Nature Reserve and Ojibway Park (recommended)
- Walpole Island First Nation (recommended)
- High Park, Toronto (oak savanna)
- Turkey Point Provincial Park (oak woodland)
- St. Williams Forest, near Long Point (oak savanna)

dwindle in performance the next year as they get squeezed out by invasive weeds.

The situation is not helped by the unrealistic expectations promoted by the creators of such tinned meadows: too often they give the idea that all you need to do is sprinkle the seeds and then sit back and enjoy, with no weeding, no fuss. (They usually add exclamation marks to their promises of carefree, low maintenance, season-long colour, low cost, less mowing, more beauty.)

An unfortunate side effect of meadow-in-a-can promotion is that many people who buy and use such mixtures are under the mistaken (but understandable) impression that they are gardening with native species. This is in part because of the pervasive confusion about terms: the tin says "wildflowers" and one assumes native plants, which is rarely the case. Instead, most versions include mainly naturalized alien plants such as cornflower, daisy, cosmos, sweet William, California poppy, baby's breath, rocket, and red poppy. Beautiful plants all, and naturalized, introduced species, not native to Ontario. When one considers the fact that, in the past, non-native and highly invasive purple loosestrife was often included in these wildflower mixes, you can see that not only were they not delivering on their promises, but they had the potential to actually do great damage to natural habitat. Obviously, the naturalized, non-native species included in these packages have the potential to insinuate their way into native plant communities.

An equally insidious problem of such mixes is that they often disappoint. I hate to think of the number of potential native plant gardeners who have been discouraged by their meadow-in-a-tin experiences, only to give up on gardening with wildflowers altogether. If you've had one showy year, then weeds forever after, you might be nervous about gardening with true native meadow and prairie species. But don't let the meadow-in-a-

tin dissuade you. If you forego the convenience of an "all-purpose" mixture and instead choose your seeds carefully (see the "Plant Choices" section above and "Native Plant Sources" in Further Reading and Resources), follow the soil preparation instructions for this chapter, and accept that you'll

---

And finally, when with calloused hands and bent back you are standing admiring the breathtaking beauty of your meadow in full bloom, someone will walk by and say 'Isn't it amazing that all these wildflowers just popped up here this summer!' Take it as a compliment. After all, in planting a meadow we are trying to mimic nature, and the highest praise for a mimic is to be taken for the real thing.

—Laura C. Martin, Wildflower Meadow Book

---

need to be diligent about weeding and that all native plant meadows require an approximate three-year start-up period before they start to look natural, then you will create a truly native wildflower meadow.

CHAPTER REFERENCES

"Social Change and the Prairie Movement: Roots of Future Culture." Neil Diboll. Westfield, Wisconsin: Prairie Nursery, n.d.

"A Survey of the Prairies and Savannas of Southern Ontario." Wasyl Bakowsky and John L. Riley. In *Thirteenth North American Prairie Conference*. Windsor: Corporation of the City of Windsor, 1994.

Wildflower Meadow Book: A Gardener's Guide. Laura C. Martin. Charlotte, North Carolina: East Wood, 1986.

Chapter 6

WETLAND AND POND GARDENS

hough I'm working on a much smaller scale than his 20-foot-deep (6-m), 130-foot-wide (40-m) pond project, I found great reassurance in Timothy Findley's poetic faith in the power and presence of water: "If you dig it, the water will come. But only if you dream it first" (*Harrowsmith*, March 1994).

My pond dreams were modest: a simple 6- by 8-foot (1.8- by 2.4-m) kidney, 2 feet deep (0.6-m), in the middle of my sister's backyard. No pump—neither of us is electrically inclined. No fish—too small for them and, besides, too many neighbourhood cats and raccoons. No waterfall—in her flat backyard, it would end up looking more like a waterslide at an amusement park than an intelligent addition to the landscape. And no maintenance—I live too far away for regular care and she works long hours.

In preparation, I read dozens of books but somehow they all made it sound either too easy or too difficult. And few answered the tricky questions my sister and I came up with: can you cover the pond liner with soil and plant in that instead of in pots? If we use pots and submerge them in water, as directed, what keeps the soil from becoming suspended and the water a murky mess? How will the frogs and toads find the pond?

As ponds go, it's about the simplest you can possibly make. In late spring, my mother and I spent an afternoon with buckets and shovels excavating the hole. (We marked the shape with a hose first.) It didn't take long, mainly because the size shrank to 5 by 7 feet (1.5 by 2.1 m) in the heat of the sun and an obstructing tree root. We put the huge tarp of 35-mil black polyvinylchloride (pvc) plastic over the hole and started filling it with water, allowing the plastic to settle to the bottom slowly, ironing out kinks as it filled. (It seemed as if the water filling took longer than the digging.) When the hole was finally full of water, we cut around the edges of the plastic and covered it with old cobblestones. That was all there was to the hard labour part.

As for the plants, I waited a week (to let the

chlorine evaporate), then planted (in submerged pots) a native waterlily as the centrepiece, some marsh marigolds on the inside edges of the pond, along with arrow arum. The oxygenating plant, put in to replenish oxygen in the absence of a pump (see later in this chapter), was Canadian pondweed. Around the outside of the pond went cardi-

---

According to the Federation of Ontario Naturalists, one-third of Ontario's mammals and half of Ontario's bird, fish and plant species depend on wetland habitat for survival.

---

nal flower and blue flag. Later in the summer, my sister put in some cattails, which were the perfect striking addition: there's now no doubt that what you're looking at from the kitchen door down the long yard is indeed a pond.

A few creatures have made their way to the pond: fairy shrimp, waterstriders, and many other insects. There are no frogs or toads yet, but I hear that the local cats have a communal stare into the littoral depths first thing every morning—some kind of feline rite.

Actually, ritual is exactly what many water gardeners talk about when discussing their ponds. There seems to be something repetitively calming about water in the garden, soothing to all the senses.

❀   ❀   ❀

Along with their undeniable beauty and tranquil effects, water features in the garden are very important for wildlife, serving as a drinking source, a bathing place and, in some cases, breeding grounds or permanent habitat. Dragonflies, for example, lay their eggs in ponds and spend their nymph stage underwater. (So do mosquitoes, which dragonflies eat.)

The small-scale, local action of building a pond also connects with broader environmental issues. With the shrinkage of wetland habitats, scientists have raised the alarm about a corresponding worldwide decline in amphibian populations. Although species numbers naturally fluctuate, there is concern that amphibian numbers are in general decline. According to the Metro Zoo's Adopt-a-pond project, "Scientists suggest that the sensitive skin of larval and adult amphibians makes them vulnerable to changes in air and water, including exposure to herbicides and pesticides, acid rain, and increases in ultraviolet light [caused by ozone depletion]." While creating a pond in your backyard will not address the complex environmental problems affecting amphibian populations, it will help to create habitat for them. If homeowners across the province were involved, think of the enormous difference it could make: toads and frogs would have places to lay their eggs; frogs would have the permanent water source they require.

If you want to build a pond as frog or toad habitat enhancement, follow the instructions below, with a few slight modifications: include a gradually sloped edge in the pond for amphibian access (this can be covered with small gravel and rocks); make the pond at least 2 1/2 feet (0.75 m) deep; place a few broken clay flower pots, turned upside-down, around the garden in shady spots for toad protection after they leave the water (fancy—and expensive—"toad homes" are also available at some nurseries); and *never* use pesticides or herbicides anywhere in your garden, as amphibians are highly sensitive to these toxins.

❀   ❀   ❀

MAKING A POND

Depending on the size of your property, you can make anything from a small, no-pump pond— the simplest—right up to an elaborate watercourse with layers and falls. You may want to consult water gardening books, specialty nurseries and other gardeners who have had experience building ponds, but the general guidelines are relatively straightforward.

It's a good idea to check your city's bylaws before you begin to make sure that you're allowed to put in a pond. If you're particularly cautious, you may also want to let your insurance agent know, in case there are liability issues of which you need to be aware.

THE SITE

You can build your pond in either a sunny or shady spot, and the amount of sunlight will dictate the species of plants you can use. If you want water lilies and lotuses, for example, the pond should be in full sun for at least five hours a day. If, on the other hand, you want a cool retreat edged with jewelweed and ferns, shade is fine. If your shade is created by nearby trees you'll need to clean fallen leaves and debris out of the water every once in a while, but this is not much of a problem.

Tree roots and underground rocks can present a challenge when digging out the pond, but again, it's not insurmountable.

If you already have a boggy or wet site, this is the obvious place to build on the natural features of your property.

THE SIZE

Decisions about whether or not you want fish or plan to overwinter plants in the pond will affect the final size you choose. If you don't want fish and you're happy to bring plants indoors, then the pond can be as small and shallow as you wish. However, fish and overwintering plants both require a depth of at least 2 to 3 feet (60 to 90 cm). (And with this depth, you'll probably want a width of approximately 7 feet/2.1 m or more, so you've got a pond rather than a pothole!) Shape is up to you, though it's a good idea to create a partial ledge in at least one area of the pond so that you can accommodate those plants that need shallow sub-

---

Water is compulsive; it draws each of us to gaze transfixed in a becalmed state which few other things induce so forcibly.

—*Mirabel Osler*, A Gentle Plea for Chaos

---

mergence. And if wildlife habitat is important to you, a gentle slope in one area of the pond will provide access for frogs, toads, turtles, and crayfish.

Even if you don't have room for a pond, you can still have a water feature of some kind. For example, a half barrel or a metal (but not copper) tub can be sunk into the ground or used above-ground. Scrub first with vinegar, then rinse. Put in about 10 inches (25 cm) of well-soaked soil, then slowly add water. After it has settled down, which will take about a week, you can add plants. Or, if you'd prefer to use pots in the tub, submerge them to the appropriate depth, adjusting the height with bricks if necessary.

THE LINER

If you're putting in a pond on anything other than the hardest, non-porous clay soil, or if you're not going down deep enough to reach hardpan, then you'll need some kind of liner to retain the water. I found pvc very easy to work with—flexible, easy to cut, and available in large sheets. Butyl rubber is reputedly longer-lasting (thirty years to pvc's ten to twenty years), but it is more expensive, and if you can't find a large enough sheet, you'll need to heat-fuse the seams. Whatever the material, use the following equation to determine the correct size of sheet to buy: the length of the pond plus twice the depth by the width of the pond plus twice the

---

The 1,235,000 acres [499,805 ha] of wetland that remains today south of the Precambrian Shield is only between 13% and 22% of the original area before settlement. The losses are continuing at the rate of 1–2% per year.

—*Wildlife Habitat Canada, "Wetland Stewardship in Ontario 1990–1993"*

---

depth; add one foot (30 cm) to both length and width. For example, suppose you want to make a pond that's 6 feet (1.8 m) long, 8 feet (2.4 m) wide, and 2 feet (0.6 m) deep. You'll need a liner that's 11 feet by 13 feet (3.3 m by 3.9 m).

DIGGING AND FILLING

Once you've outlined the shape and started digging, the most important thing to watch out for is roots or rocks around the walls of the pond that may weaken or puncture the lining. If it's impossible to create a completely smooth bed, free of obstruction, then you should line the hole with something like a thick layer of sand before you put in your plastic or rubber lining.

Align the lining over the hole, anchoring it with a few bricks, and slowly start to fill with water,

smoothing out kinks and folds as you go. When the pond is full, bury the liner under whatever rock, stone, or paved edging you're using. Let the water sit for approximately a week before you start adding plants.

You have two choices about the growing medium for plants: you can either plant them in soil-filled baskets sunk into the pond, or you can cover the pond liner with soil to a depth of 6 to 8 inches (15 to 20 cm) and plant directly in the soil. Obviously, if you decide on the latter, you should take the added depth into account when digging out your pond. As well, the latter option may lead to clogged pumps and filters. If you choose baskets (commercially available from water garden stores), add some fine gravel to the top of the soil to keep it from muddying the water.

COPING WITH ALGAE

When I think of algae not as pond scum but as some kind of primordial ooze, a primitive form of plant life, I don't feel so bad about having it in the pond. But too much algae is a sign of an imbalance and it can cause further problems by depleting the water's oxygen. An algae bloom in the spring, when the water first warms up, is not a problem, but if it doesn't disappear on its own you'll need to add more oxygenating plants or pump more oxygen into the pond.

MAINTENANCE AND WINTER CARE

Along with keeping an eye out for algae blooms, you should try to keep dead leaves and debris out of the pond, as their decomposition will use up valuable pond oxygen. If a tree overhangs the pond, you may want to cover the water with mesh in autumn to keep it free of leaves.

If your pond is 2 1/2 feet (0.8 m) deep or more, you can leave your plants out over the winter, though marginals should be moved to the deepest part of the pond to prevent their roots from freezing. An alternative method is to cover the pond with boards and mound insulating straw on top.

If your pond is too shallow for overwintering plants, bring them inside in their baskets to a cool basement, and store them in plastic bags, making sure they never dry out.

If you've got frogs, fish, newts, or turtles in your pond and it's at least 2 1/2 feet (0.8 m) deep with mud on the bottom, the animals should be fine as long as you keep part of the surface ice open to allow gasses to escape. If your pond is shallower than this, bring the animals inside for a winter aquarium retreat.

If you live in an agricultural area, where fertilizers are regularly added to the soil, or if you maintain a fertilizer-fed lawn right up to the pond, you may run into problems with run-off causing nutrient-overloading (and thus algae blooms) in your pond. There are a few ways to deal with this: create a berm around the pond, so that run-off doesn't reach the water; put marginal plants around the outside edge of the pond to absorb nutrients; or stop fertilizing the lawn.

POND AND WETLAND PLANTS

For the native plant gardener, there is an abundance of beautiful water plants to choose from. The native water lily, for example, offers all the gorgeous blooms of the tender tropical varieties without the fuss. Marsh marigolds make for an exuberant display of yellow in spring, then go dormant in summer, allowing other blooms to take over. If interesting foliage textures and combinations are what you're looking for, there are countless sedges, grasses, ferns, and rushes that can be used for graceful accents. Your water garden can take on any mood you choose: from formal severity to calming softness to chaotic wildness. It's up to you and how you arrange the plants.

Water plants are generally divided into a number of categories and these designations relate to their moisture needs: submerged oxygenators; deep-water aquatics; marginals; and moisture-loving plants. Submerged oxygenators are fast-growing plants that live below the surface of the water and don't add ornamental value but do important work for you in keeping the pond balanced (and

One lone toad will eat tens of thousands of insects a year—up to three times its weight in slugs, beetles, cutworms, flies, grasshoppers, gypsy moths, sowbugs, pill bugs, centipedes, millipedes, mole crickets and ants every day!

—Organic Gardening, *May-June 1994*

thus free of excessive algae). Deep-water aquatics are plants, such as water lilies, that need to be planted deep in the pond (1 to 3 feet/30 to 90 cm below the surface). Marginals are those plants that require shallow water above their crowns (3 to 6 inches/7.5 to 15 cm) and are thus best planted on ledges around the pond. Bog and moisture-loving plants do best in water-logged soil, not directly *in* the pond, or in soil that is kept moist. Many, such as Joe-pye weed, are familiar sites in moist fields and ditches; others, such as cardinal flower and great blue lobelia are common garden plants.

In choosing the plants for your pond, consider the natives in the following list (for more information about colour, height, and requirements, see the pond and wetland plant list in Chapter 9 for those plants marked with an asterisk), but also take a look at wetlands and ponds in your area. These will give you many good design ideas and clues about combining water plants in a naturalistic arrangement.

SUBMERGED OXYGENATORS

As already stated, the primary function of these plants is to oxygenate the water and compete with

---

Who can guess how many salamanders, on returning to their natural pond to breed, have found a condominium instead.

—*Sara Stein*, Noah's Garden

---

algae for the dissolved nutrients, thus preventing excessive algae growth. In the absence of a pump, these plants keep your pond from becoming a riot of algae. Oxygenators are sold at nurseries in clumps held together with a small lead anchor; count on approximately five bunches for every square metre of water surface. Keep them in a water-filled plastic bag when transporting them home from the nursery; remove the lead if your pond is stocked with fish. One of the best oxygenators for native plant ponds is Canadian pondweed (*Elodea canadensis*). It has a bad reputation because it's a major invasive plant pest of waterways in Europe, but in its native environment it's a great oxygenator, contributing to the health of ponds. Water milfoil (*Myriophyllum alternifolum*) is another native to try.

DEEP-WATER AQUATICS

For many people, lilies and lotuses are the show-stoppers of the water garden: the sweet-smelling white flowers of the native waterlily (*Nymphaea*

odorata)*, for example, can be 6 inches (15 cm) across. And their leaves are equally decorative, floating pads on the water's surface. All should be planted deep—from 1 to 3 feet (30 to 90 cm) deep in the pond. (When they're young and small, place the pots up on bricks and then gradually lower their depth, by taking off bricks, as they grow bigger.) Other native deep-water aquatics include floating heart (*Nymphoides cordata*); American lotus (*Nelumbo lutea*)*; water-stargrass (*Heteranthera dubia*); and bullhead-lily (*Nuphar variegatum*).

MARGINALS

These are very versatile water garden plants: they may be planted in pots placed in the water to a depth of 3 to 6 inches (7.5 to 15 cm) or they may be placed around the pond. Some attractive natives include bog arum (*Calla palustris*)*, with heart-shaped foliage and white blossoms; marsh marigold (*Caltha palustris*)*, with lovely yellow saucer-shaped flowers in spring and dark green leaves; arrow arum (*Peltandra virginica*)*, mainly an interesting foliage plant though it does send up whitish green spathes in summer; arrowhead (*Sagittaria latifolia*)*; blue flag (*Iris versicolor*)*; pickerelweed (*Pontederia cordata*); cattail (*Typha angustifolia*); and sweetflag (*Acorus calamus*).

MOISTURE-LOVING PLANTS

These plants flourish in the moist soil around ponds or in other moist areas of the garden. Most require sun, though the ferns, jewelweed, cardinal flower, bee balm, Jack-in-the-pulpit and lilies will do well in the shade. Natives to try include cardinal flower (*Lobelia cardinalis*)*; jewelweed (*Impatiens capensis*)*; swamp milkweed (*Asclepias incarnata*)*; Joe-pye weed (*Eupatorium maculatum*)*; boneset (*Eupatorium perfoliatum*); ostrich fern (*Matteuccia strathiopterus*); sensitive fern (*Onoclea sensibilis*); cinnamon fern (*Osmundus cinnamomea*); sedges (*Carex* spp.); bottle gentian (*Gentiana* *andrewsii*)*; skunk cabbage (*Symplocarpus foetidus*)*; turtlehead (*Chelone glabra*)*; swamp aster (*Aster puniceus*); royal fern (*Osmunda regalis*); Canada lily (*Lilium canadense*)*; ironweed (*Vernonia altissima*)*; bee balm (*Monarda didyma*)*; Jack-in-the-pulpit (*Arisaema triphyllum*)*; horsetail (*Equisetum hyemale*).

TREES

Trees for Planting Near Water
willow (*Salix* spp.); pin oak (*Quercus palustris*); eastern hemlock (*Tsuga canadensis*); red maple (*Acer rubrum*); silver maple (*A. saccharinum*); trembling aspen (*Populus tremuloides*); white ash (*Fraxinus americana*); white oak (*Quercus alba*); tamarack (*Larix laricina*); eastern white cedar (*Thuja occidentalis*); speckled alder (*Alnus rugosa*)

Wetland Shrubs and Small Trees
chokeberry (*Aronia melanocarpa*); large cranberry (*Vaccinium macrocarpon*); red-osier dogwood (*Cornus stolonifera*); partridgeberry (*Mitchella repens*); elderberry (*Sambucus canadensis*); nannyberry (*Viburnum lentago*); swamp rose (*Rosa palustris*); buttonbush (*Cephalanthus occidentalis*); riverbank grape (*Vitis riparia*)

BIG-SCALE COUNTRY PONDS

While urban ponds, due to their size and the way they're constructed with liners, don't generally have an impact on groundwater, if you're considering pond-building in the country, you should first contact the local office of the Ontario Ministry of Natural Resources. Permits are required if you are changing the course of a stream or affecting natural water courses, or even adding fish stocks to your pond. (In fact, permits are no longer issued for the building of ponds connected with cold-water streams or creeks, since the ponds raise the temperature of the water course and thus affect fish populations, especially our native brook trout.)

In rural areas, ponds are usually created by digging and letting a spring fill them up, or by connecting the pond through channels with a natural water source, or by filling them with well water. All of these methods affect groundwater supplies and, in turn, local wetlands, so check with the OMNR before you embark on a pond project.

As with any naturalization project, you should consider whether or not ponds are an indigenous feature in your area. You may be doing more harm than good by introducing habitat that has not evolved over time in your region.

ONTARIO'S WETLANDS

Wetlands are areas where water is the primary factor controlling the environment and the associated plant and animal life.
> —William A. Niering, Audubon Society
> Nature Guides: Wetlands

They have often been called the most productive life-support systems in the world. Among the essential ecological functions they provide are the dilution and detoxification of wastes, the storing of groundwater, the recharging of aquifers, temperature amelioration, and protection from erosion. Yet wetlands have long been denigrated as "unimproved" sites just waiting for the builder's fill or the

---

OUTSTANDING WETLAND SITES

- Point Pelee National Park
- St. Clair National Wildlife Area
- Long Point
- Southern James Bay Migratory Bird Sanctuary
- Polar Bear Provincial Park
- Alfred Bog
- Purdon Conservation Area
- Rattray Marsh, Mississauga

farmer's drainage. Things are changing, however. Even Holland, that triumph of engineering over ecology, the country built on reclaimed wetlands, is starting to stop the fight against water with a plan to return approximately one-tenth of its farmland to marshlands and lakes.

Here in Ontario, the Ministry of Natural Resources has been studying and classifying the province's wetlands in an effort to evaluate their importance to local ecosystems and to afford them some level of protection. But groups such as the Federation of Ontario Naturalists are alarmed that southern Ontario continues to lose 1 to 2 percent of its remaining wetlands every year. They urge people to become better informed about wetlands in their areas and threats to these ecosystems; they suggest that people learn about local planning laws and lobby to include wetland protection in these laws. In short, they see public participation and public valuing of wetlands as the only hope for their survival. For more information about how you can help, contact the Federation of Ontario Naturalists, 355 Lesmill Road, Don Mills, Ontario M3B 2W8; (416) 444-8419.

THE BIG FOUR

Marshes These are treeless wetlands dominated by herbaceous plants such as cattails and reeds, with areas of standing water. The soil is rich and productive, and the area is often flooded. They are primary nesting, feeding, and nurturing places for many forms of wildlife.

Swamps Swamps are dominated by trees and woody shrubs adapted to periodic flooding, such as maples, ash, and cedar, combined with various other types of vegetation that flourish in waterlogged soils.

Bogs Covering huge areas of northern Ontario, and also existing in central Ontario and as far south as St. Catharines, bogs are found on ancient substrata of peat. Soil is acidic and waterlogged,

with poor drainage. Trees such as black spruce and larch are common.

Fens Primarily a northern habitat, fens are similar to bogs but instead of being based on peat, they are formed in areas of calcareous rock. Grasses, sedges, and reeds are common, as are tamarack trees and cedars.

Source: Federation of Ontario Naturalists

ADOPT-A-POND

The Metro Toronto Zoo has an excellent program designed for school groups to adopt, create, and restore local wetlands. They provide information on all aspects of pond creation and habitat enhancement, with a particular emphasis on the connection between loss of wetland habitat and the decline of amphibian populations. They have produced an excellent book on wetland creation and protection, which includes activity suggestions for teachers and students. And—my favourite—they have put together a tape of Ontario frog and toad calls. For more information on the project, contact the Amphibian Interest Group, Metro Toronto Zoo, P.O. Box 280, West Hill, Ontario M1E 4R5.

CHAPTER REFERENCES

A Gentle Plea for Chaos. Mirabel Osler. New York: Simon and Schuster, 1989.

Noah's Garden: Restoring the Ecology of Our Own Back Yards. Sara Stein. Boston: Houghton Mifflin, 1993.

"Wetland Stewardship in Ontario 1990–1993." Ottawa: Wildlife Habitat Canada, 1994.

Wetlands. William A. Niering. New York: Knopf, 1985.

Chapter 7

DESIGN AND THE
NATIVE PLANT GARDEN
OBSERVATIONS FROM THE FIELD

I f there are just two primary anthems in naturalistic gardening, they are: identify and
understand the habitat model to which
your garden refers or which you're trying to re-create, and know your site. In other words, know what
you want your garden to be and know what *it* wants
to be. All the rest—the plants you choose, your
design aesthetic, and other variables—can be cele-
brations of individual expression, but only if you
start from a clear and well-thought-out understanding of these two basics.

Site evaluation involves everything from
identifying existing vegetation to learning what is
underground; from discovering clues about the
site's historic vegetation patterns to considerations
of abiotic factors such as rock formations; from seeing the cycles at work in your landscape—the
hydrological and nutrient cycles, for example—to
exploring its oddities; from knowing its soils to
feeling its wind patterns. While the ideal situation
is that of knowing all these variables before you
design your naturalistic garden, for many of us,

such knowledge only comes after years of experience in a particular place. Not to worry—the garden will evolve and gradually be enriched as you
develop your understanding of the site. (And, of
course, it is always changing, so this is an ongoing
project.)

Site evaluation is necessarily a process of inter-
rogation, of asking questions about your landscape.
One of the first is: what kind of habitat is your
landscape leaning towards or what is the vegetation history of the site? There are many subtleties,
but a broad characterization might include woodland (if the site contains rich soil and is predominantly shaded), meadow or prairie (if the site is
sunny with well-drained soil), or wetland (if there
are areas of periodic flooding and poor drainage).

These categories can be further broken down
into increasingly specific evaluations. For example, what is the nature of the existing woodland? Is
it a dry, upland forest or a lowland forest with
greater moisture? Are there layers of woodland
vegetation: an overstorey canopy of taller trees, a

midstorey of shade-tolerant trees, and an understorey of shrubs and herbaceous plants? Where I garden, in Toronto, for example, there used to be a mixed deciduous and conifer forest of maple, beech, ash, pine, and hemlock. But this was not the only landscape throughout the area. According to the descriptions of Toronto's natural history in Bill Ivy's book *A Little Wilderness*, someone gardening near the lower Don River in Toronto may be cultivating what was originally part of the floodplain; near the mouth of the Humber, a marsh; an alder grove along Etobicoke Creek; a sugar maple, hemlock, white pine, white cedar forest near the Little Rouge; near Toronto's High Park, an oak savanna community. And on and on, increasingly specific.

To evaluate a meadow, determine if there are any woody species, such as small shrubs, or if the site is composed of only grasses and forbs. Is it a dry meadow or moist? (The presence of moisture-loving species, such as Joe-pye weed, swamp milkweed or gentians, will indicate a moist meadow.) What is

the percentage of grasses and what is the percentage of forbs? Are they distributed randomly or are there pockets of particular kinds of vegetation indicating slightly different conditions? Are there edges—or ecotones—where one kind of vegetation gives way to another, where grassland meets forest? What changes occur in the vegetation as sun becomes shade in these edge areas?

If the site is a wetland, is there an existing pond or marsh or swamp or bog or fen? Are parts of the landscape permanently covered with water or subject only to periodic flooding? In what season(s) does flooding occur and how long does it last? Is the wet area sunny or shady? Are there any moisture-loving trees? Are there any plant indicators that can tell you if the soil is acidic? How close to the surface is the water table? Are there seasonal springs or streams?

These questions are all a part of the process of understanding the ecology of your landscape: its geology, its soils, its basic landforms, its water cycles, its light patterns and light intensity, its wind patterns, its climate and microclimate, the plants and the animals it supports. Whether your existing landscape is a thriving woodland or an expanse of lawn, you'll need to explore these variables. The answers you come up with won't fit into some kind of generic plan; rather, they'll help you to use your site's characteristics to their best advantage, working with those features you've been given.

GEOLOGICAL CONSIDERATIONS

How far do you need to go down to reach bedrock? Are there places in which the bedrock literally heaves out of the earth, providing you with spectacular rocky features to use in your design? (Rocks, because they absorb heat and release it at night, create warmer microclimates in the garden.) What kind of rock is common to your area? (This will tell you the kind of soil you most likely have:

In the highly disturbed landscapes of populated areas, where the natural plant communities have been altered over generations, you won't achieve a naturalistic garden or habitat restoration just by sitting back and "letting things go." If you do, what will "go"—as in go gangbusters, not go away—is alien weed species. They'll merrily move in and colonize at a great rate, and you'll be watching for years before any kind of natural succession to native species kicks in—and even then, only if native seed sources somehow become available.

The road to native plant gardening is a consciously constructed one—through design.

limestone-based soils are generally neutral to alkaline; sandstone- or granite-based soils, usually acidic.)

SOIL CONSIDERATIONS

Soil is considered to be one of the big three (light and moisture being the other two) that determines what plants you'll be able to grow. Although we tend to think of soil as a solid mass of matter, it is in fact half composed of air—that is, the spaces between its particles, which are filled with air and water. The other half is mainly mineral particles from the breaking down of bedrock, with a relatively small percentage (approximately 5 percent) of organic matter, which is formed from the decomposition of once-living things. And, of course, there are also many living things in soil: worms, nematodes, fungi, bacteria, insects, millipedes, centipedes, and many more.

Soil types are classified according to the size of the mineral particles: sandy soil has the largest particles, clay the smallest, with silt in-between. The "ideal" garden soil—loam—is approximately 20 percent clay, 40 percent silt and 40 percent sand. Sandy soil tends to warm up faster in the spring but doesn't hold much water. Clay soils hold nutrients well but are poorly aerated and can easily get waterlogged or baked dry.

You can do a home test to determine the relationship of various sized particles in your soil. Collect about a cup of soil from your garden, put it in a quart (litre) jar, fill it with water, shake, and then leave it to settle for about a day. Sand will settle to the bottom, and silt will be the next layer, with clay on top (organic matter will float on the water's surface). Compare the percentages of each layer to determine whether you've got loam (20 percent clay, 40 percent silt, 40 percent sand), clay (60 percent clay, 30 percent silt, 10 percent sand), or sand (5 percent clay, 10 percent silt, 85 percent sand).

Soil pH also determines the kinds of plants you can grow. The pH scale (from 0 to 14) measures the acidity or alkalinity of soil.
- pH 8 and over: very alkaline soil
- pH 7.4 to 8: alkaline
- pH 6.6 to 7.3: neutral
- pH 6.0 to 6.5: slightly acidic

The most complex way [to use native plants] is to reconstruct a plant community, or a significant part of one. The least complex is merely an "affirmative" action program to include more of the best native plants in nursery lists and in the palettes of landscape designers.

—*Brooklyn Botanic Garden*, Gardening with Wildflowers and Native Plants

- pH 5.5 to 5.9: moderately acidic
- pH 5.0 to 5.4: strongly acidic
- pH 4.3 to 4.9: very strongly acidic

You can do a pH test at home using kits available from nurseries or you can send soil out to a professional lab (some garden centres, universities, government ministries, and arboreta will provide this service for a small fee). Although it is possible to adjust soil pH through additions of lime (to raise pH) or sulphur or organic matter such as peat moss (to lower pH), it makes more sense to work with what you've got, matching plant selection to existing soil pH. (Most plants in the plant listings in Chapter 9 will tolerate conditions in the slightly acidic to slightly alkaline range, unless otherwise noted. If your soil is moderately to strongly acidic, see the plant suggestions listed at the end of this chapter.)

Soil drainage is determined by the interaction between soil type, slope, and geological and hydrological considerations—that is, what size particles the water is moving through, how close the water table is to the surface, and whether or not the land

---

A naturally occurring group of organisms living in a particular habitat, depending on and sustaining each other, is termed a biotic (living) community. Such a community cannot exist in a vacuum. It is influenced by and dependent upon abiotic (non-living) factors such as sunlight, soil, topography, wind, temperature, moisture, and minerals. The interaction of biotic and abiotic factors creates what is called an ecosystem.

—*William A. Andrews et al, A Guide to the Study of Terrestrial Ecology*

---

is subject to flooding. As already noted, heavy clay soils tend not to drain well, whereas sand drains quickly, sometimes too quickly. If the water table is close to the surface, the soil will tend to be saturated.

To find out the drainage capacity of your soil, do the following test. Dig a hole 1 foot (30 cm) deep and approximately 1 foot (30 cm) wide. Fill it with water, let it drain completely, then fill again until the soil is saturated. Depending on how long it takes for the last batch to drain, you've either got

adequate drainage (less than two hours), or poor drainage (more than two hours). Again, although there are methods of improving drainage, such as digging out the soil and installing French drains or drainage tiles (yikes!) or adding organic matter to clay soil, you can work with poor drainage using the many moisture-loving plants.

The major soil nutrients are nitrogen, phosphorus, and potassium. Each affects plant growth in different ways: nitrogen promotes healthy leaves and stems; phosphorus, root growth and the size and quantities of fruits and flowers; and potassium, root growth. If your soil has a serious deficiency of any of these nutrients, it will show up in the plants. However, regular additions of compost will go a long way towards preventing any problems.

If you live in an area once devoted to industrial or agricultural uses, you may want to consider having your soil tested for contaminants. (If you're growing food crops, this is a must.) While the results may not affect your decisions about the kinds of non-food plants you grow, it is important for health reasons to know the state of the soil in which you're digging, the dust you're breathing, and the dirt you're trailing into the house.

LANDFORM CONSIDERATIONS

The shape of your land—its dips and rises, its slopes or lack of them, its hills and valleys, or its uniformity—not only gives it one of its most immediate visual characteristics, but it also has a strong impact on plant life. (Mirabel Osler has called the shape of the land its "bossy geography.") You'll probably notice, for example, that depressions in the land tend to be cooler—because cool air sinks. Hills that slope to the south tend to warm up faster in spring. And the higher the elevation, the cooler the temperature. (Henry Art, in his book *A Garden of Wildflowers*, notes that "For each 100-foot [30-m] increase in elevation, the air temperature is only three-tenths of a degree [F] cooler, but flowering is delayed by about one day.")

Landforms will also tell you something about the possibility of erosion: if a steep slope is free of vegetation, erosion by wind and rain will most certainly be a problem. Get some kind of quick-growing groundcover on there to hold the soil as fast as possible; the idea is to stabilize the slope so that the soil bed is secure and precious soil is not lost to erosion.

WATER CYCLES

I've already touched on the issue of drainage in the soil section, but a consideration of hydrological features on your land involves much more than that; it also involves, for example, looking at surface drainage from rain and melting snow. (These are greatly influenced by the slope of the land.) Do drainage patterns create temporary streams, following the same route to some kind of drainage ditch, or does the water percolate slowly through the earth without run-off? (If there is a seasonal stream, is it bordered with moisture-loving vegetation that provides a clue?)

What amounts of rainfall does the area generally receive and at what times of the year? Are plant communities predominantly dry (xeric), moderately moist (mesic), wet (hydric), or somewhere in between, such as dry-mesic? Do these conditions vary across the site, signalling different water conditions you should exploit in your plantings?

LIGHT (SUNLIGHT OR SOLAR ACCESS)

It always surprises me that as gardeners we have not collectively developed an adequate vocabulary to describe the qualities of light with the subtlety of, say, northern inhabitants' descriptions of snow. We tend to coast with impoverished terms such as sun, part shade, and shade, and leave it at that. But, of course, late afternoon light is radically different from midmorning sun, winter light from

summer light, and so on. And it all makes a difference to plants.

The general descriptions of light levels are: full sun (eight hours a day or more of full sunlight), partial sun (six hours a day of sunlight), partial shade (three hours a day of sunlight with the rest of the day in shade—either indirect or filtered light), and

---

Your garden will not be an exact reproduction of a natural wild area, but rather the distilled essence of its beauty.

—*Frances Tenenbaum*, Gardening with Wild Flowers

---

deep shade (no direct sun, like that found in the densest forest or between two close, tall buildings).

To these I would add killer shade—mostly deep shade except for a devastating few hours of direct afternoon sun, which can wreak havoc if you're not careful in your woodland plant choices (and I wasn't, my wild ginger was *fried*); urban episodic shade (created and uncreated according to whims of neighbours pruning what's rightfully theirs but influencing your solar access); and catastrophe sun—the abrupt introduction of sunny conditions caused by an unexpected tree fall. (I thought I had my shade figured out until a neighbour lost not one but two mature trees during one year's storms; instantly, a whole new garden situation for me. These sudden "light gaps" occur in natural woodland settings, of course.)

At any rate, evaluating the conditions of light on your property involves more than just counting the hours. You'll also need to take into account the intensity of the light; how the light changes throughout the year; the quality of light (is it dappled and filtered or strong and direct?); the fact that an area may be in full sun but that taller plants shade out smaller ones, creating tiny zones of shade; and the nature of the shading agent (a solid stone fence as opposed to chain link, for example).

Light conditions can, of course, be manipulated to a degree. Trees and shrubs may be pruned to allow in more light or, more drastically, cut down; the same can be added to create shade. As plants grow and change, so will the conditions of light in your garden.

WIND

In an exposed site, wind can have a surprisingly limiting effect on plants. To evaluate your landscape in terms of the wind's influence, you'll need to observe how wind moves through your landscape. Are wind tunnels created by buildings and trees? Does vegetation, such as a line of shrubs, serve as a windbreak? What is the vegetation like in the windiest spots? Does your site make the most out of the energy-saving possibilities of trees? For example, are deciduous trees positioned near the

house, where they can cool in the summer yet not obstruct the sun's rays in winter? (For more information on designing with plants for energy efficiency, see "Design for Energy Conservation" later in this chapter.) Wind also affects moisture loss in plants. Thus, plants should be mulched in windy locations.

MICROCLIMATE

The climate of an area is determined by the overlapping factors of sun, topography, orientation to the sun, wind, precipitation, and temperature. But landscapes are rarely uniform; in addition to the dominant characteristics there are local, specific variations. These site-specific variations are known as microclimates.

The microclimates in your landscape may be caused by any of the factors listed above, and they offer opportunities to exploit their qualities for design purposes. For example, on a south-facing slope that warms up early in spring, you may want to plant spring-blooming species, rather than summer-flowering plants, so that you can enjoy a head start on spring colour.

This is a different use for microclimate than that normally suggested in gardening books; traditionally, microclimates are used to "push" the zone (what Des Kennedy has called, in his book *Crazy About Gardening*, "a form of horticultural bungee-jumping") so that, for example, you can plant a species hardy to Zone 6 in what is essentially a Zone 5 garden. In the naturalistic garden, however, you are not planting according to the horticultural system of zones, which relates only to cold hardiness, but rather to the indigenous properties of plant communities specific to a particular geographic region. Thus, the naturalistic gardener doesn't ask if wild ginger is hardy to Zone 5 but instead whether or not it's indigenous to the floral region—and if it is, you'll know that it's hardy. So although microclimates are generally not used in

---

VARIABLES IN PLANT CHOICE

- the plant's cultural requirements
- its size
- its rate of growth
- its overall form
- the shape and texture of its foliage
- the shape and size of its flowers
- the colour of the flowers
- the colour of the leaves
- the fragrance of the flower or foliage
- fall colour
- winter interest
- the plant's pollution tolerance

---

the native plant garden to introduce plants that wouldn't normally be hardy in the area, they are used to manipulate design goals, such as an early splash of colour, to evaluate plants appropriate for edge zones (or ecotones), or to augment plant health. A pocket that gets deeper snow cover, for example, might be a good place for a plant that requires a heavy winter mulch.

Consideration of microclimates is an essential part of gardening with native plants: learning the subtle variations in your landscape will allow you to grow the plants most appropriate to those conditions.

PLANTS ON THE SITE

The goal of evaluating the plants already at home in your landscape is to determine, as Richard Austin puts it in *Wild Gardening*, "how they live, where they live and why they live the way they do." These are, of course, connected with all of the above considerations. In other words, the presence of certain plants can be read as indicators of the conditions in which they're growing. This applies equally to native and non-native plants. For example, let's suppose that your existing landscape is one of non-native Queen Anne's lace, chicory, and various grasses. This would tell you that the land is highly disturbed, has been recently cultivated, and that the normal plant succession to woody species has not yet begun. If, on the other hand, your site is full of shrubs and small trees, it is already in the early stages of woodland succession. Many mature trees, of course, signal the potential for woodland habitat.

Your plant inventory should also include a consideration of factors such as diversity, distribution, and abundance. Are there many different species in your plot, or is it dominated by relatively few? (Remember that a lack of diversity, in general, signals poor environmental health and an invitation to weed invasion.) How are the species distributed throughout the landscape? Do they occur

in clusters, and do these clusters relate to some underlying environmental factor, such as the presence of moisture? What are the most abundant species and what can they tell you about the habitat? A healthy stand of royal ferns, for example, might tell you that the soil is rich and moist; dandelions, on the other hand, that the soil is com-

---

Returning your landscape to a healthy, biologically stable environment may be one of the greatest contributions you can make to future generations.

—*Carol A. Smyser*, Nature's Design

---

pacted. Plants don't just react to conditions; they also actively affect landscape conditions: certain decomposing leaves, such as oak, create more acidic conditions than those of maple or beech; some plants, such as black walnut, release chemicals that impede the germination of plants near them. How are the existing plant communities shaping the landscape?

Along with determining what you've already got comes the most difficult decision of choosing what to keep and what to remove. This will depend on whether or not you want a purely native garden or a garden that combines natives with exotics. If you go for the former, your decision of what to keep is straightforward: keep all the natives, assuming they're there because they like it, unless experience over time proves otherwise. (At the design stage, you might decide to move them around.) If you've chosen a combination garden, your decision regarding what to keep should be based both on your aesthetic preferences and on the plants' cultural requirements. You'll be letting yourself in for no end of bother if, for example, you try to keep moisture-loving exotics, such as astilbe, in dry conditions.

POLLUTION CONSIDERATIONS

No matter where you live, but particularly if you live in a city, some unfortunate conditions that impinge on the garden must also be taken into account: air pollution and salt contamination. These are just as much a part of our ecological reality as water cycles and soil profiles.

The impact of air pollution on plants is a problem with a dirty, long history. The effect of sulphur dioxide on the vegetation of Europe was first studied a hundred years ago; in Ontario, scientists turned their gaze to SO_2 in Sudbury in the 1940s. Add to the list ground-level ozone pollution (not the ozone layer, but the pollutants caused when sunlight reacts with car exhaust and industrial emissions), lead, nitrogen dioxide, and fluorides, and it starts to seem amazing that anything grows.

In areas with high sulphur dioxide pollution, the following plants will be difficult to grow, because of their sensitivity: eastern white pine, white birch, white ash, trembling aspen, and bracken fern. (This last tells you something dire about air pollution, since the fern is otherwise a sturdy colonizer.) In such areas you may choose to grow some of the relatively SO_2-resistant trees, most of which are not native to Ontario. In descending order of tolerance: tree of heaven, the native pin oak, ginkgo, Carolina poplar, and London plane.

If you suspect that vegetation is being affected by air pollution (leaves are developing lesions, turning yellow, or there's a reduction in growth and eventually death), contact the Ontario Ministry of Environment's Phytotoxicology Section.

Road-salt contamination has a more immediate and local effect on vegetation; you can be sure, for example, that if you're shovelling salt-contaminated snow into the garden or around the root zone of trees, then you will be causing stress to plants and soil microorganisms. The injury takes many forms: salt creates drought conditions for plants (since salt absorbs water); it can accumulate to toxic levels in a plant's growing sections; it can cause potassium and magnesium deficiencies in plants; and it can cause soil to compact, thus making less air and water available to plant roots.

According to Cornell Cooperative Extension studies, salt injury resembles the symptoms of drought or root injury: "stunted, yellow foliage, premature autumn leaf coloration, death of leaf margins (scorch), and twig dieback." Plants are most sensitive in spring, as they are breaking dormancy.

George W. Hudler, in his bulletin "Salt Injury to Roadside Plants" for the New York State College of Agriculture, lists the following native trees as being salt-tolerant: paper birch, white ash, honey locust, white spruce, white poplar, cottonwood, red oak, and bur oak.

You can, of course, keep salt out of the garden by using sand or gravel on sidewalks and paths in winter.

With much in the way of simplification, all of the factors in site evaluation relate to the ecological make-up of a place—in other words, to the study of the relationships between organisms and their environments.

If you are going the habitat restoration route in your native plant garden (as opposed to simply using native plants as part of a collection of ornamentals), then ecological considerations will be paramount in every step you take. No one book will be able to tell you all you need to know— which is as it should be when you consider the enormous complexity and variation in native plant communities. Only you—or a gang of borrowed ecologists and naturalists, brought in for the express purpose—can learn all the variables at work in your plot. It is for you to, as Alexander Pope put it so long ago, "consult the genius of the place in all."

❦   ❦   ❦

Questions that relate less to plant choices and more to human use considerations include: how big a garden do you want; where do you want it; do you want paths and movement through the garden; who will use the garden and how; are there any structures you want to screen out visually or neighbouring views you'd like to hide?

The design stage is the point at which you should consider how much maintenance you want to do and then plan your garden around that. In general, the more formal your design, the more upkeep it requires. Informal designs, on the other hand, tend to demand less upkeep because you are not maintaining rigid separations between plants—you're allowing organic patterns to change.

DESIGN FOR ENERGY CONSERVATION

Money doesn't grow on trees, but savings do.
  —*Wayne Roberts, NOW, April 15–21, 1993*

According to Environment Canada, on a per capita basis, Canadians use more energy than any other country in the world except Luxembourg. Along with the massive changes we will need to make to alter this profligacy, there is something that we can do in our gardens: utilize trees and shrubs in such a way that they moderate the climate around our houses and thus reduce our heating and air-conditioning needs. In other words, landscape for energy efficiency.

For example, a windbreak of trees or shrubs that buffers against winter north winds will protect against some heat loss—up to 22 percent, says Landscape Ontario in their publication *Plants: Their Role in Modifying Our Environment*. The environmental group Friends of the Earth has also studied the effect of trees in reducing energy needs and their report, *The Tree-House Effect*, concludes that heating energy needs can be reduced by 10 percent

A single isolated tree can transpire 100 gallons of water per day (Kramer and Kozlowski, 1960). It takes 230,000 Kcal. to evaporate this much water, so a tree can be equated with five average room air conditioners, each running 20 hours a day.

—A Symposium on Trees and Forests
  in an Urbanizing Environment,
  August 18–21, 1970

in urban residential neighbourhoods, and cooling needs by 40 percent, by planting approximately three trees per house and by increasing the surface albedo of buildings (from moderate-dark to medium light colour) by 20 percent.

Landscape Ontario concludes that deciduous trees provide shade that can reduce air-conditioning needs up to 75 percent. If planted on the southwest or southeast sides of the house, deciduous trees will protect from morning or late afternoon sun in summer, yet allow in winter sun, so you can take advantage of passive solar benefits. Vines grown on west walls can also protect against summer heat build-up.

DESIGN AESTHETICS

The aesthetics of native plant garden design is such a personal thing that I find it difficult to suggest even the most basic rules. Most advice starts from the premise that you should design your "natural" landscape using the shapes found in natural plant communities. This seems fine until I start to think about all of the formal ponds I've seen: you won't find many perfectly square ponds in the wild and yet there are many in garden situations that look wonderful. The same is true for garden beds of wildflowers: I've yet to see spherical beds with abrupt and consistent delineations between different species in the wild, but have seen many gardens in which native plants are treated in this way—and the overall effect works. And paths: dozens of writers warn against straight paths in the woodland garden, calling them "unnatural." Big deal—this is a garden, not Algonquin Park! If you want to get from A to B with exigency, resort to the heretical straight line.

The best advice I can offer is this: look for aesthetic guidance in wild native plant communities, see what combinations and associations appeal to you, consider the colours and textures and shapes that evoke pleasing sensations for you, define what it is exactly that causes you to react in specific ways to the plant communities you see, keep all of your senses open and receptive to the information before you, then do what it is that gardeners are meant to do (and indeed what defines the whole enterprise): that is, pick and choose. Make informed decisions about the elements you want to include in your design, and be ruthless about rejecting what you don't like. This isn't a test—and it's also not some theoretical experiment on paper. It's a landscape you're going to live with.

Any discussion of aesthetics, I think (though this might be a minority position), hinges on preferences, which vary greatly. There aren't any fixed rules—only convention. Take colour, for example.

Gardening books are full of dicta, such as never plant pink and red flowers side by side or you'll create a ghastly, jarring explosion of clashing colour. Which is fine if you think jarring explosions of clashing colours are ghastly. But maybe you find this combo pleasing. Who's to judge? You are—but only in your own garden, where personal taste rules. Frankly, I think most anything goes as long as you like it.

If you desire universal praise and approval, then by all means follow the established rules of conventional colour theory. For example, plant flowers of complementary colours together for pleasing matches of vivid contrast. Be wary of too many shades of one colour as they tend to even each other out and flatten the overall impression, though this same effect might be used to soften the garden, soothe the senses. Use white colours as accents, dotted around the garden to knit the whole thing together. (White flowers make neighbouring colours seem more intense.) Avoid close contact between sisters on the colour wheel. Keep in mind the perceptual trick that makes cool colours seem to recede and thus create a feeling of distance, and hot colours seem close up, shortening space. Such rules are the stuff of familiar fashion and style dictates: would you wear it, would you plant it?

Things get a bit murkier in the realms of harmony, unity, balance, rhythm, and all those other design terms. You might recognize a harmonious and unified design when you see one in the garden, but how and why does it work? Where does contrast stop and chaos begin? When does balanced stability ooze into boring monotony? How exactly does one go about creating that elusive but much-celebrated "cohesive whole"?

Again, there are some conventional rules, such as plant for a progression of heights, from low in the front to tall in the back; or use juxtaposition to create dynamic contrasts. Consider planting in

COMBINATIONS FOR SHADY SITES WITH WELL-DRAINED, WOODLAND SOIL

- wild ginger, Jack-in-the-pulpit, Dutchman's breeches, trillium
- wild geranium, eastern columbine, bloodroot
- wood phlox, wood poppy, trillium, baneberry
- foamflower, Christmas fern
- bellwort, Virginia bluebells, trillium
- mayapple, Solomon's seal, blue cohosh
- wood poppy, Virginia bluebells, ostrich fern, violet
- hepatica, trout lily
- Canada anemone, mayapple
- bloodroot, hepatica, wild ginger, maidenhair fern

COMBINATIONS FOR ALKALINE WOODLANDS

- maidenhair fern, eastern columbine, goldenseal, twinleaf
- wild ginger, bloodroot, sharp-lobed hepatica, foamflower

COMBINATIONS FOR ACIDIC WOODLANDS

- Canada mayflower, wintergreen
- bluebead lily, bunchberry, creeping snowberry, twinflower
- partridgeberry, winterberry
- round-lobed hepatica, barren strawberry

COMBINATIONS FOR SHADY AND DRY SITES

- wood phlox, white wood aster
- foamflower, hay-scented fern
- large-leaved aster, New York fern

COMBINATIONS FOR SUNNY AND WELL-DRAINED, MOIST SITES

- wild geranium, blue flag
- wild bergamot, coreopsis, blazing star
- beardtongue, evening primrose
- bee balm, cardinal flower, beardtongue
- swamp milkweed, ironweed, culver's root
- bottle gentian, false dragonhead
- spiderwort, coreopsis

COMBINATIONS FOR SUNNY AND WET SITES

- marsh marigold, blue flag
- swamp milkweed, turtlehead
- Joe-pye weed, eupatorium, Canada lily

COMBINATIONS FOR SUNNY AND DRY SITES

- butterfly milkweed, purple coneflower
- gray-headed coneflower, little bluestem, black-eyed Susan
- Canada goldenrod, New England aster, heath aster
- blazing star, cup plant, nodding onion, coreopsis

COMBINATIONS FOR SUNNY AND ACIDIC SITES

- bearberry, cinquefoil
- swamp milkweed, butterfly milkweed, Canada lily

The New England Wild Flower Society has produced an excellent and inexpensive booklet called *Garden in the Woods: Cultivation Guide*, which lists hundreds of combinations for all types of soil.

clumps or drifts rather than in single pockets; exploit the design possibilities of undulating edges in your planting; and consider using different sizes of woody plants of the same species to create a naturalistic look. Use coarse-textured foliage to draw and hold the eye's attention. Use accent plants to draw the eye to some focal point. Or—much vaguer—match foliage textures with each other.

But what if you like extreme contrasts of ferny, lacy foliage with broad coarse leaves? I'm loathe to dictate the acceptable and the outrageous. Indeed, I think it's our responsibility and pleasure to push at received wisdom and accepted norms. Experi-

---

GARDEN AREAS

One authority on native plant gardening in the U.S., Ken Druse, suggests in his book *The Natural Garden* that gardeners divide their landscapes into three distinct areas: the inner, the in-between, and the outer. While I wouldn't go as far as he does—his suggestion sounds more like a rule—it does offer an interesting design possibility for native plant gardeners: the inner area is the most formal section of the landscape, usually close to the house, to be admired close up, fully under control; the in-between area is a transition zone in which formality slowly gives way to wild growth; and the outer area is the wildest section, "the last place in earth to grow lawn." I've seen a number of native plant gardens structured around this design philosophy and they work well, particularly for people who want to include some lawn (in the inner or in-between sections).

---

ment on your own, be gracious about your mistakes (and hope that others will be too—if they're not, don't invite them back), and move things around until you're happy.

❀   ❀   ❀

How do you feel when you read in books and magazines that to properly plan your plot you need the stationery hardware of a graphic design firm and the drafting skill of a professional engineer? If the challenges posed by multilayered graph paper, with separate sheets for the different seasons, for the permanent fixtures, for wind direction and soil types, for blooming schedules, and on and on—if these things make you itch for pencil and ruler, then go back to those books and magazines and have a pleasant winter on paper. There are many books that describe the process quite thoroughly and well (see "Design" in Further Reading and Resources).

I suspect, however, that most gardeners secretly have no use for such elaborate paper designs. It takes so many years to get to the point at which all the information is in your head and all you have to do is press the retrieve button and out it comes onto the graph paper . . . but by that point, the design stage is usually over, and the gardener is just tinkering with the fine details.

Or maybe I'm projecting my own inadequacies and you actually want to do all the drawings. Maybe you're a *very organized person.* And maybe you have the room to give over at least one full working surface to the trappings of the garden design trade. Okay. If you want to go this route, I highly recommend Carol Smyser's *Nature's Design.* There are hundreds of pages full of every possible detail you should take into account, and it's an excellent guide for the Virgos in the crowd. You deserve our respect, and your garden will, I'm sure, benefit from your advance planning and care. But I just want to make a plea for acceptance of the wingit, do-as-you-go kind of garden designer using what might be called the immersion method—there are many of us who have rejected the tyranny of the plan, and we're no less gardeners for it.

❦ ❦ ❦

Before I am accused of a totally cavalier approach, I should say that although *aesthetic* preferences are all over the map, ecological dictates are comfortably stable. Nature's rules don't go in and out of fashion, and the naturalistic gardener needs to pay attention to them. I can't stress enough that nature's plant communities are the native plant gardener's guide. You can't force a prairie species to thrive in a densely shaded woodland plot no matter how much coddling you give it. Plants and their associated communities have evolved together over thousands of years and no amount of weekend tinkering will change the ecological imperatives that guide them. Instead, let yourself be guided by them.

First of all, learn as much as you can about where and how native plants grow in the wild. Take big bluestem, for example. It's a tall-grass prairie plant, which any reference book should tell you. Thus, you know that it needs lots of sun and is drought tolerant. Because prairie environments don't naturally receive massive amounts of rich organic matter through fallen leaves, you also suspect that it will do well in nutrient-deficient soil. Because prairie plants require good drainage, you know that drainage is important for this plant. And, as a warm-season grass, you know that it won't really get going until the soil has warmed up in late spring. Its prairie provenance also tells you to expect that a larger percentage of its growth takes place underground, in the roots, than above ground, so you know that big bluestem will do great work for you in holding the soil together. All this information is gathered from an understanding of its ecological community.

Each and every plant is equally rich in the information it reveals—though some plants, such as cedar, bur oak, and red maple, will grow in many different conditions. Part of the trick of learning is to look at and observe plants in the wild, not just as single specimens, but as members of plant communities. Spend time exploring forested areas nearby. Watch wetlands, ponder prairies, meditate in meadows—just spend time in these habitats. Learn their language, interpret their clues. Speculate on why they are the way they are. Develop theories, indulge in outrageous ideas, then test them against what information you can find in books or from other naturalists. Go on organized walks (disorganized walks can be fun too . . .); most naturalist organizations hold tours of local areas. Ask silly questions. Pick people's brains. It's amazing how quickly such field identification and learning imprints itself—and this advice comes from a self-confessed bookworm. (I betrayed my bias for book learning when I asked a native plant gardener how non-botanists could get information about plants native to their location. Visit remnant natural areas, he suggested. With a good field guide, I piped up enthusiastically. No, no—to soak up the ambience, the tremendous spirit of the place, he corrected. And I realized that he's absolutely right. You can't read the nature of a place in a field guide.)

And sometimes, you can't even identify plants with a field guide! I, for example, can spend the winter looking at photos and drawings of some species in a book and not recognize it in the wild until someone points it out—but once I've seen it (and felt it and touched it and smelled it and sometimes even tasted it), it's hard to forget.

In other words, there is no substitute for the real thing: even just one woodsy walk with wide-open senses will tell you enough about gardening with native plants to get you started. And your gardening spirit will keep you going.

CHAPTER REFERENCES

Crazy About Gardening. Des Kennedy. Vancouver: Whitecap, 1994.

Garden in the Woods: Cultivation Guide. William E. Brumbrack and David L. Longland. Framingham, Massachusetts: New England Wild Flower Society, 1986.

Gardening with Wild Flowers. Frances Tenenbaum. New York: Charles Scribner's Sons, 1973.

Gardening with Wildflowers and Native Plants. Claire E. Sawyers, ed. Brooklyn: Brooklyn Botanic Garden, 1990.

A Garden of Wildflowers: 101 Native Species and How to Grow Them. Henry W. Art. Pownal, Vermont: Storey, 1986.

A Guide to the Study of Terrestrial Ecology. William A. Andrews et al. Scarborough: Prentice-Hall, 1974.

A Little Wilderness. Bill Ivy. Toronto: Oxford University Press, 1983.

The Natural Garden. Ken Druse. New York: Clarkson N. Potter, 1989.

Nature's Design: A Practical Guide to Natural Landscaping. Carol A. Smyser and editors of Rodale Press. Emmaus, Pennsylvania: Rodale, 1982.

Plants: Their Role in Modifying Our Environment. Mississauga: Landscape Ontario Horticultural Trades Foundation, 1981.

"Salt Injury to Roadside Plants." George W. Hudler. Ithaca: New York State College of Agriculture, n.d.

A Symposium on Trees and Forests in an Urbanizing Environment. Amherst, Massachusetts: University of Massachusetts Press, 1970.

The Tree-House Effect. Hashem Akbari and Haider Taha. Ottawa: Friends of the Earth, 1991.

Wild Gardening. Richard L. Austin. Scarborough: Prentice-Hall, 1986.

Chapter 8

PROPAGATION AND ACQUISITION OF NATIVE PLANTS

One of the biggest frustrations in native plant gardening is that after you've decided to take the plunge, after you've done your research, evaluated your conditions, decided the kind of habitat you want to create, and chosen the plants for your garden, you encounter the problem of where to *get* the plants. Too few nurseries sell them (though this is changing) and some nurseries that do sell them get their plants from distant sources (or worse, through wild collection) instead of collecting and growing local seeds. So you're left with the will but not the way.

However, you can easily turn this frustration into an adventure in seed starting—a logical next step in your gardening life, especially for native plant gardeners. Along with the satisfaction that comes from seed starting, there are also very important environmental considerations: by growing plants from seed, you are increasing the gene pool and thus the diversity of plant populations. When you propagate by division, on the other hand, the offspring plants are clones, which have the same

genetic make-up as the parent and are vulnerable to the same pests and diseases and weaknesses as the parent plant. Such asexual cloning narrows the genetic base of plant populations, limiting their ability to adapt to changing conditions or environmental stresses. Thus, plants started from seed are, in general, stronger and will be better adapted to the conditions of your site, particularly if you collect seeds from local sources; and they increase the diversity of the available genetic stock.

GROWING FROM SEED

Although there are relatively few sources of locally grown native plants for sale, there *are* some great sources of seed: the Canadian Wildflower Society, for example, operates the unparalleled Seed Exchange (see "Native Plant Sources" in Further Reading and Resources). Once you join, you receive a list of seeds available (published twice a year in *Wildflower* magazine), and information about where the seed was collected, so you can try to propagate indigenous stock appropriate for your location.

This is by far the best source of native seed, and you'll be connected with a network of people who are willing to share information and expertise.

Some commercial nurseries also offer native seed for sale, though sometimes it's difficult to get information about the seed's provenance. And, of course, other gardeners, gardening groups, local arboreta, and universities are also possible sources.

If your plant identification skills are honed, you can also collect seeds from the wild. One obvious benefit of wild seed collecting is that you can observe the plant in its native habitat and use this information later in your garden to create beneficial plant associations. (If you observe the same species when it is in bloom, you will also learn which insects it attracts.) However, there are a few

CANADIAN WILDFLOWER SOCIETY *Gardener's Guidelines*

1. Do not disrupt native plant communities.
2. Obtain native plants from seed, garden, or nursery.
3. Buy only wildflowers and ferns certified by the vendors as: "Nursery Propagated."
4. Use plants and seeds which have originated in your immediate bioregion. Such plants and seeds are best adapted to the local climate, soil, predators, pollinators, and disease.
5. Give preference to bioregionally native plant species in your garden, rather than naturalized or exotic species. The latter group may escape to wild habitats and interfere with the growth and spread of native flora and fauna.
6. Promote the cultivation and propagation of bioregionally native plants as an educational and conservation measure to supplement the preservation of natural habitat.
7. Keep accurate records of any bioregionally rare flora which you are growing to increase our understanding of the biology of the species.
8. Transplant wild native flora only when the plants of a given area are officially

slated for destruction: e.g., road construction, subdivisions, pipelines, golf courses, etc. Obtain permission before transplanting.
9. Collect no more than 10 percent of a seed crop from the wild. Leave the rest for natural dispersal and as food for dependent organisms.
10. Use natural means of fertilizing, weed and predator control rather than synthetic chemical means.
11. Consider planting native species attractive to native fauna, especially birds, butterflies and moths uncommon to your bioregion.
12. Exercise extreme caution when studying and photographing wildflowers in order not to damage the surrounding flora and fauna.
13. Co-operate with institutions such as arboreta, botanical gardens, museums, and universities in the propagation and study of rare species.
14. Openly share your botanical knowledge with the public but ensure that native plant species or communities will not be damaged in the process.

caveats to keep in mind. For example, seed collection should not be done in a way that disrupts native plant communities. If you're going to have to stomp through a carpet of orchids to get at that gentian, forget it. As well, you shouldn't collect more than 10 percent of a plant's seed crop. It takes very few seeds (Gail Rhynard of Otter Valley Native Plants suggests twenty-five to thirty seeds per species) to grow a few—four to five—plants for the garden. And finally, stick to seeds that have originated in your area. By collecting local seeds, you'll be helping to maintain the appropriate gene pool for plants in your bioregion—one of the best reasons, after all, for gardening with native plants in the first place.

SEED COLLECTION

Collecting your own seeds from local wildflowers is one of the most satisfying ways to increase your knowledge of plants and increase your gardening stock. It's an activity that's not without heartbreak, but that, too, is an integral part of gardening.

First, you'll need to identify the plant and choose your particular seed source: pick the most vigorous grower, as chances are that it will produce the healthiest seed. Mark the plant for future seed collection.

In general, ripe seeds will be available about a month to six weeks after the flower appears. There are a few clues that indicate seed is ripe: the pods are dry; the seed seems to fall away from the seed head; the seed is no longer green, and it is hard and firm. For seeds contained in berries, the berries usually turn a darker colour when mature. Remember: collect no more than 10 percent of the plant's seed.

After collecting the seed, you should let it dry out for approximately two weeks in a dry, airy place. Clean away or separate any chaff or debris from the seed once dry. Then it's ready to be stored in an airtight container in the refrigerator; only store *thoroughly* dry seed, otherwise it may rot. Seeds

that are produced in fleshy berries, such as Jack-in-the-pulpit, are an exception to the above rule. They should be cleaned—the pulp removed—and stored, if not planted immediately, in moist sand in the refrigerator. Don't let them dry out.

SEED-COLLECTING TIPS

- Seed of most native spring ephemerals (for example, trout lilies, spring beauties) should not be dried out, but rather should be stored immediately in the refrigerator in moist sand.
- If the summer is very hot and dry, seed tends to set and ripen more quickly.
- Put loose netting such as cheesecloth over the seed heads of plants that expel their seed rapidly so you're sure to collect some.
- To determine whether or not seeds of fleshy or pulpy fruit are sound, place in water and stir: sound seed sinks to the bottom and unsound seed rises to the top.
- To start trees such as oaks, hickories, beech, and walnut, collect acorns or nuts when they are ripe (from September to November). Fill a bucket with water and add nuts. Those that float to the top should be discarded as nonviable. Place acorns or nuts in moist perlite (equal parts acorns and perlite) and store in the refrigerator in a polyethylene bag at 38°F (3°C) for thirty to ninety days, or plant directly outside, allowing them to go through natural stratification.

Source: Canadian Wildflower Society, *Wildflower*

The Life of a Seed

Think of someone building a kit that would include all of the parts and the directions for building a celery plant. Think of being able to do this, then offering it so that the entire package—parts, directions, and container—weighs but 1/70,000 of an ounce. Nature has designed such a kit—a celery seed.

—Marc Rogers, Saving Seeds

In the category of things you can see with the mechanically unassisted eye, seeds are truly amazing. One gains a renewed sense of awe just by looking at each tiny grain and considering that such a compact bundle contains all the genetic information a plant needs for its life journey. You can balance a potential forest in the palms of your hands.

Consider the myriad routes that lead each seed to maturity: some travel great distances by wind and sea; some need fire or freezing to release their plant potential; some require sandblasting from wind; some require a brief stint in a bird or animal intestine so those gastric juices can weaken the seed coat; some laze happily underground for a decade before conditions are right for germination.

A Few Myrmecophytes

- *Anemone quinquefolia* (wood anemone)
- *Asarum canadense* (wild ginger)
- *Corydalis* spp. (corydalis)
- *Hepatica americana* (round-lobed hepatica)
- *Jeffersonia diphylla* (twinleaf)
- *Sanguinaria canadensis* (bloodroot)
- *Trillium* spp. (trillium)
- *Viola* spp. (violet)

Source: Jim Hodgins, *Wildflower*, Summer 1985, adapted from A.J. Beattie and D.C. Culver in *Ecology*, 62(1);107–115

Seeds are as various as the plants they produce, and their structures are important clues, full of information about how the seed will germinate, what it needs, how the seed will get to where it grows, and so on. There are winged versions, assisted in their journeys to hospitable places by the breeze. There are hooked versions, which hitchhike on animal coats and find their homes via the wanderings of their host. There are daintily weightless seeds, dispersed by the faintest rustle. And there are impossibly protected seeds, armoured by hard coats that can withstand the toughest boot. Some plants are profligate in their seed production; others have just one chance to produce offspring. Getting to know seeds, listening to what they tell us, experimenting with starting your own seedlings—all are natural progressions for the native plant gardener.

The relationship of seed to environmental conditions is endlessly fascinating and full of complexities we're just beginning to understand. Take ants and their role in seed dispersal, for example. On the same day that I visited a major nursery and saw ant killer for sale by the cash register (to induce panic purchases, I suppose), I read an article by Jim Hodgins in *Wildflower* magazine that concludes: "If you want to help wildflowers spread, don't swat those ants on your next picnic; don't spray insecticides on your garden." According to Hodgins, some 30 percent of North American spring-blooming woodland plants are myrmecophytes, or plants whose seeds are dispersed by ants. Attached to the seed is something Hodgins calls an "ant snack" (actually, he also calls it an aril, caruncle, or elaiosome, but snack it is), which is filled with an oily fluid that may attract the ant to the seed. Hoarded and transported back to the nest, sometimes as far as eleven yards (ten metres) away, the ants feast on the oil and then discard the seed, where it can germinate more quickly as a result of the ant action. How's that for symbiosis?

Before you start luring ants indoors to Hotel Peat Pot, rest assured that there are simpler ways to induce germination. The most important point to keep in mind is that for successful propagation, you need to closely mimic the natural processes that cause seeds to germinate in the wild.

Plants produce their seed after flowering and then go through a long and, in Ontario, usually cold period of dormancy. This means that for most native plants you'll need to reproduce those cold conditions before the seed will germinate. This process is called stratification. (Exceptions to this rule are some plants that produce their seed in spring or early summer; some, such as eastern columbine, will germinate and grow without a period of cold treatment.)

Although there are whole books written on the subject of seed starting and which plants require what conditions for germination, take your cue from nature: native Ontario plants that produce seed in late summer and fall in all likelihood *require* a period of cold stratification, otherwise they would send up tender growth just in time for winter's chill. Their natural inhibitors prevent such self-destructive behaviour.

The easiest way to stratify seeds is to do what nature does without human intervention: plant seeds in potting mixture in fall and leave them outside over the winter. (It's fine to let the snow cover the pots.) Germination will usually occur in spring, though some plants, such as blue cohosh, may go through this cycle twice or more before germinating.

Sounds straightforward, right? It *is* straightforward. I have no idea why commercial seed packets very often don't divulge this most basic of germination information, setting you up for failure right from the start. One year, early in my gardening life, I bought a package of black-eyed Susan seeds, sowed them in April, observed no action whatsoever in May, went away in June and expected to return in July to dazzling parades of yellow flowers. Nothing. The seeds were languishing in the soil, waiting for winter to come and go, and set their inner time to the Ontario cycle. Without cold stratification, they weren't going to budge.

As with many things in gardening, however, there are ways to cheat a bit. Say you haven't had time in fall to sow the seeds, or you don't get them from a seed exchange until late winter or early spring. You still need to create the cold conditions, so make room in your refrigerator for next year's woodland or meadow. Package the seeds up in an airtight container (though big seeds, such as acorns, need some air outlet; for these, use a polyethylene bag) and place in the fridge (38°F/3°C) for a period of six to eight weeks, then plant them out as you would any seed. This will work for seeds that have a short dormancy period.

For many native trees and shrubs, which go through a deeper dormancy, dry stratification alone will not work; these seeds need moist stratification. The Canadian Wildflower Society's Seed Exchange recommends that you mix seed with one part peat moss and one part sand, moisten just slightly until damp but not soggy, and place in a

> For a concise chart of propagation requirements for hundreds of North American native plants, consider ordering the *Directory to Resources on Wildflower Propagation*, compiled by the Missouri Botanical Garden and available free with a small shipping charge from the National Council of State Garden Clubs (4401 Magnolia Avenue, St. Louis, Missouri 63110-3492). Harry Phillips' book *Growing and Propagating Wild Flowers* is also an excellent resource, as is Maria Sperka's *Growing Wildflowers*.

plastic bag in the refrigerator at 38ºF (3º C) for 60 to 150 days. (If a root emerges while in the refrigerator, take the seedling out and pot it up.)

Some seeds require a process called scarification, in which the seed coat is scratched or nicked to induce germination—examples include hoary puccoon and slender bush-clover. You can use a

---

A seed is latent, intelligent energy waiting for the right time and place to express itself. A seed knows exactly what it has to do and exactly how to do it.

—*Jamie Jobb*, The Complete Book of Community Gardening

---

knife or razor blade to do this, or, if the seed is small, some fine sandpaper. Softening the seed in a hot water bath for a few hours will often achieve the same effect.

PLANT DIVISION

Obviously, starting plants from seed is an investment of time. A faster way to increase your clump-forming plants is through division: dividing the parent plant into several pieces, which then grow into new plants. Indeed, many plants should be divided just to prevent overcrowding and die-back in the centre of the plant.

Division can be done either in early spring or fall. The general rule is that spring-flowering plants should be divided in fall and fall-flowering plants in spring. Though I find it a wrenching experience (there's something anti-growth about the ripping noise), the plants do bounce back. Simply dig out the clump and with two gardening forks, or a sharp shovel, tease the clump into two

sections. If the clump is large, you can cut it into more pieces. Discard any woody bits from the centre and replant the new sections. Don't let the clumps dry out at all—treat them like the recovering patients they are.

ROOT AND ROOTSTOCK DIVISION

In the plant listings in Chapter 9, you will notice that root or rootstock division is often recommended as a propagation method. This is because it is often faster than seed-starting and is generally foolproof, if a few precautions are taken. The most important thing is that root cuttings should only be made when the plant is dormant.

For plants with fleshy roots, dig out the plants, rinse the soil off the roots, and cut off a section close to the crown. This section can then be cut into smaller pieces, each with a bud or eye, making sure that you cut on an angle to designate either the top or bottom of the root. Plant root cuttings right side up, at or just below the soil surface.

Division of tubers and rhizomes is also done when the plant is dormant. Simply dig them up and make a clean cut, making sure that each portion has a bud. Replant the sections at the correct depth.

Plants with runners (above-ground stems that "run" along soil, from which new plants emerge) or stolons (below-ground stems) can be divided by cutting the horizontal stems, ensuring that each cut has at least one plant. Mature bulbs and corms often produce small bulblets and cormlets, which can be broken off when the plant is dormant and replanted to the correct depth. Aerial bulblets can be planted even when the parent plant is actively growing.

STEM CUTTINGS

Trees and shrubs are often propagated by stem cuttings taken from the parent plant: a section is cut and planted in the ground, where it develops roots.

This method is also used for propagating hardy perennials. Softwood cuttings are those taken from young pliant growth in spring.

SOFTWOOD CUTTINGS

In the early morning of a cloudy day, before plants start to dry out in the sun, prepare the potting mixture and flats or containers that will house your cuttings. A mixture of sand, peat moss, and compost works well. Choose a healthy-looking young shoot and, using a knife or razor blade, cut off a 6-inch (15-cm) piece. Remove the lower leaves from the stem and, after dipping the planting end in rooting hormone powder, place the cutting into the potting mixture, firming it down well. Enclose the pot in a clear plastic bag to retain moisture. Keep the mixture moist at all times, never allowing it to dry out, and place the cutting in indirect light. Roots will take anywhere from a few weeks to longer to form.

This is just a brief introduction to plant propagation, and is meant primarily to encourage you to explore these methods. There are many excellent books on the subject in general and on wildflower propagation in particular; some go into great detail for each plant species.

GARDENER BEWARE: WILD COLLECTION OF NATIVE PLANTS

Perhaps it's placing a hefty demand on a simple purchase, but when contemplating a plant transaction involving many native wildflowers at nurs-

---

SEED-STARTING TIPS

- Store completely dry seeds in a sealed plastic bag in the refrigerator, not the freezer, until ready to use.
- For moist seed stratification, use a half-and-half mixture of dampened sand and peat moss.
- Observe your fridge specimens regularly. If germination has occurred and you can see roots, pot up the plants.
- After dry or moist stratification, pot the seeds in your favourite soilless potting mixture, commercial or homemade. The mixture should be porous.
- A sterilized potting mixture will prevent damping off of seedlings, which is caused by a soil fungus.
- Plant seeds to correct depth: a general rule is two or three times the diameter of the seed. However, some seeds that need light to germinate, such as columbine or foamflower, should be placed on the soil surface.
- After you've potted up stratified seeds, place outside (if spring) in indirect light, or place under growing lights (if late winter and you're getting an early start). You can put clear plastic over the pots to prevent the surface of the soil from drying out, but remove the plastic when the seeds germinate.
- Keep the pots moist but don't drench them. It's a good idea to water from the bottom (that is, put the pots on a tray) or mist the surface.
- When the seeds have germinated, place the pots in direct light for a few hours each day, gradually increasing the time they're exposed to direct light.
- Transplant to 4-inch (10-cm) pots when seedlings have four to six leaves.

---

eries, one should have the tenacity of a detective rather than the timidity of your regular garden-variety consumer. Too often your queries will be fobbed off with a reassuring but glib response. Dig deeper.

A case in point: I received my catalogue from a thriving, fancy bulbhouse and was immediately struck by its photos of the toad trillium (native to Pennsylvania and south), with its maroon flowers poking up from mottled leaves. I phoned the company to ask if the trilliums were nursery propagated. Oh yes, came the response, we state that right in the catalogue. Across the phone lines, we flipped pages together, looking for that reassur-

---

WILD COLLECTION WORLD-WIDE

The problem of wild collection extends far beyond North American native plants. Faith Thompson Campbell of the Natural Resources Defense Council in the U.S. has compiled data on the staggering numbers of wild-collected plants from Turkey and Asia, such as sternbergia, cyclamen, anemone, and winter aconite. Botanists in these countries charge that these plants are being overexploited in the wild and that they may become endangered in their native range.

For people who want to buy such exotic bulbs, consumer choice in this matter is getting much more clearcut: as of 1995, all bulbs from the Netherlands (this includes plants that originate elsewhere but are then sent to the Netherlands for world-wide distribution) are labelled so as to indicate whether the plants are propagated ("grown from cultivated stock") or of wild origin ("bulbs from wild source").

---

ing phrase. Oops, not in this issue for some reason, but rest assured, there are no wild-collected plants. I held off on my order, not feeling flush that day, and called a few days later. A different person was on the phone this time and we ploughed through my list. Visions of spring ephemerals were within reach, but just to confirm, I asked the same question regarding nursery propagation. The answer: Well, we don't start them from seed but we get them from a reputable American dealer. Does *that* dealer start them from seed, I asked. No, but he collects them from his property; it's just like raising beef cattle, you know. Suddenly, the thought of people digging up colonies of trilliums from their land to feed the catalogue's demand seemed less and less appealing. Yes, they own the land so it's not like some midnight raid on a park, but it's still a matter of denuding wild colonies, and when that colony is gone, moving to another dealer. I cancelled my order, with regret for the next spring's bare patches in my garden, but hopes for fewer bare patches somewhere in Tennessee.

If this sounds a bit Pollyanna-ish, consider the Canadian Wildflower Society's hard line: Do not purchase bird's foot violets, yellow trout lilies, orchids, trilliums, walking ferns, Jack-in-the-pulpits, pitcher plants, and hepaticas unless the vendor marks your bill of sale with "NURSERY PROPAGATED" and his/her signature.

Maybe this seems like an extreme injunction and even contradictory—on the one hand, to encourage gardeners to use native plants and on the other, to issue strict warnings about plant sources—but it is necessitated by the destructive pillaging that has gone on in the name of commerce. Through the years, the nursery trade, whether deliberately or unknowingly—and the gardeners who buy from them—have participated in the wild-collection of native plants, sometimes to the point of severely threatening populations and disrupting native plant communities.

According to Mary Pockman, past president of the Virginia Native Plant Society, wild collection for the horticultural trade is cited as the main reason for the decline of the white fringeless orchid in the U.S. The plant is now listed as endangered in Tennessee. Jane Scott, writing in *Wildflower* in 1987, notes that "it has been estimated that well over 100,000 herbaceous plants are removed from the mountains of North Carolina and Tennessee every year," and "a sizeable portion of the native North American species offered for sale through nurseries have been collected from the wild." We may feel that our one purchase can't possibly matter, but the same explosive power of numbers that brings us the "fifty simple things you can do to help the environment" also brings us endangered and threatened plants. Multiply your desire across the continent and that purchase may no longer seem benign.

The problem with commercial collection to feed the gardener's demand is that entire populations of an existing species may be harvested from a particular location, as this is often the most expedient and profitable method. Once that community has been depleted, collectors move on to another location, and so on and so on. Even if the collectors claim that the plants have been harvested sustainably, who's to tell? Where are the studies that identify the numbers and conditions needed for wild populations to regenerate? Where's the documentation to prop up the claim that if you take a certain percentage of trilliums from a plant community, the remaining plants will set seed and reproduce, keeping the population stable and healthy? As Nina T. Marshall, in her exhaustive study *The Gardener's Guide to Plant Conservation*, concludes: "The vast majority of plants currently collected from the wild are harvested without any management plan or monitoring system."

❦   ❦   ❦

So what's the native plant gardener to do? Starting plants from seed is one obvious option, particularly for those species commonly wild-collected: trilliums, trout lilies, lilies, Jack-in-the-pulpits, bellwort. If the time involved is too much for you, then you can buy these plants from native plant society sales; very often, they have been rescued from

> *Terrestrial orchids have never been propagated successfully in the quantities necessary for commercial trade; therefore, virtually every plant offered for sale has been dug from the wild. No responsible gardener should ever buy one of these plants.*
>
> —Jane Scott, Field and Forest

development sites, raised from seed by members, or divided from plants in members' gardens. If you're considering a purchase from a commercial nursery, try to determine the plant's origin. Nurseries that are propagating their plants rather than collecting them from the wild will most likely be proud of the fact and advertise this to consumers. Look for the phrase "nursery propagated"—and don't be misled by ambiguous and confusing terms such as "nursery grown" (this *could* mean that the plant was originally wild-collected then stuck in a nursery bed for one season or less). Be particularly cautious about the many woodland plants that take a long time to reach flowering size from seed; rarely do nurseries invest the time necessary to propagate these plants. As well, most native orchids (*Cypripedium* spp.) have yet to be propagated successfully from seed to flowering, so you can be almost certain that any for sale have been collected from the wild. Some require a particular fungus in the soil in order to grow, so not only will the purchase deplete native populations, but it will be doomed to failure in the garden. (One expert who has been studying native orchids for years, Frederick W. Case, Jr.,

---

It seems likely that wild collection will eventually be replaced by propagation, but "eventually" may be some time in coming. In the meantime, through care in acquiring plants, gardeners can both add to their own pleasure and take a stand with all who are working to ensure that wildflowers and native plants remain part of a treasured living heritage.

—Mary Pockman, in Gardening with Wildflowers and Native Plants

---

concludes in his book, *Orchids of the Western Great Lakes Region*, that "native orchids are quite susceptible to fungus rot and leaf spot diseases under cultivation.") Given their extensive wild-collection and difficulty of cultivation, it seems prudent to forego orchids.

In her book *The Gardener's Guide to Plant Conservation*, produced jointly by the World Wildlife Fund and the Garden Club of America, Nina T. Marshall suggests the following consumer tips for purchasing wisely.

• Before buying a plant, look for information about source.

• Critically evaluate the information about plant origins.
• If there is any ambiguity, question the vendor.
• Consider growing plants from seed rather than purchasing plants of uncertain origin.
• Voice your concerns.
• Be aware of . . . legislation protecting plants.
• When in doubt, contact plant societies, botanical gardens, and other conservation organizations to determine which nurseries or vendors sell propagated plants.

One final note: while all the above might mitigate against the destruction of native plants being carried out in your name for your garden, the only long-term and truly meaningful way to protect native plants and perpetuate native plant communities is to protect their habitats. The growing of rare or endangered plants in gardens across the continent will produce only the botanical equivalents of zoos—guarded enclosures, not thriving wild communities.

PLANT RESCUES

In some cases—when a site is being developed, for example—it may be appropriate to dig plants from the wild after permission is received from the landowner. Since the transplanting will most likely be done in non-optimum conditions (plants in flower, for example), it makes sense to contact organizations with expertise in this area before embarking on a project alone. Try the Canadian Wildflower Society or a local arboretum, particularly if the site contains rare species.

CHAPTER REFERENCES

The Complete Book of Community Gardening. Jamie Jobb. New York: William Morrow, 1979.

Field and Forest. Jane Scott. New York: Walker & Co., 1984.

The Gardener's Guide to Plant Conservation. Nina T. Marshall. Washington: World Wildlife Fund and the Garden Club of America, 1993.

Gardening with Wildflowers and Native Plants. Claire E. Sawyers, ed. Brooklyn: Brooklyn Botanic Garden, 1990.

Growing and Propagating Wild Flowers. Harry R. Phillips. Chapel Hill, North Carolina: University of North Carolina Press, 1985,

Growing Wildflowers. Maria Sperka. New York: Charles Scribner's Sons, 1973.

Orchids of the Western Great Lakes Region. Frederick W. Case, Jr. Bloomfield Hills, Michigan: Cranbrook Institute of Science, 1964.

Saving Seeds: The Gardener's Guide to Growing and Storing Vegetable and Flower Seeds. Marc Rogers. Pownal, Vermont: Storey, 1990.

Chapter 9

PLANT LISTINGS
A DETAILED GUIDE

I have been greatly assisted in the compilation of this specific plant information by Gail Rhynard, who runs a native plant nursery in Eden, Ontario, called Otter Valley Native Plants (see "Native Plant Sources" in Further Reading and Resources). Gail has been growing, propagating, and working with native plants in restoration projects for five years, and she has amassed a great deal of practical knowledge about landscaping with native plants. Her comments and observations are identified by the initials "GR" at the end of relevant plant entries.

❋ ❋ ❋

The plant lists are arranged according to habitat: sunny meadow and prairie; shady woodland; and wet sites (including ponds).

Where plants are adaptable to a range of habitats, this is noted. However, keep that inquisitive gardening spirit alive by experimenting: for example, while New England aster is a sunny meadow plant (indeed, it brightens fields through-out Ontario in the late summer and fall), I've bent the rules a bit by growing two healthy clumps in what is essentially a woodland habitat, in an area of light shade. Such a compromised condition keeps the rampant aster in check and allows me to enjoy the stunning purple in autumn out the front window—something I wouldn't be able to do if I were to slavishly follow habitat rules to the letter.

However, just so you are aware of the rules before you start to twist them:

- The plants listed under the sunny meadow and prairie habitat section all do best in full sun—that is, sun for at least five hours a day.
- When all the experts say you don't need to enrich the soil for meadow and prairie plants, they mean it: these plants don't need rich soil. In fact, highly fertile soil will in most cases produce more vegetative growth and fewer flowers. And sometimes monster plants!
- The plants in the shady woodland section, obviously, prefer shade, but this is by no means a uniform term. Even a forest has many shades of shade:

from the dense darkness of a coniferous forest to the airy shade produced by many urban street trees. As well, your particular microclimate will greatly affect the plant's adaptability to the site. Detail is provided in the plant lists, but again, experiment, bend, twist, and possibly break...

- Some of the plants listed for wet sites want sun and some want shade, but they all require more moisture than is usually available in a regular garden. These plants are perfect for "problem" sites (in fact, turn problem to advantage), such as places where the water table is close to the surface, places that flood in spring, or places that border permanent watery sites such as ponds. The pond plants include species that live in the water and plants that thrive along pond margins. If you don't yet have a water feature in your garden, you might be inspired by these plants to try one out.

- Gardening books often resemble science textbooks when they get going about soil pH. I'm of two minds on this matter: on the one hand, it's necessary to be in intimate contact with your soil, which includes knowing its pH; on the other hand, intimate doesn't mean intimidated! For the most part, unless you have dramatically acidic or alkaline soil (below 5 or above 7.5), you can make use of any of the native plants in these plant listings. Exceptions to this are noted in the list.

- Southern Ontario is home to an ecosystem known as the Carolinian life zone. If you live in this area (see map in Chapter 4), you have a great opportunity to specialize in a garden of native Carolinian plants, identified in Chapter 4.

- Remember that there are approximately two thousand native plants in Ontario—the following is necessarily a highly selected list! All the plants outlined here will reward you with interesting textures, foliage, flowers, and seedheads. But it's just a start. See Further Reading and Resources for wildflower guides and reference books on native Ontario plants that will help you expand your garden palette. The cardinal rule in gardening: experiment.

- The plants listed are native to many regions of Ontario, but of course this is a huge province. Within your area there will be typical plant communities and plant associations that you may want to replicate in your garden. The best source of local plant information is, of course, in remnant wild areas and parks. Many naturalist groups also publish very specific lists of plants native to the region. These groups often conduct walking tours of wild areas where you can experience first-hand the diversity of your specific ecological zone. In general, the more widespread in distribution a plant is, the more adaptable it is; conversely, the more specific a plant is in its ecological requirements, the more difficult it will be to cultivate in the garden.

- For more detailed habitat and plant range information, consult a field guide, such as *A Field Guide to Wildflowers of Northeastern and North-central North America* by R. T. Peterson and M. McKenny.

- Unless otherwise noted, the plants are perennial.

- Plants described as "spring ephemerals" appear in spring, then go dormant in midsummer. Don't be discouraged by this disappearing act—many make up for their short show with great spring beauty and exuberance. You'll just need to be careful to design your garden so that the bare spots fill in with other plants during the summer. It's a good idea to mark the spot with a small twig or stone so that you don't inadvertently damage spring ephemerals by digging when they are dormant.

- Although the plant listings provide information about heights and blooming dates, please note that there may be some local variation.

- For information on plant propagation of most plants in the listings, see the general guidelines outlined in Chapter 8. Any exceptions—plants that require or benefit from a particular method of propagation—are noted in the listings.
- Plants marked with an "R" are designated as rare in the wild in Ontario by Argus and Pryer in *Rare Vascular Plants in Canada*.
- Plants marked with a "W" are listed in Nina Marshall's *The Gardener's Guide to Plant Conservation* as being either primarily wild-collected or having some wild collection in North America. Gardeners should be particularly cautious about determining the plant's origin when buying these species from nurseries.

SUNNY MEADOW AND PRAIRIE PLANTS

Beardtongue (*Penstemon digitalis*) W

With foliage clustering low to the ground, this plant sends up a tall, 2- to 4-foot (0.6- to 1.2-m) flower stalk in May to June. The tubular white flowers last for several weeks. It attracts hummingbirds, and tolerates dry soil and light shade. It readily self-sows or can be divided in spring or fall.

GR: A wonderful plant with long-lasting blooms that range from white to white tinged with purple and even lavender, it's definitely a favourite for early summer colour. Though it blooms early in the season, the seed isn't ripe until late September to mid-October.

Bergamot (*Monarda fistulosa*)

This plant has several quirky features that make it a real treat to the senses: its leaves smell like Earl Grey tea; its tubular flowers manage to look both regal and silly at the same time; its stem is square rather than round; and if you spend any time listening to this plant, you'll hear the busy buzz and hum of many bees. It grows to over 3 feet (1 m) and bears lavender-coloured blooms in July and August. It's easy to propagate from seed, which ripen in September; you should also divide clumps in spring to prevent dieback in the centre. Give it lots of room as it gets quite bushy. Mine gets mildew every year but is robust as anything, so instead of worrying I sit back and enjoy the fortuitous grey foliage. It does well in poor or rich soil—and heavier soil—and is drought tolerant. It attracts butterflies as well as bees and looks fabulous with black-eyed Susans and coreopsis.

GR: Seedlings of monarda are easy to identify as they have that Earl Grey tea scent even at the four-leaf stage.

Black-eyed Susan (*Rudbeckia hirta*) R

Probably the most familiar wildflower, this biennial self-sows readily so you have blooms year after year, though it does wander throughout the garden. Drought tolerant, the yellowy orange flowers appear from June until frost and the dark brown seedheads provide bird food throughout the winter. Butterflies also visit the flower. Plants are 2 to 3 feet (60 to 90 cm) tall. If you have lots of room, plant in huge drifts for a stunning display, especially when mixed with purple coneflower or bergamot.

GR: Watch for seedlings when weeding (even at the four-leaf stage they're recognizably hairy), as these are next year's flowering plants.

Butterfly milkweed (*Asclepias tuberosa*) W

Brilliant orange flower clusters from July to September attract butterflies, hummingbirds, and

---

Goldenrods do produce pollen but only in small quantities, and their pollen is heavy and sticky. It is not carried on the wind and . . . . must not be blamed as the source of irritation for ragweed hay fever sufferers.

—J.F. Alex, Ontario Weeds

---

bees. It grows to 1 to 3 feet (30 to 90 cm) and thrives in dry sandy soil with good drainage. It can cope with moderately acidic conditions. Give it room as it gets bushy. It has a very long tap root, so it's best to transplant seedlings to a permanent place. If starting from seed, which ripen in mid- to late October, sow in deep pots in late fall and mulch over winter. Established plants may need mulching in a cold winter. This is one of the host plants for monarch butterfly larvae.

Canada goldenrod (*Solidago canadensis*)

Please don't call this native wildflower a weed or blame it for causing hay fever—two common burdens it doesn't deserve. In fall, you just can't beat the yellow plumes and welcome glow of this tall grower (up to 5 feet/1.5 m). It self-sows readily, spreads by underground stems, and has a tendency to flop, but it is drought tolerant and very showy.

It's easy to divide clumps. Goldenrod is a victim of our tendency to prize the exotic over the common.

GR: Also try gray goldenrod, which is clump-forming, prefers well-drained soil, and is good for xeriscaping. It is short-lived but self-seeds readily and will grow in semishade to full sun. The tips of its flowering stalks nod. Another favourite is blue-stemmed goldenrod: it grows in semishade to light shade; is a good woodland edge plant; is not aggressive; and withstands dry soil.

Compass plant (*Silphium laciniatum*)

This conversation-starter orients the edges of its deeply cut leaves on a north-south axis (so the flat surfaces don't get scorched by midday sun), hence the name. It grows very tall, up to 12 feet (3.6 m), with yellow daisylike flowers in July to September. It's drought tolerant, with a very deep tap root.

GR: If you're starting it from seed, it may take up to five years to bloom; cold-moist stratify the seed.

Culver's root (*Veronicastrum virginicum*) R, W

A tall and graceful plant (2 to 7 feet/0.6 to 2.1 m), each stem has many white flower spikes that bloom from late July through early fall. The pointy leaves grow in whorls all around the stem.

GR: It prefers moist to average soil. Since I'm gardening in sand, I've planted culver's root with cup plant beside a rock; the roots travel under the rock where they find more moisture.

Cup plant (*Silphium perfoliatum*) R, W

Often denigrated as "coarse," the upper leaves of this interesting prairie species grow around the square stem, creating a cup. It's a tall grower (4 to 8 feet/1.2 to 2.4 m), with yellow flowers that appear in July to September.

GR: Cold-moist stratify the seed.

Dense blazing star (*Liatris spicata*) R, W

An interesting and dramatic plant with smooth slender foliage and a flower spike that grows from 1 to 5 feet (0.3 to 1.5 m). Small lavender flowers bloom from the top of the spike down, from July to September. It doesn't mind the heat but likes moisture. It's easy to propagate from seed.

GR: Seedlings bloom in the second year. Two other *Liatris* species for drier soil are *L. aspera*, 1 1/2 to 4 feet (45 to 120 cm), and *L. cylindracea*, 8 to 18 inches (20 to 45 cm). They are great butterfly plants.

Evening primrose (*Oenothera biennis*) W

This biennial has small, 4-petalled yellow flowers. Many books say that the flowers open in late afternoon or dusk, for night pollination, but I've found that they open during the day. Attractive to birds (for its seeds) and butterflies, it grows from 1 to 5 feet (0.3 to 1.5 m) and thrives in dry soil. The flowers bloom from July to September. It's considered by some to be too rampant, but why complain?

Gray-headed coneflower (*Ratibida pinnata*) R

Though not as showy as *Rudbeckia*, this fine prairie plant produces yellow ray flowers that droop around a distinctive, tall centre cone. (Don't be misled by the name: the ray flowers are yellow, the cone is greyish.) The leaves are deeply cut and airy, and the plant is 3 to 5 feet (0.9 to 1.5 m) tall. Long-lasting flowers appear from late June to August. It's easy to start from seed.

GR: Gray-headed coneflower is a great plant for xeriscaping—it thrives in arid soil.

Ironweed (*Vernonia altissima*) W

Purple fans take note: the vivid flower clusters of ironweed appear from August through October on stems that grow from 3 to 7 feet (0.9 to 2.1 m) tall. It does best in moist to average soil, and it attracts butterflies.

GR: Plant ironweed with Culver's root for a striking combination of colour and flower form.

Jerusalem artichoke (*Helianthus tuberosus*)

Also known as sunchoke, the tubers of this rapid spreader are edible. It grows very high (up to 10 feet/3 m) and may need staking. Individual flowers are small and yellow, appearing in late summer and lasting through the fall. Leaves are rough; stems are hairy.

GR: Plant a patch of Jerusalem artichokes in a corner where tubers can be dug easily every fall without disturbing the plants around them. Dig all you can find—you never get them all—to keep the patch from growing out of bounds.

Lance-leaved coreopsis (*Coreopsis lanceolata*) R

Also known as tickseed, this plant is a meadow favourite with slender leaves and glowing gold flowers throughout the summer. It grows to 1 to 2 feet (30 to 60 cm) and is very easy to start from seed. It's an obliging plant that does well in poor soil, tolerates drought, and attracts butterflies.

GR: Coreopsis grows lanky by midsummer. I cut mine back in mid-July; it grows back and flowers furiously until late fall.

Lupine (*Lupinus perennis*) R

I love everything about this plant: its leaves (palmately compound and a gorgeous forest green), its flowers (spikes of blue pealike blossoms in May to July), and its easy nature (as long as it's happy, it will self-sow). It grows 1 to 2 feet (30 to 60 cm) high in nice full mounds. It's leguminous, so its root nodules and bacteria enrich the soil with nitrogen while enlivening the garden. Lupines don't respond well to transplanting, but they're easy to grow from seed, especially if you soak the seed for a day before planting. It likes well-drained sandy soil. Although *Lupinus perennis* is now rare in the wild in southern Ontario, there are a few gorgeous stands in High Park, Toronto, and in Pinery Provincial Park, where it serves as the host plant for the provincially rare Karner blue butterfly.

GR: Like other leguminous plants, lupines need the proper inoculant in the soil, so inquire at a nursery before trying to grow them.

New England aster (*Aster novae-angliae*)

Tall slender and leafy stems, up to 7 feet (2.1 m) though usually 3 to 4 feet (0.9 to 1.2 m), bear gold-centred violet-purple flowers in late summer through fall. It's a vigorous grower, so prune it back in spring if you want a bushier plant. It should be divided every few years, and readily self-seeds. Seeds ripen in November. Lower leaves tend to look straggly if there is not enough moisture. Bees and butterflies love this plant. It's a must for a meadow, especially when combined with certain goldenrods. It also grows in light shade and prefers moist conditions.

Left to right: panicled, heath, and New England asters

GR: Ontario is fortunate to have many species of asters blooming from mid-August until late October. With asters for both sun and shade, native plant gardens can be as colourful in October as they are in May.

Native plants, when grown in gardens and given better soil and less competition than in the wild, will often surprise us with their vigorous growth. I saw an *Aster macrophyllus* (large-leaved aster), which in the woods grows 1 1/2 to 2 feet (0.45 to 0.6 m) and sends up two or three unimposing stems, in a garden, where it was 3 feet (0.9 m) tall with a spread of 2 1/2 feet (0.75 m).

Nodding wild onion (*Allium cernuum*) W

Feathery, ribbonlike foliage to 1 foot (30 cm) supports hanging clusters of pinky white flowers in July and August. It's easy to start from seed. It also grows in open woodlands, though it doesn't bloom as much in shade. The closed flower buds, covered in a white tissuelike sheath, are also attractive.

GR: Flowers are long lasting, and stems are wiry and strong. Bulbs can be divided in spring or fall just as the leaves are beginning to show. It prefers well-drained soil.

Obedient plant (*Physostegia virginiana*) W

Spreading by underground running stolons, this plant (also known as false dragonhead) does well in moist, fertile, sunny conditions. Lavender, sometimes white, flowers resembling snapdragons appear in late summer, last well into fall, and are borne atop 2- to 4-foot (0.6- to 1.2-m) stems. The stem dies back after flowering, but new shoots are sent up in spring. It's a good idea to dig out the centre clump and divide in late fall or early spring.

Prairie smoke (*Geum triflorum*)

Also known as purple avens, this early bloomer flowers in April to June, then produces its most interesting feature: long feathery hairs or puffs of grey mauve seeds and fruits. It grows to 6 to 18 inches (15 to 45 cm) in dry soil, making it a good plant for rock gardens. The foliage is interesting, deeply cut, almost fernlike.

GR: Seed can be sown fresh or after cold dry stratification. Prairie smoke will bloom the second year from seed. Plants can be readily divided.

Purple coneflower (*Echinacea purpurea*) W

This is a fascinating plant that is showy throughout its many changes: in midsummer pinky white flowers emerge; as they grow they start to turn down and change from pink to purple. Likewise, the orange flower centre turns bronzy brown. Flowers last well into fall. The plant grows to 3 feet (0.9 m) tall, is bushy, and should be divided every few years. It's a profligate self-seeder. Butterflies swarm purple coneflower, which is very attractive with certain goldenrods and black-eyed Susan. It's drought tolerant and does well in many types of soil.

GR: Purple coneflower responds to good soil with adequate moisture, but prefers good drainage. I add compost or manure in light soil.

Spiderwort (*Tradescantia virginiana*) W

With its irislike leaves and violet flowers from May to July, this attractive plant is a great garden addition, though it can take over. It grows 1 to 2 feet (30 to 60 cm) tall in clumps. It is easy to start from seed or divide.

GR: Spiderwort will tolerate dry sandy soil. Cut it back after flowering (unless you want seeds) to promote new growth and flowering later in summer.

Sunflower (*Helianthus annuus*)

Its rough hairy stem and heart-shaped leaves grow quite high (3 to 10 feet/0.9 to 3 m) and support yellow flowers with brown centres that bloom from July to October. This annual produces lots of seeds, so it's easy to establish. In her book on meadow gardening, Laura Martin warns that sunflowers release an inhibitor from their decaying roots that affects the growth of nearby plants; she suggests removing the roots after flowering.

SHADY WOODLAND PLANTS

Bellwort (*Uvularia grandiflora*) W

A spring treat, especially when combined with Virginia bluebells, this plant produces nodding yellow bells that hang down from arching stems in April and June. It grows up to 2 feet (60 cm), with good bushy foliage. Plant seeds as soon as they ripen in late July through August, or divide clumps. As *Wildflower* editor Jim Hodgins first pointed out to me, this woodland plant is much more floriferous and robust-looking in the garden than it is in the wild.

GR: This handsome woodland plant looks good from spring until fall. Bellwort seems to benefit from division.

Black snakeroot (*Cimicifuga racemosa*) R, W

Also known as black cohosh or bugbane, this bushy plant is great for summer interest, when it sends up long-lasting white spikes. This tall grower (3 to 8 feet/0.9 to 2.4 m) needs lots of room, but it's dependably easy to grow. Increase through division or start from seed, which ripens in late September through October. It likes humic soil, slightly acidic, and will do well in partial sun. In her book *Growing Wildflowers*, Maria Sperka warns that seed germination is "slow and uneven."

GR: This striking plant is effective when placed against a dark background, so the white flower spikes really stand out. Black snakeroot is the host plant for the spring azure butterfly.

Bloodroot (*Sanguinaria canadensis*) W

A woodland must, this groundcover (6 to 12 inches/15 to 30 cm) is a perky charmer in early spring, when it sends up curled leaves covering the flowering stem, "much like a diva emerging into the limelight" as Peter Loewer puts it in his book *The Wild Gardener*. The starlike white flowers with yellow centres don't last long, but they're one of the first in the spring garden. Leaves unfurl a nice green, and these flat, deeply lobed saucers carpet the ground. It prefers rich soil; during dry summers, the plant will go dormant in midsummer. It's easy to propagate by rhizome division. If you're starting it from seed, which ripens in June, don't let the seeds dry out.

GR: Bloodroot seems to withstand variable growing conditions: I've seen it in both heavy clay soil and well-drained, drier soil. Divide the rhizomes in fall, or once the leaves begin to die back, treating the cut ends with a fungicide before replanting.

Blue cohosh (*Caulophyllum thalictroides*) W

This attractive foliage plant somewhat resembles meadow-rue, bleeding heart, or columbine. It grows to 1 to 3 feet (30 to 90 cm), with small greenish yellow or chocolate brown flowers in May and gorgeous blue seeds in late summer. It likes rich, moist soil. Seeds may take a few years to germinate, but the plant is easy to propagate via division.

Broad-leaved waterleaf (*Hydrophyllum canadense*)

Of interest mainly as a foliage plant for woodland groundcover, the plant grows to approximately 18 inches (45 cm) with maplelike leaves. Flower clusters are white to pink, appear in early summer, and are often obscured by foliage.

Canada anemone (*Anemone canadensis*)

Although Canada anemone is a rapid spreader, you can use this trait to your advantage in problem spots that need a quick groundcover. The plant is a delight: it grows 1 to 2 feet (30 to 60 cm) high with single white flowers in spring and leaves that surround the stem. It does well in moist, open woods and also grows well in full sun. Divide in fall if (or when, since it's inevitable) the plant becomes crowded. It's easy to propagate from seed, which ripens in July, or rhizome division.

GR: This is a good plant to use for naturalizing in damp areas—let other taller wet meadow plants grow up through it.

Canada lily (*Lilium canadense*) W

A boon to open woodland gardens for its July flowers, this tall lily (to 5 feet/1.5 m) produces many orange, yellow, or red blooms with out-curved petals. The leaves are whorled. It requires some sun, so it's best near a woodland border. It also does well in moist meadows and prefers acid to neutral soils. It's very difficult to propagate from seed, which ripens in September, and is often wild-collected; forego this plant unless you have a reputable source.

GR: Another lily, *L. michiganense*, is also good for open shady areas; it needs moisture, and is easy to propagate from seed. In the first year, the seed sends down a root and forms a bulb; the second year, the first leaf appears. To speed up propagation, give the seed warm moist stratification for six to eight weeks; when small bulbs develop, place them in the refrigerator for six to eight weeks, then plant them in pots.

Canada mayflower (*Maianthemum canadense*) W

Also known as wild lily-of-the-valley (though not to be confused with the non-native lily-of-the-valley, *Convallaria majalis*), the leaves of this low-growing—6-inch (15-cm)—groundcover are shiny and dark green. Many small white, scented flowers appear on a spike in late spring and early summer. Berries turn red in late summer. It spreads by rhizomes and creates large colonies. It needs humic soil, and prefers slightly to strongly acidic conditions.

Canada violet (*Viola canadensis*) W

This is a great groundcover that grows to 1 foot (30 cm) tall and looks best in masses. White flowers with purplish veins and yellow centres appear in early spring. Divide rhizomes in fall, or plant seeds when ripe—June through July.

GR: Watch closely for seed, as they are quickly expelled as the seed capsules dry.

Cut-leaved toothwort (*Dentaria laciniata*)

The serrated leaves of this low-growing (8 to 12 inches/20 to 30 cm) plant die back in summer. Flowers are white or pink and appear from April to May. It needs rich moist soil and can cope with acid

conditions. It spreads by rhizomes and is easy to increase by division.

Dutchman's breeches (*Dicentra cucullaria*) W

The foliage of this lovely plant is lacy and fernlike: too bad it goes dormant and disappears in early summer. However, it's gorgeous in spring when

---

Before I began gardening with wild flowers, I thought a violet was a violet was a violet. Now I know that the bird-foot violet and the dog violet are violets, but that the dog's tooth violet is a trout lily. Now I know that the stemless violets have longer stems than the stemmed violets. And now that I know all that, I am tempted to say that violets are those pretty purple-blue wild flowers that everybody knows—except that some of them are white and some of them are yellow.

—Frances Tenenbaum, Gardening with Wild Flowers

---

nodding white flowers with yellow tips hang down from arching stems—the flowers do look like pantaloons. It does well in partial shade and filtered light. You can start it from seed or divide the bulblets. It grows to 6 inches (15 cm) and is pollinated by bumblebees.

Early meadow-rue (*Thalictrum dioicum*)

With its delicate columbinelike leaves, this airy plant does well in dry, open shade. Yellowy or whitish green flowers are small and drooping and appear from April to May on 1- to 2 1/2- foot tall (30- to 75-cm) plants. Start it from seeds sown as soon as they are ripe—late May through June. Maria Sperka, in her book *Growing Wildflowers*, recommends early meadow-rue as a substitute for ferns in dryish soil.

Eastern columbine (*Aquilegia canadensis*)

Interesting flowers and delicate foliage make this short-lived perennial a must in the woodland garden (though it also does well in sun). Red and yellow flowers that hang down, with five spurs pointing upwards, appear in April to June and attract hummingbirds and bees. According to Phyllis Busch, in her book *Wildflowers . . . and the Stories Behind Their Names*, columbine is derived from the Latin for dove (*columba*), as the flower heads resemble a flock of hovering doves. Leaves are round and divided into threes—mine are often lined with leaf miner tunnels but they don't harm the plant (and I've grown to enjoy the lacy patterns they create). Columbine grows 1 to 2 feet (30 to 60 cm) and self-seeds. It also works well in the rock garden or dry areas (once the plant is established). It can be divided and is easy to start from seed, which ripens mid-June to mid-July. The seed needs light to germinate, so don't cover it with soil.

GR: Countless seedlings will pop up around the parent plants in late summer; wait until the following spring to thin them out as quite a few may die over the winter. Seeds don't need cold treatment.

Foamflower (*Tiarella cordifolia*) W

A wonderful groundcover for light shade, foamflower sends up leafless flower stalks covered with small white starlike flowers in early spring. It grows 6 to 12 inches (15 to 30 cm) high, with coarsely toothed leaves that vary from deep green in heavy shade to light green in partial sun. It's easy to divide

stolons in fall; or plant seeds as soon as they ripen in early to midsummer (do not cover them with soil; they need light to germinate).

GR: Foamflower needs rich humic soil. It can be easily propagated from runners.

Geranium (*Geranium maculatum*) W

Sometimes called cranesbill, this wild geranium looks nothing like and should not be confused with the cultivated geranium, which is a *Pelargonium*. Providing a note of pinky purple colour in the woodland garden, this plant's small but numerous flowers appear in late spring and last into summer. Keep deadheading and you'll get long-lasting blooming. The toothed, deeply lobed foliage grows 1 to 2 feet (30 to 60 cm) high. Mine tends to flop after heavy rain or strong winds. Geranium tolerates acidic soil. Propagate by division in early spring or fall. The seed pod is a beaklike capsule. According to Laura Martin, seeds usually require two winters of cold stratification before germinating.

GR: Geraniums like open shade and will also grow in full sun. If you are collecting seed, watch the plant closely: seed is dispelled suddenly as the pods dry. Collect seed when it has begun to turn dark.

Goldthread (*Coptis groenlandica*) W

This low-growing (3 to 6 inches/7 to 15 cm) groundcover has white flowers from May to July and shiny, toothed, evergreen leaves. Its common name refers to its yellow creeping rhizomes. It needs acid soil and moisture. You can start it from seed, which ripens in late July, or propagate it by root cuttings in spring.

Green dragon (*Arisaema dracontium*) R, W

This dramatic show-stopper has huge umbrellalike leaves topping a thick stem that grows 1 to 3 feet (30 to 90 cm) high. Flowers are greenish white, appear May to June, and resemble Jack-in-the-pulpit. Berries are bright orange. In the booklet *Plants of Carolinian Canada*, Larry Lamb and Gail Rhynard describe the "greatly exaggerated tapering tip of the spadix" as being "reminiscent of a large flickering lizard's tongue." It likes moist, rich, acidic soil. It takes a long time to flower from seed, but can be propagated from cormlets.

Jack-in-the-pulpit (*Arisaema triphyllum*) W

This interesting plant delights throughout the seasons: from its unique flower in spring to its bright, orange red berries in late summer. The flower invites a short botany lesson: the central column, or spadix, is surrounded by a green (though in some varieties purple and white, or green and brown) hooded sheath or spathe. It needs moist, rich soil and prefers slightly acid conditions. It grows 1 to 3 feet (30 to 90 cm) high. If you're growing it from seed, which ripens in September, remove the pulp before planting in the fall. It can also be propagated by root division or separating cormlets in the fall.

GR: Corms should be planted shallowly—1 1/2 to 2 inches (4.5 to 6 cm) deep. The richer and moister the soil, the larger the plants.

Mayapple (*Podophyllum peltatum*) W

Striking umbrellalike leaves make this plant a knockout when massed as a woodland ground cover (though it will tolerate up to three-quarters full sun). A single white flower appears in late spring, but is hidden underneath the foliage. It likes rich soil and spreads well by rhizomal growth, creating dense colonies to 1 1/2 feet (45 cm) tall. Foliage withers in midsummer.

GR: Propagate by root division when dormant.

Monarda (*Monarda didyma*) R

Sometimes called Oswego tea or bee balm, monarda has one of the most striking red flowers you'll see in woodland gardens. The plant grows to 4 feet (1.2 m), with fragrant serrated leaves. The flowers are tubular and look a little like a jester's hat; they appear in midsummer and last for quite a few weeks. Deadhead to extend blooming. Hummingbirds, bees, and butterflies are all attracted to this plant, which prefers moist conditions and light shade. Although it's rare in the wild, it's often found in gardens. Propagation is easy from seed or by division in early spring. According to Henry Art, author of *A Garden of Wildflowers*, seeds do not require cold stratification.

GR: Monarda will also do well in full sun with adequate moisture.

Sarsaparilla (*Aralia nudicaulis*)

The finely toothed leaves make this plant an attractive groundcover. In May to July, it sends up three round greenish white flower clusters, held on leafless stems 12 to 18 inches (30 to 45 cm) tall. Berries turn deep blue black in autumn. The plant spreads through seeds and underground rhizomes, which can be divided in fall. It does well in acidic, dry, woodsy soil. Roots have a root-beer flavour.

GR: When dividing sarsaparilla, be sure to get a length of stem with a visible new bud.

Sharp-lobed hepatica (*Hepatica acutiloba*) W

With its low-growing, three-lobed leaves, hepatica makes a nice groundcover. Lavender, white, or pink flowers appear before the new leaves in early spring. It likes calcium-rich soil and grows to approximately 6 inches (15 cm). Start it from seed, which ripens in late May, or divide clumps.

GR: Hepatica will tolerate relatively dry conditions, which makes it a good plant for dry shade.

Solomon's seal (*Polygonatum biflorum*) W

An interesting and easy-to-grow foliage plant that is pleasing through the seasons: in spring, it sends up pointy pokers that become 3-foot (0.9-m) arching stems with many flat leaves; flowers are white and droop underneath the leaves in early summer; in fall, the leaves turn a gorgeous yellowy gold, with hanging blue-black berries, which remain handsome throughout the winter. It does well in deep shade to partial sun and will tolerate a wide range of soil conditions—from acidic to neutral, moist to average. Seeds, which ripen in September, may take a few years to germinate (don't let them dry out) but this plant is easy to increase through rhizome division in spring or fall.

GR: Divide before the stem disappears in fall, otherwise the rhizomes are difficult to find. Rhizomes are whitish, knotted, and lie just below the surface of the soil.

Spring beauty (*Claytonia virginica*) W

This harbinger of spring carpets woodlands early in the season, then goes dormant. Leaves are narrow and flowers are starlike, pale pink, veined with a darker pink. Each corm produces many shoots, which grow 6 to 12 inches (15 to 30 cm) high.

It can be started from seed or by corm division. It needs rich woodsy soil and, like many spring ephemerals, looks best in masses.

Trout lily (*Erythronium americanum*) W

Also known as dog's-tooth violet, this spring ephemeral groundcover has two brownish spotted leaves and nodding, bell-shaped yellow flowers that appear in early spring and grow to 6 inches (15 cm) high. It likes rich soil. It takes years to flower from seed, though you can propagate it by root offshoots dug up in fall.

GR: As bulbs develop, they push themselves lower down in the soil. When they reach their desired depth, they bloom.

Twinleaf (*Jeffersonia diphylla*) W

The unique leaves of this groundcover, which grows to 1 foot (30 cm) high, provide much interest in open woodlands: many writers compare them to birds' wings because of their two lobes. Each stalk has one short-lived, starlike white flower in April to May. Also unique is the plant's fruit: a hinged, pipe-shaped capsule that contains the seeds. Propagate by division in fall or by starting seeds as soon as they're ripe and before they have dried out. Rick Imes notes in his book *Wildflowers* that seeds may take two years to germinate; and Harry Phillips in *Growing and Propagating Wild Flowers* says that seeds take four to five years to flower. It needs rich, moist soil.

Virginia bluebells (*Mertensia virginica*) R, W

This spring ephemeral produces gorgeous clusters of nodding pink buds that turn into trumpetlike blue flowers in spring. The plant goes dormant in early summer. Its leaves are pale, oval, and smooth, and it grows to 2 feet (60 cm) high. It requires moist soil and can be propagated by root division or

Confession time: I have never had much luck with ferns. While many gardeners spend their summers trying to control the monsters, I average three murders per season (but since my source for ferns is those same gardeners making gifts of their excess, I don't feel too guilty—their choice is slow death by my futile attempts or a speedy, blunt chop in the compost bin). At any rate, I think I've finally diagnosed the problem: inappropriate transplanting. In my experience, you just can't hope for fern survival if you transplant them when they're growing; it's much better to transplant them in very early spring before the fronds uncoil or in late fall.

Ferns hold much appeal, particularly in the woodland garden. Not only are they a very ancient species (350 million years by most estimates), but many also thrive in conditions that could be considered difficult—deep shade—and they create a very lush, cool retreat. They don't flower but their fascinating and varied textures easily make up for this, and their many different greens may be all the colour you want.

Most ferns do not do well in sun (exceptions are noted below); instead, they want filtered or dappled light (though many will thrive in deep shade). Not surprisingly, many require rich, humusy soil, full of leaf mould. When you're planting ferns, make sure that the base of the crown is at soil level, and supplement the soil with loads of compost. Keep well watered throughout the first growing season.

FERNS TO TRY

Christmas fern (*Polystichum acrostichoides*); lady fern (*Athyrium felix-femina*); maidenhair fern (*Adiantum pedatum*); cinnamon fern (*Osmunda cinnamomea*); New York fern (*Dryopteris novaboracensis*); ostrich fern (*Matteuccia struthiopteris*); interrupted fern (*Osmundia claytoniana*); sensitive fern (*Onoclea sensibilis*); marginal fern (*Dryopteris marginalis*); Goldie's wood fern (*Dryopteris goldiana*); oak fern (*Gymnocarpium dryopteris*); male fern (*Dryopteris filix-mas*); rock fern (*Polypodium virginianum*); bracken fern (*pteridium acquilinum*—invasive); hay-scented fern (*Dennstaedtia punctilobula*)

Ferns for Moist Places

Christmas fern; cinnamon fern; ostrich fern; interrupted fern; lady fern; sensitive fern

Ferns for Deep Shade

marginal fern; Christmas fern; lady fern; maidenhair fern; wood fern; oak fern; cinnamon fern

Ferns for Dry Places

hay-scented fern; male fern; rock fern; Christmas fern; marginal fern

Ferns for Sun

hay-scented fern; New York fern; sensitive fern; bracken fern; lady fern; ostrich fern

I have never tried propagating ferns from spores (ferns don't produce seeds), but most experts say that it's a relatively simple procedure. Dustlike spores, which develop on the underside of fronds, are sprinkled onto the surface of a commercial starting mix, misted, and kept under plastic or glass until they germinate (anywhere from a few weeks to several months). If you're interested in fern propagation, see Gail Rhynard's article in *Wildflower* (Fall 1992), H. R. Phillips' *Growing and Propagating Wild Flowers*, or the Brooklyn Botanic Garden's publication *Ferns*.

started from seed, which ripens in late May. Virginia bluebells are stunning when combined with bellwort or wood poppy, which both have yellow flowers and bloom at the same time.

GR: Virginia bluebells will self-seed and naturalize readily in a woodland garden.

White trillium (*Trillium grandiflorum*) W
The provincial floral emblem of Ontario, this gorgeous plant carpets woodlands with white blooms from March to May. A single large white flower that becomes pinkish as it matures grows above three broad leaves; red berries are produced in late summer. It needs rich moist soil and grows to 12 to 18 inches (30 to 45 cm) high. If you're planning to purchase a trillium from a nursery, only buy from a reputable source and even then, only after you have interrogated staff as to the plant's provenance. This plant is often wild-collected.

GR: Trillium is slow to start from seed, which ripens in late July. Keep the seed moist, and sow outside right after collecting. It takes at least four to five years to flower, but give it a try.

Wild blue phlox (*Phlox divaricata*) W
This great woodland garden groundcover grows to 1 foot (30 cm) high, with clusters of pinky blue flowers from April to June. Leaves are pointed; stems are hairy. Start it from seed or divide clumps in spring to late summer. It spreads by rhizomes, and likes open shade and rich soil.

Wild ginger (*Asarum canadense*) W
An excellent groundcover for rich woodland habitat, wild ginger grows up to 6 inches (15 cm) high, with hairy stalks and large, heart-shaped leaves. Search out the flowers in early spring: they're low to the ground, browny maroon, cup-shaped, and relatively small (3/4 inch/2 cm). Propagate by rhizome division in fall, or start from seed, which

ripens in June. Seeds take two years before aboveground shoot appears.

GR: Small seedlings will appear near the parent plant and these volunteers can be easily moved to another spot in the garden. Because of its large leaves, wild ginger combines well with ferns or early meadow-rue.

Wild leek (*Allium tricoccum*)
This groundcover of rich woodlands sends up 6- to 18-inch-high (15- to 45-cm) white flower clusters in early summer, after the two or three broad, smooth leaves have died back. Propagate by separating bulb offsets in summer and replanting them 18 inches (45 cm) deep, or start from seed.

Wild strawberry (*Fragaria virginiana*)
A woodland edge plant that needs sunlight, the wild strawberry makes a great groundcover: it spreads aggressively by runners and grows to approximately 6 inches (15 cm). Pretty white flowers with yellow centres in late spring to early summer give way to tasty small berries. (I find them much more flavourful than the cultivated varieties—and just as welcome is the scent of bruised or mushy berries that I've missed picking.) It's easy to propagate from new runners.

GR: Wild strawberry is excellent for poor sandy soil; place it among newly planted small trees for a quick groundcover.

Wood poppy (*Stylophorum diphyllum*) R, W
Also known as celandine poppy—and often confused with celandine (*Chelidonium majus*), a non-native rapid spreader—the rare wood poppy is excellent for the woodland garden. It has deeply lobed leaves, grows 12 to 18 inches (30 to 45 cm) tall and produces yellow flowers from March to May. If starting it from seed, don't let the seed dry out; it's easy to propagate by rhizome division.

Wood poppy looks spectacular with Virginia bluebells and trillium.

Woodland sunflower (*Helianthus divaricatus*)

If you're looking for a yellow flower that blooms in dry woodland conditions in summer (a tall order), this is it. It grows from 2 to 6 1/2 feet (0.6 to 2 m), with thin, rough leaves, and flowers July to October. It's easy to grow from seed.

GR: Woodland sunflower is a great plant to brighten a woodland garden mid- to late summer when the flush of spring bloom has disappeared. It can be easily divided.

WETLAND, POND, OR WET SITES

Arrow arum (*Peltandra virginica*) R

This swamp and marsh plant provides interest in ponds with its large, shiny, arrow-shaped leaves. The green flower, a slender spadix covered by a leaflike spathe, appears in late spring to early summer. The plant grows to 18 inches (45 cm) in sun or shade. Submerge pots just below the water's surface or plant along the pond edge.

Blue flag (*Iris versicolor*) W

Looking like a smaller version of the cultivated iris, blue flag is a stately addition to wet meadows, pond edges, and marshy areas. It grows 1 to 3 feet (30 to 90 cm) tall, with spiky leaves, and produces blue flowers from May through July. It prefers acidic conditions and likes full sun, though it will grow in light shade. It can also be planted in pots in the shallows of an artificial pond. Propagate by rhizome division in early fall; it's easy to start from seed, which ripen in September, as long as young plants are kept moist. (The seed coat is quite thick, so I experimented with scarifying some seeds and not others, and it didn't seem to make any difference to the germination rate.)

Bottle gentian (*Gentiana andrewsii*) W

Unmatched for its pure blue flowers (though they are occasionally white), the bottle gentian induces strong feelings: I fell in love with this plant the first time I saw it in the wet prairie at Ojibway Prairie Provincial Nature Reserve in Windsor—I just couldn't believe that such a blue existed. The flowers, which appear in late summer and last into October, don't ever open up; instead they retain their closed, or bottle, shape. It grows to 1 to 2 feet (30 to 60 cm) in sun to partial shade, though it needs moist soil. Propagate by root crown division or from seed. Seeds germinate best in light, so sow them on the soil surface.

GR: Plants should bloom in the second year.

Broad-leaved arrowhead (*Sagittaria latifolia*)

Another dramatic foliage plant for the pond, arrowhead has nice white flowers from July to September. Leaves are bright green, sometimes narrow, sometimes wide. The plant grows 1 to 4 feet (0.3 to 1.2 m) tall in the shallow water at pond edges. It will tolerate partial shade. Propagate by rhizome division in fall or start from seed. Submerge the pots just below the water's surface.

Cardinal flower (*Lobelia cardinalis*) W

I have the death of many cardinal flowers on my conscience; my garden just isn't moist enough. However, I planted one on the edge of my sister's pond and it bloomed almost immediately. Prized for the intense red of its tubular flowers, which appear from July to September, the cardinal flower must have average to moist soil, and does well in full or half-sun. It's a spiky plant that grows to 2 to 4 feet (0.6 to 1.2 m); the leaves are narrow and serrated. The red flowers attract hummingbirds. It's easy to start from seed, which ripens from September through October, though seeds need light to germinate.

GR: Some seedlings may even bloom the first year.

Forget-me-not (*Myosotis laxa*)

Similar to the European *Myosotis scorpioides*, which is often cultivated in gardens, this native plant works well as a groundcover in moist areas. It is 6 to 18 inches (15 to 45 cm) tall with tiny pale blue flowers from spring though summer. It likes full sun to light shade and is best grown at pond edges. Propagate through division.

Jewelweed (*Impatiens capensis*)

Also known as spotted touch-me-not, this annual provides a rare orange in partially shady areas. Its main requirement is moist soil. It grows up to 5 feet (1.5 m) tall, with loose and airy leaves, in colonies.

Tubular, lipped flowers appear in July and last through the summer. It looks best in large groupings. Hummingbirds love this plant, as do bees and butterflies. You *can* touch it—the name derives from the fact that mature seeds are expelled (with surprising force the first time you encounter this phenomenon) from the capsule upon contact. It self-sows with abandon in moist sites. *Impatiens pallida*, the pale touch-me-not or jewelweed, is similar to spotted touch-me-not but with pale yellow flowers.

Marsh marigold (*Caltha palustris*) W

Colonies of this bright yellow wetland plant carpet wet forests in spring, then go dormant and disappear by midsummer. It grows 1 to 2 feet (30 to 60 cm) tall, with a flower that looks like a large buttercup, and dark, glossy, heart-shaped foliage. Propagate by division after flowering, or sow ripe seed (don't let them dry out). Grow it around a pond or in standing water in a pot, submerged to the top of the soil.

Skunk cabbage (*Symplocarpus foetidus*)

Skunk cabbage is an unfortunate name for a fascinating plant. One of the first plants to appear in wet woods and along streams in early spring, skunk cabbage pushes its way up through the soil with a thick spadix and mottled spathe that twists and curls. Leaves are large and appear after the flower dies back; the plant grows to 1 to 2 feet (30 to 60 cm). It needs damp, rich soil and plenty of room, and will grow in sun or partial shade. Try it around a pond, or along the banks of a stream if you're lucky enough to have one. Propagate by rhizome division or start from seed.

GR: This is another early-blooming plant whose seeds don't ripen until October. Seeds are contained in the blackened spadix and must be planted, when fresh, in pots to overwinter outside.

Spotted Joe-pye weed (*Eupatorium maculatum*)

This is a tall stunner in moist to wet sites like damp meadows, marshes, or shorelines, though it is not for the totally refined, under-control-type garden.

Clusters of purple pink flowers appear in midsummer and last through early fall, borne on top of 2- to 6-foot-tall (0.6- to 1.8-m) purplish stems. Leaves are pointy and coarse, and grow in whorls around the stem. It needs sun. Propagate by division; seeds need moist stratification.

GR: Spotted Joe-pye weed is sometimes even higher in rich soil—I've seen it up to 10 feet (3 m) tall in gardens.

Swamp milkweed (*Asclepias incarnata*)
Swamp milkweed does best in moist sites, though it will tolerate regular garden soil. It grows up to 4 feet (1.2 m) tall, with purple pink flower clusters from June to August. Lance-shaped leaves are narrow and dark. It needs full sun. Propagate by division of clumps in spring or start from seed in fall. It looks great with Joe-pye weed.

GR: Swamp milkweed is a larval food plant for monarch butterflies; mine have had caterpillars on them all summer: one plant in an open area is a veritable monarch caterpillar hotel.

Waterlily (*Nymphaea odorata*)
If you read water gardening books or talk with water gardening aficionados, they make it sound like waterlilies are the *only* reason for creating a pond, which is easy to understand once you see the gorgeous blooms. Saucer- or platter-like leaves float on the water's surface, and large (3 to 5 inches/ 7 to 13 cm) white flowers appear from June to September, and are very fragrant. They open in the morning and close in the afternoon. Waterlilies need full sun, calm water, and fertile soil. Submerge the pots at least 12 inches (30 cm) below the pond's surface. Propagate by rhizome division in fall.

White turtlehead (*Chelone glabra*)
At the edge of a pond or in a damp spot, turtlehead provides a great accent from late summer through fall, when the intriguing white flowers appear (yes, they look a bit like open-mouthed turtles in profile). It grows to 3 feet (0.9 m) tall, with dark, lance-shaped serrated leaves. It does well in sun or partial shade, and will self-sow in a good location. Seeds require moist stratification. You can also propagate by division in late fall, and stem cuttings can be made in spring or summer.

GR: White turtlehead will also grow well in average (mesic) soil. Seeds are not ripe until late October. Look for brown seed capsules; the seed inside should be tan with a black centre. Turtlehead is the host plant for the caterpillar of the Baltimore butterfly.

Wild calla (*Calla palustris*)
Also known as bog or water arum, this plant grows in shallow water or along moist, calm shores with peaty, acidic soils, in good sun. It grows to 1 foot (30 cm), with attractive heart-shaped leaves and white flowers (actually a white spathe that covers a yellow-flowered spadix) in early to late summer. Clusters of red berries are produced in fall. Propagate by root cuttings or from seed sown upon ripening. If growing in a pot in a pond, submerge the pot just to the top of the soil.

Yellow lotus (*Nelumbo lutea*) R
Large (6 inches/15 cm across) yellow flowers rise out of the water on stalks in mid- to late summer. Blossoms are fragrant and close at night. The matte leaves are also large, sometimes up to 2 feet (60 cm) in diameter, and they, too, stand above the water. The seedpod is equally fascinating—a round head with many seed chambers—and is often found in dried flower arrangements. Submerge pots 4 to 10 inches (10 to 25 cm) deep in the water. Propagate by rhizome division in fall.

GRASS AND GRASSLIKE PLANTS FOR PRAIRIES AND MEADOWS

Big bluestem (*Andropogon gerardii*)

A dominant tall-grass prairie plant, big bluestem needs space but is a stunning plant if you have the room. Clump-forming, it grows from 3 to 8 feet (0.9 to 2.4 m) tall in full sun. Thin grassy leaves are bluish green and turn bronze in fall. Flower clusters that appear in July and August look a bit like turkey's feet, giving the plant one of its common names. It's drought tolerant and easy to start from seed. Here's how the authors of *Wild Wealth* describe a field of big bluestem on a sunny summer day: "beneath a bowl of azure, they have the endlessness and sweep of the sea."

Blue-eyed grass (*Sisyrinchium montanum*)

A member of the iris family, blue-eyed grass forms 1- to 2-foot-high (30- to 60-cm) clumps of grassy foliage. Star-shaped, blue to violet flowers with yellow centres are borne in late spring through early summer. Each flower lasts for a day, but the plant flowers abundantly. It likes moist to average soil with a high lime content, and sun to partial shade. It's easy to start from seed or by division.

GR: Divide in spring, carefully separating the crowns, then replant. It also self-seeds readily and seedlings will be found near the base of the parent plant; move them in the fall.

NATIVE VINES TO TRY

virgin's bower (*Clematis virginiana*); wild cucumber vine (*Echinocystis lobata*); Virginia creeper (*Parthenocissus vitacea*); wild grape (*Vitis* spp.); moonseed (*Menispermum canadense*); bittersweet (*Celastrus scadens*)

Indian grass (*Sorghastrum nutans*)

Another striking plant of the tall-grass prairie, Indian grass looks wonderful when grown as a specimen or focal point in the garden. It forms clumps that reach 3 to 6 feet (0.9 to 1.8 m) in full sun, with bronzy flowers in summer and bronze leaves in fall. It's easy to start from seed.

GR: The seed heads are beautiful—shiny golden brown, which gleam in the sun—but the plant can be aggressive in some soils.

Little bluestem (*Andropogon scoparius*)

A backbone of the mixed-grass and short-grass prairie, little bluestem is a grass of choice for the sunny garden. A clump-former that grows 1 1/2 to 2 1/2 feet (45 to 75 cm) tall, it looks great in summer, with its bluish foliage, and then turns bronze with fluffy seed heads in fall that provide winter interest. It's drought tolerant and does fine in poor soil. Little bluestem is easy to start from seed.

GR: Little bluestem can also be propagated by division in spring or fall. One clump can be pulled apart into many smaller ones, though large plants are harder to divide because of the deep root system.

Panic grass (*Panicum virgatum*)

Panic is no stranger to the garden, though some people might balk at the idea of inviting it in. However, this switch grass is a fine, easy-going plant for marshy to dry sites. It reaches 3 to 5 feet (0.9 to 1.5 m) in full sun, turning gold in the fall.

GR: Panic grass can be aggressive in rich moist soil, but in dry soil doesn't spread as quickly. It has a very tough root system.

Pennsylvania sedge (*Carex pensylvanica*)

This low-growing sedge (to 1 foot/30 cm) works well as a groundcover in dry, shady areas, though it also does well in sun. The leaves are fine; purplish seeds are borne at the top of the stem in spring. Sedges look like grasses but if inspected closely have triangular rather than round stems in cross-section. They are drought tolerant and easy to start from seed.

GR: Pennsylvania sedge can also be divided in spring. It sends out rhizomes that produce new plants; separate these once they've developed roots, and replant.

Plantain-leaved sedge (*Carex plantaginea*)

In a shady, moist woodland, this sedge does well as a groundcover. It grows to 1 1/2 feet (45 cm) tall, has wide leaves, and is evergreen. It's easy to start from seed.

GR: This is a spring-flowering sedge; watch for the seed early in the season.

Sideoats grama (*Bouteloua curtipendula*) R

This bunchgrass has attractive oatlike seeds that droop on the stem and rustle in the breeze. It grows to 3 feet (0.9 m) in sun or partial shade. A bluish green in summer, it turns gold in fall. It's drought tolerant and easy to start from seed.

GR: Watch for the flowers: tiny, brilliant, red orange and purple flowering parts, with purplish seed heads.

CHAPTER REFERENCES

Ferns. C. Colston Burrell. Brooklyn: Brooklyn Botanic Garden, 1994.

A Field Guide to Wildflowers of Northeastern and Northcentral North America. R. T. Peterson and M. McKenny. Boston: Houghton Mifflin, 1968.

A Garden of Wildflowers: 101 Native Species and How to Grow Them. Henry W. Art. Pownal, Vermont: Storey, 1986.

The Gardener's Guide to Plant Conservation. Nina T. Marshall. Washington: World Wildlife Fund and the Garden Club of America, 1993.

Gardening with Wild Flowers. Frances Tenenbaum. New York: Charles Scribner's Sons, 1973.

Growing and Propagating Wild Flowers. Harry R. Phillips. Chapel Hill: University of North Carolina Press, 1992.

Growing Wildflowers. Maria Sperka. New York: Charles Scribner's Sons, 1973.

Ontario Weeds. J. F. Alex. Toronto: Ministry of Agriculture and Food, 1992.

Plants of Carolinian Canada. Larry Lamb and Gail Rhynard. Don Mills: Federation of Ontario Naturalists, 1994.

Rare Vascular Plants in Canada. George W. Argus and Kathleen M. Pryer. Ottawa: Canadian Museum of Nature, 1990.

The Wild Gardener. Peter Loewer. Harrisburg, Pennsylvania: Stackpole, 1991.

Wild Wealth. Paul Bigelow Sears et al. New York: Bobbs-Merrill, 1971.

Wildflowers. Rick Imes. Emmaus, Pennsylvania: Rodale, 1992.

Wildflowers . . . and the Stories Behind Their Names. Phyllis S. Busch. New York: Charles Scribner's Sons, 1977.

Part 3

OF WEEDS, LAWNS, AND WILDLIFE

Chapter 10

WEEDS ARE US, BUT THEY'VE GOT ME STUMPED

Sometimes it's not the thing itself that causes distress, but what we name it. I had my lesson in the problems of labels at Pat's new house. We were wandering around the garden and she pointed to some healthy, tall foliage. Is that a weed? she asked, because in her experience of this relatively young garden, healthy and tall meant one thing: weed.

It's goldenrod, I offered. Stall, stall. Isn't that a weed? she pressed. I opted for obfuscation. Well, I've got some in my garden, in fact I planted it on purpose. Yes, but *is it a weed*?

I'd like to say that I had an answer, but I let Pat down. Instead of launching into a spiel on the hermeneutics of plant status and the ontological difficulties of names, we decided to repair to the deck with our wine. Much safer than weed discussions among friends.

Indeed, it seems that weed discussion and definitions are the most clearcut when they're being debated by enemies. Feuding neighbours admit no fuzziness in *their* fights about weeds: each has a firm position re weed or not weed. They may be diametrically opposed, but there's no prevarication. I wish I felt the comfort of such certainty, but in my search for the meaning of weeds, I've come up a blank.

A short tour of the canon of weed literature may be helpful here to explain my impasse. First, the dictionary definition, courtesy of the *Shorter Oxford*: "a herbaceous plant not valued for use or beauty, growing wild and rank, and regarded as cumbering the ground or hindering the growth of superior vegetation." Slippery on many counts. Not valued by whom? for example. I value the autumnal verve of goldenrod's spikes, as do all those British gardeners who pay good money to include this North American import in their blooming borders. (Not that I subscribe to the prevalent attitude that the British gardener's stamp of approval equals value, but it does provide some context.)

"Herbaceous" leaves out all those woody plants, such as Norway maple and European buckthorn, that could qualify as weeds if you used eco-logical criteria as the basis for your definition. Many ecologists view the Norway maples that are taking over the indigenous plant communities in Toronto's ravines as little more than weeds—indeed, weeds that should be yanked out.

"Growing wild and rank" seems particularly

The more disturbed or the more simplified a site, the more susceptible it becomes to the colonization of weed seeds.

—*Carol A. Smyser*, Nature's Design

---

sticky to me. The first part would relegate *all* of our native and naturalized wildflowers to the position of weeds, equating wildness with weediness; the second part, too vague to be useful. Flip to "rank" in the dictionary and along with words like coarse and gross are words like luxuriant, rich, and fertile —for every put-down is a gardener's dream. Judging by its rampant lustiness, I'd have to say that fertile appropriately describes my goldenrod, but its feathery leaves are anything but coarse.

It's in the phrase "hindering the growth of superior vegetation" that I become unhinged. Since when did anyone have the chance to vote on this hierarchy? Weeds may be opportunistic, but does that necessarily make them inferior? If any-thing, their adaptation to human disturbance shows a wily fitness for survival in this world. They've made their peace with us; why can't we show a reciprocal tolerance? Just to confound the issue, the hierarchy is inverted in my garden, where the so-called superior vegetation of the rasp-berries hinders the growth of the goldenrod by

flopping over the straight tops, and I'm not entirely sure that I approve.

If dictionaries are muddy on this one, what do the botanists say? What sorts of value judgements seep into their weed-view and inform their prac-tice? Interestingly, botanists tend to avoid the term weed altogether, using instead the non-judgemen-tal term ruderal, which is used for plants that grow in disturbed soil. They tend not to blame the weeds themselves for their weedy characteristics, but rather position them in relation to humans: weeds are plants that move into and colonize land that has been disturbed by human agency. In other words, weeds are inevitable and they're our fault. There's no such thing as a weed in a virgin forest (though, of course, there's probably no such thing as a virgin forest left in North America either). Weeds are the result of cultivation—once we start turning over the soil, we create the conditions for the very things we're trying to obliterate, inviting invaders into an unstable land community, spread-ing out the red carpet for monoculture. We set our-selves up for failure.

While botanists hedge their bets with a human-centred definition, refusing to load down their object of study with any intrinsic original sin, locating it instead with the plough and trowel, most gardening books and field guides are more declarative. Weed lists invigorate the gardener with purpose and mission: don't get wimpy and rel-ative and philosophical, they imply, just get on with the deed. Then they outline with the preci-sion of a military strategy all the steps necessary for triumphant weed eradication.

Which is fine if you're willing to turn som-nambulist for long enough to ignore what it is that your senses might be telling you. Your eyes, for example, might be responding to the luminous blue of chicory. Your nose to the tropical fruit mim-icry of pineapple weed. Your mouth to the salad potential of lambsquarters. Your touch to the soil erosion duty done by clover. Your ears to the gentle click of field horsetail. Now, I don't mean to romanticize weeds and make them out to be benign botanical presences in your purposeful plot, but I do think we should lighten up a bit and admit to a small measure of floral confusion and even double standard. Because the whole subject of weeds is one of the last areas where gardeners (typically an opinionated and self-directed bunch) are conformists to convention. Throw out the list and decide for yourself! Yank out whatever you don't want, but be sure you know why. Not only will you be asserting your own sense of style, but you'll also be saved the embarrassment of having to admit no answer to the question, is it a weed?

❦   ❦   ❦

By now I'm sure you've noted the defensive tone of this rant and wondered about its appropriateness in a book that's essentially about wildflowers. I guess I take any discussion of weeds so personally because many people lump the two w's together: wildflowers and weeds. If wildflowers could talk or at least afford PR agents, I suspect that their first campaign would be an all-out verbal volley against this indiscriminate association. They might begin their assault with the claim that weeds and wildflowers have as much in common as guns and peace rallies, cars and bike lanes; they might assert that their only connection is that they're both green and grow in soil. This would be an effective tactic, but not necessarily true.

The reason they're commonly put together is that weeds and wildflowers share an ability to grow with no human intervention. You no more have to coddle columbine than pamper purslane. Since even the thought of being relegated to the role of unnecessary observer is distressing to gardeners, this might explain why many people dismiss wildflowers as readily as they fight weeds. The gardener needs to be needed, or what's the point?

Yet again I think this is as much a terminology problem as it is a gardening problem. We need to be more specific in our categories. Let's side with the botanists and keep value judgements out of our weed definition: a weed is an opportunistic plant that follows human disturbance and colonizes cultivated land. A very few are native plants but

---

Not to be overlooked are the often maligned weeds or ruderals that have tagged the steps of man in his wanderings over the earth. Whatever unpleasant qualities they have are balanced by their virtues, for they are nature's scar tissue, the first steps in healing broken and idle land.

—*Paul B. Sears et al*, Wild Wealth

---

they've become "weeds" as a result of our actions. Most (80 to 95 percent, depending on which source one consults) are not native but are here because we introduced them. (I doubt that accepting responsibility will make any of us feel better about chickweed, but it's a start—and if it worked for the self-helpers, maybe it will work for gardeners.)

As for wildflowers, I think it's imperative that we be more specific, though it does require a bit of work and research. For one, we should be careful to distinguish between native and naturalized wildflowers. Both will grow without deliberate cultivation in the wild, but one side of the equation gives us the lady's slipper orchid (native) and the other purple loosestrife (non-native, introduced, naturalized). The distinction is significant to our wetlands.

Interestingly, it is almost always the naturalized, non-native wildflowers that are called weeds. The native goldenrod and ragweed are obvious exceptions to this, however. Maybe if we are careful to make distinctions when talking about wild-

---

In the rough corners of the garden we allow the local dandelions to grow and prosper. This may sound like madness, but for our interests, dandelions are of great value. They can produce nectar at very low temperatures and so are an important source of food for our early butterflies.

—Bernard Jackson of Memorial University Botanical Garden, St. John's, Newfoundland, in Wildflower, *Summer 1985*

---

flowers, our natives will not all be tarred with the broad weed brush.

❦   ❦   ❦

I admit that the following observation has lost some of its revelatory glow, but when it first occurred to me it seemed a startlingly definitive and clear way out of the conundrum caused by weeds: next time you're travelling in a foreign country and find yourself in a nice open field (without field guide, no cheating), try to distinguish between weeds and wildflowers. It's next to impossible. I tried this in Morocco and was struck by the realization that weeds are inherently contextual (an oxymoron, but appropriate). Weeds

are, by nature, of the "it all depends" variety. Depends on the country, depends on the ecosystem, depends on the backyard, depends on the gardener, and on and on until one gets lost in relational and associative ifs, ands, or buts.

Such slipperiness finds its way into field guides, so you can't count on them for unambiguous declarations. I tried looking up the native field horsetail in two very different books—*Common Weeds of Canada* and *Canadian Wildflowers Through the Seasons*—and discovered the rhetorical power of word choice. From the description in *Common Weeds*: "Perennial, spreading by spores and by creeping rootstocks; not a flowering plant . . . a common weed in all provinces . . . a poisonous plant particularly affecting young horses; unbranched stems ending in a cone appear by the middle of April and soon wither." Reinforcing this unflattering verbal portrait is a photo of horsetail growing in gravel.

If not glowing, the picture that emerges from *Canadian Wildflowers* at least piques one's interest: "The Horsetails are the only survivors of a group of plants that grew on the earth 250 million years ago. In those far-away times, some Horsetails were tree-size. . . . From March to June, the brown fertile stems push up through the ground in great numbers. . . . On top of each is a cream-colored fruiting cone. . . . These hold the spores, which are released and under the right conditions grow into the small, green, lobed prothalliums." The photo is coffee-table-book gorgeous.

So on the one hand, a notorious and sneaky equine killer that withers; on the other, a fertile oddity with a mysterious prothallium and a Jurassic past. It all depends.

One more example. I'm waging a constant and losing battle with Japanese knotweed in the northwest corner of my backyard. I suppose I should be relieved that it's relatively confined to a small section, but even so it has sorely tempted the organic pulse of my gardening policy. As anyone who has been burdened with this green scourge knows, the more ruthless you are with knotweed, the happier it is. Its delight in S&M practice knows no bounds —cut it down, try to pull it out, and it springs back with umpteen new shoots, scattered even farther afield. A kinky plant. But it turns out that the whole reason why we *have* knotweed in the first place is that it was introduced to North America as an exotic garden ornamental and it escaped cultivation. People actually coveted it. Tastes change. Styles come and go. This decade's weed was last century's wonder. Or dinner: Queen Anne's lace and dandelion were both grown for food in New England prior to 1700. Or forage: crab grass was introduced to the United States and promoted by the government as a forage plant for animals. Or remedy: plantain was brought to New England by the puritans, who used it to treat cuts and festering wounds. All is contextual.

Unfortunately, while contextuality might be of sociological interest to the historian, it's not much comfort to the gardener. I'm afraid that it's almost inevitable that in the course of gardening with native plants, you will be confronted with the insidious charge of promoting, nurturing, spreading, and infecting other gardens with weeds. This could be considered benignly naive if it weren't also entrenched in a popular aesthetic that's too often propped up with legal conformity bylaws.

So try to take comfort in the irony of the situation. Here are native plant gardeners, trying to restore landscapes to the kind of health and stability that precludes weeds from growing—that is, landscapes in which non-native interlopers aren't able to gain a foothold and crowd out the indigenous plant community. On the other hand are weeds—evidence of a disturbed landscape, one that has been degraded, in most cases, by humans. There's nothing natural or inevitable about this. Our impact does not need to be destructive.

Let's hope that native plant gardeners will gradually be recognized not as weed workers but as active participants in the dynamic process of trying to knit plant communities back together again— in essence, trying to find a healthy, healing, natural place for humans in the ecosystem.

If we confine the concept of weeds to species adapted to human disturbance, then man is by definition the first and primary weed under whose influence all other weeds have evolved.

—Jack R. Harland, Crops and Man

WEED IDENTIFICATION

If you're looking for a good weed book, I highly recommend *Ontario Weeds* by J. F. Alex, put out by the Ontario Ministry of Agriculture and Food. It's a definitive source that has information for everyone—from the browser to the Ph.D—and covers in detail, almost all with drawings or photographs, 315 of the most prevalent weeds in the province. Of particular interest to the native plant gardener are the sections on plant origin. There is also plenty of information on the most successful eradication methods.

Here's the "official" definition from the book, which notes that a whopping five hundred species of plants have been considered weedy, in one way or another, in Ontario: "Weeds are ordinary plants which have some undesirable features. They may grow where people do not want them. They may disfigure lawns (dandelion) and gardens (redroot pigweed), interfere with crop production (field bindweed), reduce crop yield (wild mustard), reduce crop quality (wild garlic), lower feed palatability (wormseed mustard), reduce visibility along roadsides (nodding thistle), poison livestock (water-hemlock), or cause prolonged human discomfort by contact (poison ivy) or by inhalation of their pollen (common ragweed)."

A weed is a plant that is not only in the wrong place, but intends to stay.

—Sara B. Stein, My Weeds

For a crash course in relativity, I also recommend going through this book while shopping at your favourite garden centre: I counted thirteen widely available plants, such as dame's rocket, St. John's wort, yarrow, and cornflower, that I have bought over the years, and another nine, including wild garlic and white snakeroot, that are on my list. Only a minor weed-identity crisis.

WHAT WEEDS CAN REVEAL

Just as we learn to read the habitat clues provided by plants in the wild, so too can we glean information from the so-called undesirables.

The following is a sampling of what weeds indicate about garden soil, culled from a variety of sources.
- nettles: rich moist soil
- smartweed: poor drainage
- dandelions and plantain: compacted soil
- sorrel, horsetail: acidic soil
- chamomile, bladder campion: alkaline soil
- Canada thistle: clay soil

- lamb's quarters: fertile soil
- burdock, pigweed, purslane: fertile, well-drained soil
- moss (though I would *never* call it a weed): wet soil, possibly acidic

WEEDS AND THE LAW

If you relax your standards too much in Ontario, you might have to pay for it: while milkweed might be your idea of a good native meadow plant (and the monarch butterfly would agree, since *Asclepias* spp. is the only known larval food for the monarch caterpillar), the Weed Control Act begs to differ. All milkweeds are on the list of twenty-three plants identified as noxious weeds under the 1988 (revised) legislation. (So young, so ecologically outdated . . .) You are required by law to destroy these plants on your property—and if you don't do it, an official can, and then charge you for it: common barberry (non-native, introduced as an ornamental shrub); European buckthorn (ditto); wild carrot (aka Queen Anne's lace); colt's foot (introduced from Europe); dodder (several species native to Ontario); goat's beard (non-native); poison hemlock (introduced from Eurasia); Johnson's grass; knapweed; milkweed (native); poison-ivy (native); black-seeded proso millet (introduced from Europe); ragweed (native); yellow rocket; sow thistle; Cypress spurge; leafy spurge; bull thistle; Canada thistle; nodding thistle; Russian thistle; Scotch thistle; tuberous vetchling.

I find it highly ironic—and evidence of the Act's shortsightedness—that another Ontario government publication called "Environmental Living" recommends that homeowners plant a border of Queen Anne's lace in order to encourage beneficial bugs in the garden. I wonder if this would stand up as a reasonable defense in court? Let's hope that a piece of legislation that in theory would obliterate the monarch butterfly from Ontario would *not* stand up!

It's important to note that some municipalities in Ontario have bylaws restricting the use of other plants as well. You might want to check with City Hall.

CHAPTER REFERENCES

Canadian Wildflowers Through the Seasons. Mary Ferguson and Richard Saunders. Toronto: Van Nostrand Reinhold, 1976.

Common Weeds of Canada. Gerald A. Mulligan. Toronto: NC Press, 1987.

Crops and Man. Jack R. Harland. Madison, Wisconsin: American Society of Agronomy, 1975.

"Environmental Living." Toronto: Ontario Ministry of the Environment, nd.

My Weeds. Sara B. Stein. New York: Harper and Row, 1988.

Nature's Design. Carol Smyser. Emmaus, Pennsylvania: Rodale, 1982.

Ontario Weeds. J. F. Alex. Toronto: Ontario Ministry of Agriculture and Food, 1992.

Wild Wealth. Paul Bigelow Sears et al. New York: Bobbs-Merrill, 1971.

Chapter 11

SHAMED INTO DECENCY, FORCED INTO FESCUE

THE LAWN

In 1958, an Augusta, Georgia, company sold 20,000 gallons (75,700 L) of artificial colouring to turn brown grass green. In 1965, an American company marketed Neo-turf, a plastic grass promoted with the tag line: "grasslike surfacing of Polyloom III really does look like real grass, only it never grows." These products have faded into the gloom of consumer culture, but the "better living through chemistry" ingenuity that led to their invention still applies to the modern lawn. Genetically altered, forced to grow in conditions hostile to its atavistic inclinations, coddled, cosseted, urged into lush spurts through fertilizing and watering only to be sheared before it can set flowers or seed, bombarded with chemical cures for its every whimpering malaise, the lawn is more Product than plant.

Yet the strange thing about lawns is that despite the fact that they're North America's dominant landscape fixation and that inordinate amounts of energy and time go into producing them, there's still so much hostility towards them.

Even the people who profess to love them also seem to hate them: the work, the bother, the ever-elusive perfection.

Like any other object of worship, they've become subject to public mood swings of sanctified reverence and grumbling vilification. Some are strident in their animosity. If you have a lawn and a short fuse for criticism, you may want to skip over the following invective from Lorrie Otto who, not surprisingly, has been called the high priestess of the antilawn movement: "Today I think that maintaining a lawn is one of the most evil practices of the upper and middle classes. It continues with government support in spite of being flagrantly wasteful of drinking water and our non-renewable resources, irresponsibly destructive of our native plant and animal species, cognizant of the defiant and dishonest use of chemicals which are far more threatening to human health than any weed pollen, ignorant or disrespectful of air and water pollution, and finally, because officials are paralysed by the thought of any economic impact, they condone the inexplicable rudeness of noise pollution." (*Wildflower*, Winter 1994) Law-abiding, civic behaviour labelled as evil? Fighting words indeed!

Others, indeed *many* others, cherish the lawn. A Manitoba man, for example, took his love to extreme lengths when he specified in his will that

---

Lawns, I am convinced, are a symptom of, and a metaphor for, our skewed relationship to the land. They teach us that, with the help of petrochemicals and technology, we can bend nature to our will. Lawns stoke our hubris with regard to the land.

—*Michael Pollan*, New York Times, 1989

---

after his death a neighbour should mow his lawn regularly so that when he returned from the dead, he could reclaim his green carpet. Now that's eternal devotion. And if not devotion, then how else to explain the fact that in 1991 in the U.S. alone, there were 45 million lawns covering approximately 30 million acres (12 million ha) of the country. (Picture the provinces of New Brunswick and Nova Scotia combined into some kind of fuzzy green parking lot and you get the idea of what those abstract figures mean.)

One could, of course, opt for somewhat less reverential reasons and propose a more cynical critique. Perhaps the modern lawn speaks not to some innate landscape preference (as has been suggested by some researchers, who find our lawn-desire roots in the savannas of Africa, encoded in our genes), but rather speaks about corporate manipulation and engineering based on that most modern of motivations: the desire for profit. This view, expressed most thoroughly by the scholar Virginia Scott Jenkins in her book *The Lawn*, sees the lawn as an industrial product made possible by colliding developments in technology and science such as the mower, petrochemicals, genetic engineering, and modern irrigation. Add the vested interests of a massive lobby and advanced marketing and advertising, and what you get is precisely what we've got: the largest single crop of exterior decoration in North America.

✤   ✤   ✤

The success of the lawn is built on shaky, even unpalatable, foundations—for it began as a snobbish import of what itself was an exclusive, privileged feature. The English estate lawn of the eighteenth century was made possible—for a few—only by the wealth that could sustain it and the legion of cutters and weeders, including sheep and goats, it demanded. While this kind of landscape made some sense in the wet, cool climate of Britain, the early American champions of the lawn imported only the status symbol and forgot about the ecology.

The grasses they promoted and, as Michael Pollan has pointed out in *Second Nature*, eventually democratized, simply didn't want to grow in the varied climates and conditions of North America. Thus, the stage was set for a monumental battle between the forces of lawnification and the finickiness of fescue. Guess which won? Not too surprising, really, when you consider that the armaments included at least fifty years of genetic tinkering, decades of chemical assault, and massive doses of advertising—in short, the preferred pampering techniques of the nuclear age.

Somewhere along this jumbled path, though, democratic acceptance and celebration of the lawn turned into rigid idolatry. Not only have we inherited the biological homogeneity of monoculture, but it's propped up with enforcement. To question the lawn, even tentatively, to reject it, to replace it, is to threaten the very collective code of our conformity. Lawns aren't just the struggling sprouts of 30 million blades per acre (0.4 ha), they're a cultural institution, worthy of a capital letter. The Lawn: homogeneity imprinted right on the landscape. Defy at your own risk.

The coercive side of this status symbol is externally regulated by hundreds of bylaws across the country that demand lawn conformity and punish any deviance, but we can't blame it all on *them*. We've also internalized the code to such a degree that it seems lawns are a kind of atavistic response to bare patches. As if we have no other options.

This perceived lack of choice would not be of particular concern if it didn't also come with an enormous environmental price-tag. From the mini to the macro, the bill is expensive. The "perfect" lawn ideal of a single grass species, when multiplied by millions of homeowners, has created a monocultural nightmare—the antithesis of all we have learned about the need for biodiversity. These millions of missed opportunities—for diverse plantings of natives or exotics, for wildlife habitat, for ecological restoration, for personal expression of any kind—do more than just deaden the vista; they affect the whole complex web of the ecosystem, taking strands out of circulation as it were, replacing cyclical and connected parts of the whole with biological dead-ends. Imagine being a song bird, for example, looking for a place to build a nest, and encountering lawnified North America? Or a butterfly looking for nectar? A toad in search of a pond? About all we've done with our lawns is create cinch bug habitat, take away the conditions that would encourage their predators, and then complain about the damage.

This circular trap is enacted over and over in almost all of our dealings with the lawn. We go through what Michael Pollan has called the absurdist drama of lawn mowing, spewing the pollution equivalent of driving 350 miles (563 km) after just one hour with the power mower. We rake up approximately 4 1/2 tons of grass clippings per half-acre (0.2-ha) lawn per season (that's about 334

For as soon as someone decides to rip out a lawn, he or she becomes, perforce, a gardener, someone who must ask the gardener's questions: What is right for this place? What do I want here? How can I go about creating a pleasing outdoor space on this site? How can I use nature here without abusing it?

—*Michael Pollan*, in Keeping Eden

---

large yard bags full), and send their 121 pounds (55 kg) of nitrogen, 38 pounds (17 kg) of phosphate, 122 pounds (55 kg) of potassium and other nutrients to already overburdened landfills (a graphic demonstration courtesy of Rodale research reported in the April 1994 issue of *Organic Gardening* magazine). Then we buy fertilizers ($75 million worth in 1990, according to Statistics Canada; a million tons in the U.S. in 1984, more than that applied to food crops in India the same year), which have the effect of creating fast green growth of succulent tissue—insects' favourites. So we need to do something about those bugs (even if most of them are beneficial, who can tell the difference?), and what a third of Canadians do is use pesticides, on average more than farmers do. Weeds are considered equally a blight on the lawnscape, so down goes more kill-all, though it turns out that weeds may in fact have something to do with our mowing practices—the aesthetic that demands short-cropped grass also produces more weeds than longer cuts, according to a 1990 report from the Cornell Cooperative Extension. Everything other

---

With everything else exploding— population, culture, fashion—so has grass. It is literally spreading all over and has become, in fact, much more than a ground cover. It is an emotion that has blossomed into a status symbol.

—James A. Skardon, Saturday Evening Post, *March 17, 1962*

---

than that single species of grass must be eradicated. Why is nitrogen-fixing clover not allowed? Beats me, though I'm sure it has something to do with the anti-clover campaign launched by the lawn seed companies. They tried the same tactic with earthworms in the 1950s, actually saying their castings were a problem, but gardeners were too smart for that.

Then there's the water. Although an alien being tromping through suburbia one summer afternoon might speculate that it's the concrete that grows since so many people seem to be watering it, lawns do in fact gobble up a great deal of H_2O. Environment Canada says that water use increases 50 percent during the summer and they attribute this to lawns and gardens. It is easy to agree, since lawns require about an inch (2.5 cm) a

week; as Virginia Scott Jenkins has calculated in her book *The Lawn*, that means 10,000 gallons (45,500 L) a summer for a 25- by 40-foot (7.6- by 12.2-m) lawn. It's not that lawns would die without water; they naturally go dormant during a long dry spell, responding to nature's cycles with a protective mechanism, but we want them green instead of brown so we pour on the water.

Isn't it about time we let these dinosaurs go or at least did a bit of strategic lawn population control? Not everywhere, all the time, of course. Lawns are incontestably great for some things, and if you truly, actively love your lawn, then you won't hear one peep out of me. It's all in the "why" of your desire for it (and any thoroughly examined lawn desire is a good one as far as I'm concerned—it's the mindless mimicking that causes problems simply because there are so many of us doing it) and the "how" of your upkeep.

LAWN CARE TIPS

Love your lawn? Want to retain some grassy mown area for kids, dogs, and more adult pleasures? In many ways, it's not the plant choice that causes problems but our maintenance practices. So if you're looking for a guilt-reduced grassy groundcover, consider the following.

- For new lawns, shop around at knowledgeable nurseries for a grass variety that's best suited to your particular conditions. We tend to be lazy with the terminology, yet there are over ten thousand named species of grasses, and the most popular, Kentucky bluegrass, isn't necessarily the best in every situation. Consider some of the recent varieties of North American native buffalograss that are being developed; they require less water and fertilizer, and are relatively pest free. Some perennial ryegrasses and fine fescues on the market have been selectively bred for their naturally occurring pest-resistant characteristics. (They contain microscopic fungi that repel pests such as aphids and cutworms.) Shop around with your priorities—drought tolerance, low maintenance, low fertility requirements—on your sleeve.

- Relax the single-species rule. What's the problem if other hardy growers invade? The main idea is green, relatively short, and able to withstand foot traffic. Clover, yarrow, chamomile all fit the bill—why not live and let live? Relax the fight for what D.R. Otis has called "immaculate monotony."

- Keep your lawn high—at least 2 1/2 inches (6 cm)—and don't cut more than a third of its total height in one mowing. Don't cut during periods of drought, when the lawn is already under stress.

- Leave the clippings on the lawn (you can buy fancy mulching attachments if expensive technology makes you feel better about such a retro-manoeuvre). Recycle the nutrients back where they belong—on *your* lawn or in plant beds, not in landfill.

- Don't overfeed with fertilizers as the lawn will then require more water. Top-dress with compost, which will improve soil fertility. And encourage nitrogen-fixing clover.

- Can you live with a little brown in your life during drought? The grass won't die; it simply goes into a protective state of dormancy. If you must water, water intelligently (people who set up the sprinkler to mainly irrigate the sidewalk, then disappear for hours, should have their hoses revoked). Irrigate in the morning; give the lawn a good and thorough soaking (1 inch/2.5 cm at least, which will penetrate about 6 to 8 inches/ 15 to 20 cm in loamy soil) rather than frequent shallow watering, which just encourages shallow, thirsty roots. And appreciate every drop: Michael MacCaskey calculates (in *All About Lawns*) that 1 inch (2.5 cm) for a 1,000-square-foot (93-square-m) lawn is a whopping 625 gal-

lons (2,841 L)—and under average water pressure and with a 1/2-inch (1.2-cm) hose takes about two hours to deliver.

The *Globe* headline read "State of the grass has fans worried," and I must admit that my first thought

---

Annual pollution emissions from lawn utility machines in California are equivalent to the emissions produced by 3.5 million 1991 model automobiles driven 16,000 miles each.

—F. Herbert Bormann et al, Redesigning the American Lawn

---

was: Finally, lawns have hit the front page of our national newspaper; it's about time. Actually, the article was all about the turf health in Stanford University Stadium and its implications for the soccer game between Brazil and Russia.

No, it took Sandy Bell and the Toronto "lawn wars" for fescue to find its way to the front page. Sandy's crime was letting her grass grow. She says she did it not out of laziness but because of her environmental beliefs. The city said not in Toronto you don't and charged her with "excessive growth of grass and weeds." (There were no weeds, as defined by law, on the property, and the grass was about 1 foot high.) She went to court in 1993 to challenge the bylaw, lost, and was assessed a fifty-dollar fine. She appealed the decision on constitutional grounds, framing the issue in terms of freedom of expression and conscience.

The city, meanwhile, decided that the bylaw under which Sandy was charged was not repressive enough and passed a new one. It is now illegal in Toronto to grow a plant, in the front or backyard, over 8 inches (20 cm) high if a weed inspector arbitrarily decides that it is a weed. There is no definition of weed in the bylaw, no list of what plants are

---

The Environmental Protection Agency [U.S.] estimates that about 70 million pounds [31.7 million kg] of chemicals are applied to lawns each year, and that number is growing by 5 to 8 percent annually. By the late eighties, the average lawn owner was using a higher concentration of chemicals than farmers use.

—*Virgina Scott Jenkins*, The Lawn

---

not allowed to grow over this height—no meaningful limits or guidelines whatsoever. Anything over 8 inches (20 cm) is suspect. Take a look out your window, walk in any park, check out City Hall: if you live in Toronto, I guarantee you're surrounded by rampant floral activity of a criminal nature; if you live in another city, just hope you're not next.

While the debate was raging, I sat in on a few City Services Committee hearings and Council discussions on the matter, and I was amazed by all the subterranean fears that bubbled to the surface: rats would find a haven in the "weeds," garbage would get dumped on unkempt lawns, the whole look of the city would deteriorate, we'd be "horrified by the effects," and property values would

plummet. One deputant even brought in a video of her neighbour's backyard, looking for sympathy, when all I could see were herbs. Councillors nodded reprovingly, yet I doubt even one could have told the difference between rhubarb and burdock on the screen. Participatory democracy called for a botany class.

If I'd ever wondered what propelled the urge to regulate clipped lawns, my question was answered in that committee chamber: urban lawn conformity is fuelled by concern over money. Keep up with the Joneses through regular mowing because the Joneses are trying to keep up with their mortgage payments and keep up the value of their property investment. The whole thing works by adhesion; one dissenter and the coercive collusion collapses —along with property values. Once again we've traded aesthetic freedom and ecological health for dollars—and the debate ends up being just one more addition to the constitutional roster.

❦   ❦   ❦

If Sandy Bell's experience with the lawn police makes you nervous about contemplating even the most minor of lawn infractions, rest assured that there are thousands of dissenters across North America working for an enlightened lawn aesthetic, dragging the green carpet into the 1990s. In the U.S., a group of Yale graduate students has proposed something called the "Freedom Lawn" (and published a book about it called *Redesigning the American Lawn*), which looks something like this: plants, such as dandelion, violet, spurge, bluet, Canada mayflower, and clover, are allowed, if not necessarily encouraged, to invade the previously sacred territory of the lawn. These plants are not bombarded with chemicals; countless Saturday mornings are not devoted to their eradication. Instead, it's a live-and-let-live, equal-opportunity landscape. Amazing to say, but in contemporary North America, this is a highly radical concept—

botanical promiscuity replacing the lawn yawn. Democratic acceptance over autocratic rule.

Tom Cook of Oregon State University opts for a more managed aesthetic in his eco-lawn. According to an article in *Harrowsmith Country Life*, Cook is experimenting with lawn mixtures that include regionally appropriate grasses and broad-leaved plants, such as strawberry, clover, common yarrow, and daisies, that require less maintenance, water, and chemical inputs (mowing every two to four weeks; watering once a month).

And my favourite subversive act of lawn reinvention: in 1992, the city of Fort Saskatchewan, Alberta, used sheep to graze and thus keep clipped 235 acres (95 ha) of city grounds. The pilot project actually saved the city money in terms of maintenance and reduced the city's use of pesticides. Appropriately enough, herbivore grazing goes right back to the very roots of the traditional British estate lawn—a cyclical reinvention, you might say. And none too soon.

CHAPTER REFERENCES

All About Lawns. Michael MacCaskey. San Francisco: Ortho, 1979.

Keeping Eden: A History of Gardening in America. Massachusetts Horticultural Society. Boston: Bulfinch, 1992.

The Lawn: A History of an American Obsession. Virginia Scott Jenkins. Washington: Smithsonian Institution Press, 1994.

Redesigning the American Lawn: A Search for Environmental Harmony. F. Herbert Bormann, Diana Balmori and Gordon T. Geballe. New Haven: Yale University Press, 1993.

Second Nature. Michael Pollan. New York: Laurel, 1991.

Chapter 12

WILDLIFE ATTRACTION

If you're already gardening with native plants, you're well on the way in the wildlife attraction department. It may not have been an intentional goal, but rather something that just happened as a result of using indigenous plants that have long evolved in association with indigenous wildlife. If this is the case, or if you're just starting out with native plants, there are a number of steps you can take to increase the attractiveness of your garden to various species of wildlife. Since habitat loss is the major problem confronting wildlife, not just in Ontario but across the globe, any effort you make to enhance the value of your property as habitat will contribute one small piece to the puzzle of reconnected spaces for the creatures with whom we share this planet.

Of course, any consideration of attracting wildlife to the garden should immediately raise the question: what is wildlife? The standard dictionary definition of "wild living things" includes all manner of creatures—slugs and butteflies, skunks and birds—not just those that for whatever reasons one

may consider desirable as local neighbours. Once you make a conscious effort to attract wildlife to your space, you will be confronted with complex moral and ethical questions, as Michael Pollan, the author of *Second Nature*, discovered when he tried to justify his urge to firebomb a woodchuck burrow. Wildlife, yes, but cohabitant? Each of us will need to decide, and it's best to go into the enterprise with an awareness of our limits, zero romanticism, a good dose of humility, and a recognition of the fact that the notion of "wildlife pests" is highly subjective. And if you are going to pick and choose species to attract, you'll need to manage your habitat accordingly.

There's also the question of how much you can reasonably expect to support in your particular space. Whether you live in the city or country, are you willing to share your home, make it hospitable and safe for the creatures you are attracting? Are you putting up bird feeders only to have local cats hunt down and kill birds? Are you putting in a pond only to have young toads mowed down during grass cutting? Are you planting nectar plants only to unwittingly kill butterflies and insects through the use of chemical pesticides, herbicides, and insecticides in other parts of your property? How far are you willing to go? Planting for wildlife involves making a commitment—and if you're not willing to learn all you can about their needs and

---

But let us weave [landscapes] together into something big enough to matter by connecting each patch with others at the corners and along the boundaries. This is the rich, new landscape; this is the new kind of gardener who asks not whether he should plant this ornament or another but which patch is missing from his community, how he can provide it, and how animals will move from his patch to the next. This is the ark.

—Sara Stein, Noah's Garden

---

then perhaps make some compromises for their health and safety if necessary, then it's much better not to embark on wildlife attraction in the first place.

That said, there's no doubt that having a diversity of creatures in your local landscape makes it a much more exciting, dynamic, and interesting place. Who hasn't thrilled to the sight of a cardinal flashing its red in winter? Been charmed by the buzz of cicadas in summer? Been surprised by the darting flight of hummingbirds in their search

for nectar? All these encounters, literally and metaphorically, bring life to the garden.

❧   ❧   ❧

There's a wonderful cartoon in the book *City Critters* by David Bird that provides a sly commentary on North American wildlife appreciation: a man and a woman are sitting on a couch watching television. Outside their window are numerous animals peering in, and one of the creatures is saying "*Wild Kingdom* is their favourite show." We're a television-addicted culture and we tend to mediate our experience through the tube, to the exclusion of the world around us. Hardly a new or original observation, but one that bears repeating. But when we manage to extract ourselves from the tyranny of the box, it's astounding what we can find right outside our doors.

Granted, not everyone has the expertise of an entomologist like Frank Lutz, who identified 1,402 insect species in his 75- by 200-foot (22- by 60-m) New Jersey lot one summer, including 477 species of moths and butterflies, 259 beetles, 258 flies, and 167 ants, bees and wasps! But all we need to do is to start looking—even in the midst of the densest city. In Central Park in New York City, naturalists have observed 13 native species of mammals, 9 species of fish, 8 of reptiles and amphibians, and 268 species of birds, according to a 1983 *New York Times* report. In other words, even cities can be rich in habitat, whether the result of a connected system of parkland, fortuitous remnants of "abandoned" land, or the efforts of enlightened backyard naturalists.

HABITAT GARDENING FOR WILDLIFE

Though the specifics vary for different species, the principles of wildlife attraction are general. The key to attracting wildlife *and* maintaining the elements they need for survival is the creation of the proper habitat conditions: food, cover (that is, some kind of protection), water, and space. Any one of these without the others will not constitute a living environment, though it might provide temporary advantages (and dangers—see above). But if you want to create a home for wildlife, you'll need all four.

In broad terms, the more diverse the habitat, the more diverse the species you will attract; clumps of vegetation tend to be more useful than single plantings; and layers of vegetation—from groundcovers through to taller plants and shrubs, up to trees—tend to provide more diversity of shelter. And finally, chemicals are absolutely out: if you're gardening for wildlife, you're not using pesticides, herbicides, or any other "icide" that poisons.

FOOD

Wildlife food in the garden is in the form of plants (seeds, berries, nuts, fruit, leaves, nectar), which are eaten by creatures who themselves become food for other creatures. Dynamics of the food chain in action—nothing fancy about it. Predation will occur and should not be discouraged —except, of course, when domesticated species such as cats enter the picture.

Some creatures have extremely limited food requirements (in its larval stage, the Karner blue butterfly, for example, only eats the native lupine); others eat a wide assortment. Native plants are excellent food sources for indigenous wildlife.

SHELTER

Creatures need places to build their nests, raise their young, hide out from predators, hunt, rest, sleep, preen, breed, and whatever else it is that they do. Shelters may be constructed by the gardener (such as bird houses and brush piles) or the gardener may just provide the materials for the animals themselves to do the constructing (leaving old tree snags in the garden, for example). Some

creatures, such as insects and various birds, live close to the ground; others require high nesting grounds.

WATER

All creatures need water to drink, and some use it for cleaning (birds) or as year-round habitat

---

Let's imagine a goal: that at some time in the future, the value of a property will be perceived in part according to its value to wildlife. A property hedged with fruiting shrubs will be worth more than one bordered by forsythia. . . . Perhaps there will be formal incentives: tax abatements geared to the number of native species; deductions for lots that require neither sprays nor sprinkler. A nursery colony of bats might be considered a capital improvement. There could be bonuses for birdhouses.

—*Sara Stein*, Noah's Garden

(frogs), transient habitat (toads and mosquitoes), or for fishing (herons). Water features in the garden can range from a standing puddle to an elaborate pond.

SPACE

The size of your garden and its proximity to natural areas will determine the types and numbers of wildlife you will be able to support. Some creatures, such as a number of songbird species, need large woodlands to support viable populations; others, such as ants, can fill tiny niches.

These are the broad-brush principles, but each species has specific preferences that you can take into account when planning your native plant garden for wildlife. The following is meant as a general introduction to some of these preferences for a variety of species.

Every neighbourhood needs an entomologist who does house calls.

—Des Kennedy, Crazy About Gardening

ATTRACTING BIRDS

With their colours, songs, and calls, insect-eating capabilities, and general antics, birds are considered one of the most desired creatures in the garden. To attract them, some people build birdhouses (there are different designs, heights, and sizes for different species); some put out birdfeeders (again, different types of food attract different species); and some people have birdbaths in the garden.

To learn about birds and their habitats, consider joining a local naturalist club. If you're having trouble finding a group, contact the Federation of Ontario Naturalists.

If you're going to do any of the above, I urge you to do some research by reading any of the books listed under "Wildlife Attraction" or contacting any of the organizations in Further Reading and Resources. The subject is much too large for the scope of this book, but you should be aware of some of the dangers of attracting birds. For example, if you don't build a proper birdhouse, the nest may be invaded by predators such as rodents, English sparrows, and starlings; thus, it's important to research the kind of birdhouse that's appropriate and safe for the kind of bird you want to attract and that visits your area. Birdfeeders also require care. What kind of food is best for the species you want to feed? How will you keep predators out of the feeder? Are you willing to clean out the feeder thoroughly at least once a week, even in the depths of winter, so that the birds are not subject to diseases? Will you keep it full so birds don't starve? And with birdbaths: is the bath at least 3 feet (0.9 m) off the ground in an open shady area, away from shrubs, so that birds are not vulnerable to hidden predators? Are you willing to clean it thoroughly, in winter as well, at least once a week? Does it have a gentle slope for easy bird access?

You can also attract birds through the planting of native species of vegetation. You won't be doing any harm by planting any of the following (as you could with improper care of the above), and you could very well be doing some good. Along with the specifics listed below, a few things to keep in mind include: one tree or shrub does not a habitat make; if you want to create habitat for a particular species, you'll need to research its requirements; nonmigratory birds need plants that hold their fruit into winter; songbirds prefer berries to nut-producing plants; and evergreen trees make the best winter shelter. Leave seed heads as a food source over the winter. Clean them up in early spring.

Trees for Food and/or Shelter

eastern white pine; white, bur and red oak; white spruce; paper birch; American mountain ash; redbud; pin cherry; shagbark hickory; eastern hemlock

Shrubs and Small Trees for Food and/or Shelter

sumac; viburnum; dogwood; blueberries; serviceberry; bearberry; inkberry; winterberry; cranberry; elderberry

Vines for Food

bittersweet; Virginia creeper; grape

Herbaceous Plants

bee balm; columbine; coreopsis; aster; goldenrod

Groundcovers

bearberry; bunchberry; partridgeberry

Grasses

bluestem; Indian grass

Scientists are alarmed by the worldwide decrease in songbird populations, and many suggest that deforestation, including forest fragmentation, is a major cause for decline. (The migrating birds depend on forests from the temperate zone to the tropics.) And, of course, chemical contamination through the use of insecticides, and global warming are compounding the problem. A backyard feeder will do little to help these birds (some avoid human-disturbed areas anyway) if it's not backed up with strong conservation measures to protect habitat right here in Ontario. If you'd like to assist in conservation efforts, contact Conservation International–Canada for more information. The group has also produced an excellent, detailed guide to planting for migratory songbirds (including indispensable information regarding specific species and their use of particular plants), called *Bring Back the Birds: A Community Action Guide to Migratory Songbird Conservation (Eastern Canada Edition)*. It's available for a modest fee from Conservation International–Canada (see Further Reading and Resources).

HUMMINGBIRDS

Chances are you've already been regaled with amazing facts about these compact bundles of energy, but here goes anyway. One of the smallest warm-blooded animals, ruby-throated humming-

---

A garden without animals is like a florist's refrigerator.

—*Hortense Miller, quoted in* Fine Gardening *magazine*

---

birds reach a full flying speed of 25 to 30 miles (40 to 48 km) per hour and flap their wings at a clip of fifty times a second (females) to seventy times a second (males). They're able to fly upside-down, backwards, and sideways, and they hover to feed. They normally feed every ten minutes or so, and according to the American Backyard Bird Society, they must drink up to eight times their body weight in nectar and water every day. In one small example of nature's symbiosis, their long grooved tongue

---

BIRDS AND BUGS

Organic Gardening **magazine's Top Ten Birds for Bug-eating:**
chickadee; wren; swallow; bluebird; phoebe; native sparrows; vireo; woodpecker; nuthatch; nighthawk

allows them to extract nectar from tubular flowers (they don't need landing platforms as bees and butterflies do), and their feeding helps to pollinate flowers. They also eat insects and spiders. In short, they're marvellous.

If you'd like to attract hummingbirds to your garden, give the following natives a try. You'll

---

Like birds? Then you better get used to bugs.

—*Neil Diboll, quoted in* The Natural Habitat Garden

---

notice that most are red, orange, or yellow—these are the colours they go for. Hummingbirds also feed on tree sap, which is exposed via the holes drilled by sapsuckers in trees such as white and yellow birch and red maple. If hummingbird attraction is your goal, use the wild varieties of the following (avoid sterile, cultivated hybrids as they have little or no nectar): columbine; jewelweed; bee balm; cardinal flower; trumpet honeysuckle; butterfly weed; wild blue phlox; Virginia bluebells; turtlehead.

ATTRACTING BATS

Who knows why these creatures are so maligned; thankfully, a number of bat conservation associations have sprung up and are doing great work to counter the bad PR these small mammals have received over the years. Unfortunately, it's more than a case of bad PR; it's also a case of bad chemicals. According to an essay in *Conserving Carolinian Canada*, the government continues to approve the use of DDT in bat control; the authors conclude that "the continuing registration of DDT

for bat control in Canada clearly reflects the public's attitude towards these animals."

Why would you want to have bats around? Aside from the fact that they're losing habitat—in particular, their nesting areas—and every little bit helps, bats are great at insect control, consuming about half their body weight in bugs, such as mosquitoes, each night. So why not consider having a bat house? They're relatively small—a foot (0.3 m) long, 1/2 foot (0.15 m) wide, with the opening at the bottom—and easy to construct. (Bat houses are also readily available from conservation organizations, as are bat-house building plans.) They should be installed quite high, 10 to 15 feet (3 to 4.5 m) above the ground, on a tree or side of a house, in a spot with five to six hours of sun a day and protected from wind. You'll know your bat box is in use if there are bat droppings underneath. It may take a few years before bats move in or they may roost quickly.

ATTRACTING BUTTERFLIES

The lesson of the butterfly is something we've only half learned. Though many people love the idea of attracting adult butterflies to the garden, we're somehow less alert to the needs of butterflies in their early stages of life; the adults need nectar (and are easy to oblige with bright flowers), but at their larval stages they also need particular and highly specific host plants on which to munch. Someone who goes about raging at leaf damage and eradicating all caterpillars will not be doing butterflies a favour. We need to accept the "good" with the "bad," the youth with the adult, the "crawling beast" with the "flying beauty," as William Stolzenburg puts it in *Nature Conservancy* (May/June 1992). Thus, the butterfly gardener will plant not only the showy nectar sources, but also the larval host plants.

This dual need is particularly important in the context of habitat destruction and the corresponding (and increasing) rarity of many butterfly species, for what they're losing is precisely the specific host plants that sustain them. The book *Conserving Carolinian Canada* includes a depressing litany of such losses: for the northern zebra swallowtail butterfly, the host plant—pawpaw—is scarce in Ontario; the dog face butterfly is probably now extirpated in Ontario and its preferred host plant, false indigo, is rare in Ontario; the larvae of frosted elfin butterflies will feed only on wild lupine and wild indigo, both of which are rare in Ontario.

But gardeners have a role to play in conservation efforts. As already discussed in Chapter 3 and the plant listings in Chapter 9, monarch butterflies rely on milkweeds at their larval stage, and even though butterfly and host plant are not endangered in Ontario, they are most certainly under threat—as milkweeds (all species) are listed in the Weed Control Act as noxious weeds and, by law, are required to be eradicated on property! How ironic that on the one hand, the government applauds Mexico for protecting the monarch butterfly, yet on the other hand not only allows but requires the destruction of the host plant. Courting arrest, I urge you to plant the gorgeous garden milkweeds such as butterfly milkweed or swamp milkweed. A few other larval plants include the wild lupine (for Karner blue and frosted elfin); poplars, ash, elm, and willow (for mourning cloak); tulip trees (for tiger swallowtail); golden alexanders (for eastern black swallowtail); turtlehead (for Baltimore butterfly); spice bush and sassafras (for spice-bush swallowtail); two-leafed toothwort (for West Virginia white); violets (for fritillaries); and black snakeroot, dogwood, and sumac (for spring azure).

To attract adult butterflies, you need flowers with some kind of landing pad, such as cones, spikes, or clusters. Again, native plants are ideal for this purpose as they have evolved over thousands of years in association with butterflies—the symbiotic fit of butterfly mouth parts and corresponding nectar plants is truly incredible—and they have the perfumed nectar that has been bred out of many faintly scented hybrids. Large masses of sunny plantings work best, particularly those that bloom in late summer. Natives to try include but-

---

Good neighbours come in all species.

—*Sally Wasowski*, Requiem for a Lawnmower

---

terfly milkweed, asters, goldenrod, black-eyed Susan, gray-headed coneflower, blazing star, Joe-pye weed, cup plant, culver's root, helianthus, and coreopsis.

And remember, if you want butterflies in the garden, no chemicals, not even *Bacillus thuringiensis* (BT), a widely used biological control agent.

ATTRACTING INSECTS

On the back cover of a national gardening magazine appeared the most astounding statement in the context of, surprise, an insecticide advertisement: "Because the only good bug is a dead bug." Wrong! Imagine a world without bugs and you're also imagining a world without much of anything else. Many plants depend on pollinating insects of all kinds to produce fruit and set seed. And bear in mind that, according to a report in *Wildflower* magazine (Summer 1986), more than 99.9% of all insect species are either directly beneficial to humans or at least are not harmful to humans.

Though many people harbour not only insect fear—entomophobia—but active insect loathing, the native plant gardener will welcome such creatures in the garden, realizing that many wildflowers depend on insects.

In *Wildflower*, Summer 1986, Katherine Dunster lists the following native plants as good for attracting insects, particularly honey bees: tulip tree; basswood; asters; jewelweed; bearberry; dogwoods; blueberries; New Jersey tea; buttonbush; black-eyed Susan; honey locust; eastern redbud; serviceberries; wild grape; Virginia creeper; spring beauty; milkweeds; blazing star; Joe-pye weed; viburnums.

CHAPTER REFERENCES

Bring Back the Birds: A Community Action Guide to Migratory Songbird Conservation. Kenneth Towle. Toronto: Conservation International— Canada, 1994.

City Critters: How to Live with Urban Wildlife. David M. Bird. Montreal: Eden, 1986.

Crazy About Gardening. Des Kennedy. Vancouver: Whitecap, 1994.

Conserving Carolinian Canada. Gary M. Allen et al. Waterloo: University of Waterloo Press, 1990.

The Natural Habitat Garden. Ken Druse with Margaret Roach. New York: Clarkson N. Potter, 1994.

Noah's Garden: Restoring the Ecology of Our Own Back Yards. Sara Stein. Boston: Houghton Mifflin, 1993.

Requiem for a Lawnmower. Sally Wasowski with Andy Wasowski. Dallas: Taylor, 1992.

Second Nature. Michael Pollan. New York: Laurel, 1991.

AFTERWORD

While many people garden with native plants simply for the challenge of trying something new, I hope that the environmental reasons have added an urgent weight to the activity. If you're at all swayed by the ecological imperatives, why stop at the garden? There are literally thousands of untapped opportunities throughout our communities—areas ripe for greening with native plants. (And, indeed, many native plant proponents argue that efforts in our own yards will make little real, valuable difference to the health of ecosystems if we do not accompany them with a commitment to restoration of larger landscapes.)

As Edwinna von Baeyer has documented in *Rhetoric and Roses*, there is a long history in Canada of garden movements to "beautify" vacant lots, school grounds, and other public spaces. But what if the goal were not beautification—a relative and contested term—but rather restoration? What if our civic energies were directed towards the healing of the land that maintains us? If children had a place right outside the schools' doors to learn about natural processes through working with the land? If vacant lots were native plant meadows where we could have unstructured experiences with native flora and fauna? If the buzz and roar of lawnmowers were replaced with the hum of insects? If parks were not rigidly controlled spaces of manicured grass and single-function ornamentals? If our "landscapes without a future" (as one critic, Michael Hough, has called our big tree and grass park landscapes) were replaced with places of dynamism and change, where natural processes charge ahead with their long-evolved wisdom, and our role is one of stewardship and learning rather than control?

Perhaps it's inevitable that native plant gardening leads us out of our backyards and into the bigger garden of our shared communities.

❦   ❦   ❦

While the major international conference on population was going on in Cairo in the summer of 1994, CBC radio ran a documentary in which the scientist Paul Erlich speculated that the ecological systems of the planet would not be able to support the expected 13 or 14 billion people by the year 2050. Since I was long ago convinced by his assertion that humanity is "dangling by our fingertips," I was receptive to his argument. What I wasn't expecting, though, was to find much of a connection between his analysis and the issue of native plant gardening. After all, he was talking about global collapse and I was thinking about digging in the dirt—a wide chasm indeed!

But when Erlich gave his examples of that digital dangling, I was struck by how closely they related to the restoration issues at hand: "we are losing our biodiversity, we are exhausting our soils, and we are exhausting our supplies of groundwater." Erlich was speaking on a massive, global scale, and while I don't want to diminish the importance of what he was saying or deny the almost unimaginable social transformations his diagnosis demands, it did seem in one sense very locally relevant to me that his list of immediate ills included exactly those things that native plant gardening seeks to redress: maintaining rather than diminishing biodiversity; healing rather than depleting soils; conserving rather than wasting water.

Butterfly milkweed may not change the world, but it could certainly change your backyard—and for many of us, that's an appropriate place to start, one small bit of the biosphere, one bucket at a time.

CHAPTER REFERENCES

City Form and Natural Process. Michael Hough. London: Routledge, Chapman and Hall, 1984.

Rhetoric and Roses. Edwinna von Baeyer. Toronto: Fitzhenry and Whiteside, 1984.

FURTHER READING AND RESOURCES

T his section is divided into Books; Magazines; Native Plant Sources; and Organizations. Books have been further grouped under the main headings of Ecology and Environment; Gardening; and Native Plants and Natural History. Specific subject areas are listed under these three main headings.

For example, if you were interested in books on pond design, you would turn to the Gardening section and look under Water Gardens. Key words at the bottom of each page will help you locate the relevant section quickly.

BOOKS

ECOLOGY AND ENVIRONMENT

Biological Diversity

Biodiversity. E. O. Wilson and Frances M. Peter, eds. Washington: National Academy Press, 1988.

Challenges in the Conservation of Biological Resources: A Practitioner's Guide. Daniel J. Decker et al., eds. Boulder: Westview Press, 1991.

Conservation and Evolution. O. H. Frankel and Michael E. Soule. New York: Cambridge University Press, 1981.

Conservation Biology: An Evolutionary-Ecological Perspective. Michael E. Soule and Bruce A. Wilcox. Sunderland, Massachusetts: Sinauer Associates, 1980.

Conservation Biology: The Science of Scarcity and Diversity. Michael E. Soule, ed. Sunderland, Massachusetts: Sinauer Associates, 1986.

Conserving the World's Biological Diversity. Jeffrey A. McNeely et al. Washington: International Union for Conservation of Nature and Natural Resources, 1990.

The Diversity of Life. Edward O. Wilson. Cambridge, Massachusetts: Harvard University Press, 1992.

Earthly Goods: Medicine-Hunting in the Rainforest. Christopher Joyce. Boston: Little, Brown, 1994.

The Fragmented Forest: Island Biogeography Theory and the Preservation of Biotic Diversity. Larry D. Harris. Chicago: University of Chicago Press, 1984.

Genetic and Ecological Diversity. L. M. Cook. London: Chapman and Hall, 1991.

Ghost Bears: Exploring the Biodiversity Crisis. R. Edward Grumbine. Washington: Island Press, 1992.

The Importance of Biological Diversity. M. Holdgate et al. New Haven: Yale University Press, 1989.

Keeping Options Alive: The Scientific Basis for Conserving Biodiversity. Walter V. Reid and Kenton R. Miller. Washington: World Resources Institute, 1989.

Landscape Linkages and Biodiversity. Wendy E. Hudson, ed. Washington: Island Press, 1991.

Monocultures of the Mind: Perspectives on Biodiversity and Biotechnology. Vandana Shiva. London: Zed Books, 1993.

Systematics, Ecology and the Biodiversity Crisis. Niles Eldredge, ed. New York: Columbia University Press, 1992.

Wildlife, Forests and Forestry: Principles of Managing Forests for Biological Diversity. Malcolm L. Hunter. Englewood Cliffs, New Jersey: Prentice-Hall, 1990.

Bioregionalism

Boundaries of Home: Mapping for Local Empowerment. Doug Aberly, ed. Gabriola, B.C.: New Society Publishers, 1993.

The Dream of the Earth. Thomas Berry. San Francisco: Sierra Club, 1986.

Dwellers in the Land: The Bioregional Vision. Kirkpatrick Sale. San Francisco: Sierra Club, 1985.

Home! A Bioregional Reader. Van Andruss et al. Gabriola, B.C.: New Society Publishers, 1990.

Out of Place: Restoring Identity to the Regional Landscape. Michael Hough. New Haven: Yale University Press, 1990.

Turtle Talk: Voices for a Sustainable Future. Christopher and Judith Plant, eds. Gabriola, B.C.: New Society Publishers, 1990.

Cities, Communities, and Naturalization

"An Annotated Bibliography on Community-Based Naturalization." Ecological Outlook Consulting, Box 93, Schomberg, Ontario L0G 1T0.

Building Cities That Work. Edmund P. Fowler. Montreal: McGill-Queen's University Press, 1992.

Canadian Cities in Transition. Trudi Bunting and Pierre Filion, eds. Toronto: Oxford University Press, 1991.

The Canadian City. Kent Gerecke. Montreal: Black Rose, 1991.

The Canadian City: Essays in Urban History. Gilbert A. Stelter and Alan F. J. Artibise, eds. Toronto: McClelland and Stewart, 1977.

Cities of Tomorrow: An Intellectual History of Urban Planning and Design in the Twentieth Century. Peter Hall. New York: Blackwell, 1989.

City: Rediscovering the Center. William H. Whyte. New York: Doubleday, 1988.

City Form and Natural Process. Michael Hough. London: Routledge, 1989.

Conservation in Practice. A. Warren and F. B. Goldsmith, eds. New York: Wiley, 1974.

Conservation in Progress. F. B. Goldsmith and A. Warren, eds. New York: Wiley, 1993.

Crabgrass Frontier: The Suburbanization of the United States. Kenneth T. Jackson. Toronto: Oxford University Press, 1985.

The Death and Life of Great American Cities. Jane Jacobs. New York: Vintage, 1961.

The Ecological Greening of Southern Ontario: An Imperative for the '90s. John Ambrose, Jane Dougan and Henry Kock, eds. Guelph: The Arboretum, University of Guelph and the Ontario Society for Environmental Management, 1990.

The Ecology of Urban Habitats. O. L. Gilbert. London: Chapman and Hall, 1989.

Emerald City. John Bentley Mays. Toronto: Viking, 1994.

Environmental Restoration: Science and Strategies for Restoring the Earth. John J. Berger. Washington: Island Press, 1990.

Environmental Stewardship: Studies in Active Earthkeeping. Sally Lerner. Waterloo: University of Waterloo Press, 1993.

Futures by Design: The Practice of Ecological Planning. Doug Aberley, ed. Gabriola, B.C.: New Society Publishers, 1994.

Good City Form. Kevin Lynch. Cambridge, Massachusetts: MIT Press, 1981.

The Granite Garden: Urban Nature and Human Design. Anne Whiston Spirn. New York: Harper Collins, 1984.

Green Cities: Ecologically Sound Approaches to Urban Space. David Gordon, ed. Montreal: Black Rose, 1990.

Greening Canada: A Guide to Community Tree Planting. Chris Winter. Toronto: Conservation Council of Ontario, 1994.

The Greening of the Cities. David Nicholson-Lord. London: Routledge and Kegan Paul, 1987.

Greenways for America. Charles E. Little. Baltimore: The Johns Hopkins University Press, 1990.

Groundwork 94: A Workshop Towards Excellence in Community-based Tree Planting. Toronto: Evergreen Foundation, 1994.

Habitat Restoration: A Guide for Proactive Schools. Edward Cheskey. Waterloo: Waterloo County Board of Education, 1993.

Helping Nature Heal: An Introduction to Environmental Restoration. Richard Nilsen, ed. Berkeley: Ten Speed, 1991.

Integrating Man and Nature in the Metropolitan Environment. L. W. Adams and D. L. Leedy, eds. Columbia, Maryland: National Institute for Urban Wildlife, 1987.

Landscape Restoration Handbook. Donald Harker et al., eds. Ann Arbor, Michigan: Lewis Publishers, 1993.

A Life Zone Approach to School Yard Naturalization: The Carolinian Life Zone. S. Aboud and H. Kock. Guelph: University of Guelph Arboretum, 1994.

The Living Landscape: An Ecological Approach to Landscape Planning. Frederick Steiner. New York: McGraw-Hill, 1991.

Living with the Land: Communities Restoring the Earth. Christine Meyer and Faith Moosang. Gabriola, B.C.: New Society Publishers, 1992.

Natural Regeneration Guide for Schools. Hamilton: Hamilton Naturalists' Club. (Available from 478 Hiway 53E, R.R. 1, Ancaster, Ontario L9G 3K9.)

Nature and Urban Man. Canadian Nature Federation Conference. Ottawa: Canadian Nature Federation, 1975.

Nature in Cities. Ian C. Laurie, ed. New York: Wiley, 1979.

Nature in the City. John Rublowsky. New York: Basic Books, 1967.

Nature in the Urban Landscape: A Study of City Ecosystems. Don Gill and Penelope Bonnett. Baltimore: York Press, 1973.

The Necessity of Empty Places. Paul Gruchow. New York: St. Martin's Press, 1988.

No Place Like Home: Building Sustainable Communities. Marcia Nozick. Ottawa: Canadian Council on Social Development, 1992.

People and City Landscapes. Michael Hough and Suzanne Barrett. Toronto: Conservation Council of Ontario, 1987.

Perspectives on Landscape and Settlement in Nineteenth Century Ontario. J. David Wood, ed. Toronto: McClelland and Stewart, 1975.

The Politics of Park Design: A History of Urban Parks in America. Galen Cranz. Cambridge, Massachusetts: MIT Press, 1982.

Promoting Nature in Cities and Towns: A Practical Guide. Malcolm J. Emery. London: Croom Helm, 1986.

Public Space. Stephen Carr et al. New York: Cambridge University Press, 1992.

Regeneration. Toronto: Royal Commission on the Future of the Toronto Waterfront, 1992.

Restoring the Earth: How Americans are Working to Restore Our Damaged Environment. John J. Berger. New York: Knopf, 1985.

Schoolyard Magic: A Green-Up Guide for Outdoor Classrooms in Peterborough County. Peterborough: Peterborough Green-Up, 1992.

Shading Our Cities: A Resource Guide for Urban and Community Forests. Gary Moll and Sara Ebenreck, eds. Washington: Island Press, 1989.

The Simple Act of Planting A Tree: A Citizen Forester's Guide to Healing Your Neighbourhood, Your City and Your World. Tree People, with Andy and Katie Lipkis. Toronto: McClelland and Stewart, 1990.

The Social Life of Small Urban Spaces. William H. Whyte. Washington: Conservation Foundation, 1982.

A Symposium on Trees and Forests in an Urbanizing Environment. Amherst: University of Massachusetts Press, 1970.

Toward Sustainable Communities. Mark Roseland. Ottawa: National Round Table on the Environment and Economy, 1992.

Trees in Urban Design. Henry F. Arnold. New York: Van Nostrand Reinhold, 1980.

Urban Forestry. Gene W. Grey and Frederick J. Deneke. New York: Wiley, 1986.

Urban Forestry: Planning and Managing Urban Greenspaces. Robert W. Miller. Englewood Cliffs, New Jersey: Prentice Hall, 1988.

Urban Natural Areas: Ecology and Preservation. W. A. Andrews and J. L. Cranmer-Byng, eds. Toronto: Institute for Environmental Studies, 1981.

Urban Trees: A Guide for Selection, Maintenance and Master Planning. Leonard E. Phillips, Jr. New York: McGraw-Hill, 1993.

Welcoming Back the Wilderness: A Guide to School Ground Naturalization. Evergreen Foundation. Scarborough: Prentice-Hall, 1994.

Yes In My Back Yard: A Guide to Rehabilitating Urban Streams. Laurie Fretz. Toronto: Conservation Council of Ontario, 1992.

Conservation

The Biological Aspects of Rare Plant Conservation. Hugh Synge, ed. Toronto: Wiley, 1981.

Bring Back the Birds: A Community Action Guide to Migratory Songbird Conservation. Kenneth Towle. Toronto: Conservation International—Canada, 1994.

Building an Ark. Phil Hoose. Washington: Island Press, 1981.

Canada's National Parks. R. D. Lawrence. Toronto: Collins, 1983.

Canada's National Parks: A Visitor's Guide. Marylee Stephenson. Scarborough: Prentice-Hall, 1983.

Conservation Biology: The Theory and Practice of Nature Conservation, Preservation, and Management. Peggy L. Fiedler and Subodh K. Jain, eds. New York: Chapman and Hall, 1992.

Conservation by the People: The History of the Conservation Movement in Ontario to 1970. Arthur Herbert Richardson. Toronto: University of Toronto Press, 1974.

Conservation of Threatened Plants. J. B. Simmons et al., eds. New York: Plenum, 1976.

Creative Conservation: A Handbook for Ontario Land Trusts. Stewart Hilts and Ron Reid. Don Mills: Federation of Ontario Naturalists, 1994.

An Ecological and Evolutionary Ethic. D. G. Kozlovsky. Englewood Cliffs, New Jersey: Prentice-Hall, 1984.

Ecology of Greenways. Daniel S. Smith and Paul C. Hellmund. Minneapolis: University of Minnesota Press, 1993.

Ecosystem Management for Parks and Wilderness. James K. Agee and Darryll R. Johnson, eds. Seattle: University of Washington Press, 1988.

Enduring Seeds: Native American Agriculture and Wild Plant Conservation. Gary Paul Nabhan. Berkeley: North Point Press, 1989.

The First Resource: Wild Species in the North American Economy. Christine Prescott-Allen and Robert Prescott-Allen. New Haven: Yale University Press, 1986.

Genetics and Conservation: A Reference for Managing Wild Animal and Plant Populations. Christine M. Schonewald-Cox et al., eds. Menlo Park, California: Benjamin/Cummings, 1983.

Genetics and Conservation of Rare Plants. Donald A. Falk and Kent E. Holsinger, eds. New York: Oxford University Press, 1991.

Genetic Resources: A Practical Guide to their Conservation. Daniel Querol. Atlantic Highlands, New Jersey: Zed Books, 1993.

Genetic Resources in Plants: Their Exploration and Conservation. O. H. Frankel and E. Bennett, eds. Oxford: Blackwell, 1970.

The Gift of Good Land. W. Berry. San Francisco: North Point Press, 1981.

Green Footsteps: Recollections of a Grassroots Conservationist. Charles Sauriol. Toronto: Hemlock Press, 1991.

Green Inheritance. Anthony Huxley. New York: Doubleday, 1985.

Heritage Conservation: The Natural Environment. E. Neville Ward, Beth Killham. Waterloo: Heritage Resources Centre, University of Waterloo, 1987.

Islands of Green: Natural Heritage Protection in Ontario. Stewart G. Hilts, Malcolm D. Kirk, Ronald A. Reid, eds. Toronto: Ontario Heritage Foundation, 1986.

Islands of Hope: Ontario's Parks and Wilderness. Lori Labatt and Bruce Litteljohn, eds. Willowdale: Firefly, 1992.

Land Acquisition Alternatives—Handbook. Toronto: Land Management Branch, Ontario Ministry of Natural Resources, 1985.

Land-Saving Action. R. L. Brenneman and S. M. Bates. Washington: Island Press, 1984.

The Last Landscape. William H. Whyte. Garden City, New York: Doubleday, 1970.

The Man Who Planted Trees. Jean Giono. Toronto: CBC Enterprises, 1989.

Methods of Preserving Wildlife Habitat. B. Haigis and W. Young. Ottawa: Lands Directorate, Environment Canada, 1983.

The National Parks of Canada. Kevin McNamee. Toronto: Key Porter, 1994.

Nature Reserves Manual. M. Kirk. Don Mills: Federation of Ontario Naturalists, 1971.

Nature Study for Conservation. John W. Brainerd. New York: Macmillan, 1971.

Our Green and Living World: The Wisdom to Save It. Edward Ayensu et al. New York: Cambridge University Press, 1984.

Parks and Protected Areas in Canada: Planning and Management. Philip Dearden and Rick Rollins, eds. Toronto: Oxford University Press, 1993.

Plant Genetic Resources: A Conservation Imperative. Christopher W. Yeatman, David Kafton and Garrison Wilkes, eds. Boulder: Westview Press, 1984.

Plant Genetic Resources: An Introduction to Their Conservation and Use. Brian Ford-Lloyd and Michael Jackson. London: Edward Arnold, 1986.

Preserving Corridors and Communities. G. Mackintosh, ed. Washington: Defenders of Wildlife, 1989.

Private Options: Tools and Concepts for Land Conservation. Land Trust Exchange. Washington: Island Press, 1982.

Protected Places: A History of Ontario's Provincial Parks System. Gerald Killan. Toronto: Dundurn Press, 1993.

Protecting Ontario's Natural Heritage Through Private Stewardship. S. Hilts and T. Moull. Toronto: Natural Heritage League, 1985.

Protection of Natural Areas in Ontario. Suzanne W. Barrett and John L. Riley, eds. Toronto: Faculty of Environmental Studies, York University, 1980.

Rare Plant Conservation. Larry E. Morse and Mary Sue Henifin, eds. Bronx, New York: New York Botanical Garden, 1981.

The Redesigned Forest. Chris Maser. Toronto: Stoddart, 1990.

Saving America's Countryside: A Guide to Rural Conservation. Samuel Stokes. Baltimore: Johns Hopkins University Press, 1989.

Saving the Prairies: The Life Cycle of the Founding School of American Plant Ecology, 1895–1955. Ronald C. Tobey. Berkeley: University of California Press, 1981.

Seeing the Forest Among the Trees: The Case for Wholistic Forest Use. Herb Hammond. Vancouver: Polestar, 1991.

The Status of Ecological Reserves in Canada. P. M. Taschereau. Ottawa: Canadian Council on Ecological Areas, 1985.

Wilderness Canada. Borden Spears. Toronto: Clarke Irwin, 1970.

Wildlife 2000. Jared Verner, ed. Madison: University of Wisconsin Press, 1986.

Woodland Ecology: Environmental Forestry for the Small Owner. Leon Minckler. Syracuse: Syracuse University Press, 1980.

World Conservation Strategy. Morges, Switzerland: International Union for the Conservation of Nature, 1980.

Ecosystems

Botany in the Field: An Introduction to Plant Communities for the Amateur Naturalist. Jane Scott. Englewood Cliffs, New Jersey: Prentice-Hall, 1984.

Changing Landscapes: An Ecological Perspective. Isaak S. Zonneveld and Richard T. T. Forman, eds. New York: Springer-Verlag, 1990.

Common Landscape of America, 1580–1845. John R. Stilgoe. New Haven: Yale University Press, 1982.

Communities and Ecosystems. Robert H. Whittaker. New York: Macmillan, 1975.

Concepts of Ecology. Edward J. Kormondy. Englewood Cliffs, New Jersey: Prentice-Hall, 1969.

Ecology. Eugene P. Odum. New York: Holt, Rinehart and Winston, 1963.

Ecology and Field Biology. Robert Leo Smith. New York: Harper and Row, 1980.

Ecology of North America. Victor E. Shelford. Urbana, Illinois: University of Illinois Press, 1963.

Field and Forest: A Guide to Native Landscapes for Gardeners and Naturalists. Jane Scott. New York: Walker & Co., 1984.

Fundamentals of Ecology. Eugene P. Odum. Philadelphia: Saunders, 1971.

A Guide to the Study of Terrestrial Ecology. William A. Andrews et al. Scarborough: Prentice-Hall, 1974.

Helping Nature Heal: An Introduction to Environmental Restoration. Richard Nilsen, ed. Berkeley: Ten Speed, 1991.

The Interpretation of Ordinary Landscapes. D. W. Meinig, ed. New York: Oxford University Press, 1979.

Interpreting the Environment. Grant W. Sharpe, ed. New York: Wiley, 1982.

Introduction to Ecology. Paul A. Colinvaux. New York: Wiley, 1973.

An Introduction to Evolutionary Ecology. Andrew Cockburn. Oxford: Blackwell, 1991.

Landscape Ecology. Richard T. Forman and Michel Godron. New York: Wiley, 1986.

Landscape Ecology: Theory and Application. Zev Naveh. New York: Springer-Verlag, 1984.

Landscape Ecology and Management. Michael R. Moss, ed. Montreal: Polyscience Publications, 1988.

Landscape Ecology of a Stressed Environment. Clair C. Vos and Paul Opdam, eds. New York: Chapman and Hall, 1993.

Landscape Restoration Handbook. Donald Harker et al., eds. Ann Arbor, Michigan: Lewis Publishers, 1993.

Natural Enemies: The Population Biology of Predators, Parasites, and Diseases. Michael J. Crawley, ed. Oxford: Blackwell, 1992.

The Natural Vegetation of North America: An Introduction. John L. Vankat. New York: Wiley, 1979.

Nature's Everyday Mysteries: A Field Guide to the World in Your Backyard. Sy Montgomery. Shelburne, Vermont: Chapters, 1993.

Noah's Garden: Restoring the Ecology of Our Own Back Yards. Sara Stein. Boston: Houghton Mifflin, 1993.

Plants and the Ecosystem. William D. Billings. Belmont, California: Wadsworth, 1978.

The Plant Observer's Guidebook: A Field Botany Manual for the Amateur Naturalist. Charles E. Roth. Englewood Cliffs, New Jersey: Prentice-Hall, 1984.

The Professional Practice of Environmental Management. Robert S. Dorney and Lindsay C. Dorney. New York: Springer-Verlag, 1989.

Reading Nature's Clues: A Guide to the Wild. Doug Sadler. Peterborough: Broadview, 1987.

Reading the Landscape of America. May Theilgaard Watts. New York: Macmillan, 1975.

The Recovery Process in Damaged Ecosystems. John Cairns, Jr., ed. Ann Arbor, Michigan: Ann Arbor Science Publishing, 1980.

Restoration Ecology: A Synthetic Approach to Ecological Research. William R. Jordan III, Michael E. Gilpin and John D. Aber. New York: Cambridge University Press, 1987.

The Study of Plant Communities: An Introduction to Plant Ecology. Henry J. Oosting. San Francisco: WH Freeman, 1956.

Terrestrial Plant Ecology. Michael G. Barbour, Jack H. Burk, Wanna D. Pitts. Menlo Park, California: The Benjamin/Cummings Publishing Co., 1980.

Aquatic Ecosystems

Bogs of the Northeast. Charles W. Johnson. Hanover, New Hampshire: University Press of New England, 1985.

Common Marsh, Underwater and Floating-Leaved Plants of the United States and Canada. Neil Hotchkiss. New York: Dover, 1972.

Freshwater Marshes: Ecology and Wildlife Management. Milton W. Weller. Minneapolis: University of Minnesota Press, 1981.

Freshwater Wetlands: A Guide to Common Indicator Plants of the Northeast. Dennis W. Magee. Amherst: University of Massachusetts Press, 1981.

The Life of the Marsh. William A. Niering. New York: McGraw-Hill, 1966.

A Manual of Aquatic Plants. Norman C. Fassett. Madison: University of Wisconsin Press, 1957.

Of Men and Marshes. Paul Errington. New York: Macmillan, 1957.

The Restoration of Rivers and Streams: Theories and Experience. James A. Gore, ed. Stoneham, Massachusetts: Butterworth, 1985.

Riparian Landscapes. George Patrick Malanson. New York: Cambridge University Press, 1993.

Some Important Wetlands of Ontario South of the Precambrian Shield. M. V. Patter and S. Hilts. Don Mills: Federation of Ontario Naturalists, 1985.

The Swamp. Bill Thomas. New York: W. W. Norton, 1976.

The Water Naturalist. Heather Angel and Pat Wolseley. New York: Facts on File, 1982.

Wetland Conservation Policies in Southern Ontario. Michal James Bardecki. Toronto: Geographical Monographs, York University, 1984.

Wetland Creation and Restoration. Jon A. Kusler and Mary E. Kentula. Washington: Island Press, 1990.

Wetland Planting Guide for the Northeastern United States. Gwendolyn A. Thunhorst. 1993. (Environmental Concern, Inc., P.O. Box P, 210 West Chew Avenue, St. Michael's, Maryland 21663.)

Wetlands. Max Finlayson and Michael Moses. New York: Facts on File, 1991.

Wetlands. William J. Mitsch and James G. Gosselink. New York: Van Nostrand Reinhold, 1993.

Wetlands. William A. Niering. New York: Knopf, 1985.

Wetlands: An Approach to Improving Decision Making in Wetland Restoration and Creation. A. J. Hairston, ed. Washington: Island Press, 1992.

Forest Ecosystems

The Boreal Ecosystem. James A. Larsen. New York: Academic Press, 1980.

Deciduous Forests of Eastern North America. E. Lucy Braun. New York: Free Press, 1974.

Eastern Forests. Ann Sutton and Myron Sutton. New York: Knopf, 1993.

A Field Guide to Eastern Forests. John C. Kricher. Boston: Houghton Mifflin, 1988.

Forest Ecology. Stephen H. Spurr and Burton V. Barnes. New York: Wiley, 1980.

Forest Primeval. Chris Maser. Toronto: Stoddart, 1991.

Forest Regions of Canada. J. S. Rowe. Ottawa: Canadian Forestry Service, Department of Environment, 1972.

Forests: A Naturalist's Guide to Trees and Forest Ecology. Lawrence C. Walker. New York: Wiley, 1990.

Meadow and Prairie Ecosystems

Fire in America: A Cultural History of Wildland and Rural Fire. Stephen J. Pyne. Princeton: Princeton University Press, 1982.

The Grassland of North America. James C. Malin. Kansas: Lawrence, 1947.

Grasslands. Lauren Brown. New York: Knopf, 1985.

History and Ecology: Studies of the Grassland. James C. Malin. Lincoln, Nebraska: University of Nebraska Press, 1984.

North American Prairie. John E. Weaver. Lincoln, Nebraska: Johnsen Publishing, 1954.

The Prairie World. David F. Costello. New York: Crowell, 1969.

Siftings. Jens Jensen. Baltimore: Johns Hopkins University Press, 1990.

The True Prairie Ecosystem. P. G. Risser et al. Stroudsberg, Pennsylvania: Hutchinson Ross, 1981.

Where the Sky Began: Land of the Tallgrass Prairie. John Madson. Boston: Houghton Mifflin, 1982.

Environmental Thought

The Age of Ecology. David Cayley. Toronto: Lorimer, 1991.

Back to Nature: The Arcadian Myth in Urban America. Peter Schmitt. New York: Oxford University Press, 1969.

The Culture of Nature. Alexander Wilson. Toronto: Between the Lines, 1991.

The Ecology of Freedom. Murray Bookchin. Montreal: Black Rose, 1991.

The Experience of Landscape. Jay H. Appleton. London: Wiley, 1975.

The Experience of Nature: A Psychological Perspective. R. Kaplan and S. Kaplan. New York: Cambridge University Press, 1989.

Healing the Wounds: The Promise of Ecofeminism. Judith Plant, ed. Toronto: Between the Lines, 1989.

Home Place: Essays on Ecology. Stan Rowe. Edmonton: NeWest, 1990.

The Human Impact on the Natural Environment. Andrew Goudie. Cambridge, Massachusetts: MIT Press, 1990.

The Idea of Wilderness: From Prehistory to the Age of Ecology. Max Oelschlaeger. New Haven: Yale University Press, 1991.

The Natural Alien. Neil Evernden. Toronto: University of Toronto Press, 1985.

Remaking Society. Murray Bookchin. Montreal: Black Rose, 1989.

The Rights of Nature. Roderick Nash. Madison: University of Wisconsin Press, 1989.

Rogue Primate. John A. Livingston. Toronto: Key Porter, 1994.

Second Nature: A Gardener's Education. Michael Pollan. New York: Laurel, 1991.

Speaking for Nature. Paul Brooks. San Francisco: Sierra Club, 1980.

Wilderness and the American Mind. Roderick Nash. New Haven: Yale University Press, 1967.

Invasive Species

Biological Pollution: The Control and Impact of Invasive Exotic Species. Bill Knight, ed. Indianapolis: Indiana Academy of Science, 1993.

The Dispersal of Plants Throughout the World. Henry Nicholas Ridley. Ashford: Kent L. Reeve Publishers, 1972.

Ecological Imperialism: The Biological Expansion of Europe, 900–1900. Alfred W. Crosby. New York: Cambridge University Press, 1986.

The Ecology of Invasions by Plants and Animals. Charles S. Elton. New York: Wiley, 1958.

"Invasive Alien Plants in Ontario." Steve Smith. Toronto: Urban Forest Associates, 1994.

Invasive Plants of Natural Habitats in Canada. David J. White, Erich Haber and Cathy Keddy. Ottawa: Canadian Wildlife Service, 1993.

Native Peoples and the Environment

Aboriginal Relationships Between Culture and Plant Life in the Upper Great Lakes Region. Richard A. Yarnell. Ann Arbor: University of Michigan Press, 1970.

Changes in the Land: Indians, Colonists, and the Ecology of New England. William Cronon. New York: Hill and Wang, 1983.

The Columbian Exchange: Biological and Cultural Consequences of 1492. Alfred W. Crosby, Jr. Westport, Connecticut: Greenwood, 1972.

Enduring Seeds: Native American Agriculture and Wild Plant Conservation. Gary Paul Nabhan. Berkeley: North Point Press, 1989.

Indian Givers: How the Indians of the Americas Transformed the World. Jack Weatherford. New York: Crown, 1988.

Rivers of Change: Essays on Early Agriculture in Eastern North America. Bruce D. Smith, ed. Washington: Smithsonian Institution Press, 1992.

Songs for the People: Teachings on the Natural Way. Arthur Solomon. Toronto: New Canada, 1990.

Wisdom of the Elders. Peter Knudtson and David Suzuki. Toronto: Stoddart, 1992.

Threatened Species and Spaces

The Atlas of Endangered Species. John Burton, ed. New York: Macmillan, 1991.

Atlas of the Rare Vascular Plants of Ontario. George W. Argus and David J. White, eds. Ottawa: National Museum of Natural Sciences, 1982–1987.

Birds in Jeopardy: The Imperiled and Extinct Birds of the United States and Canada. Paul Erlich. Stanford: Stanford University Press, 1992.

Canada's Threatened Species and Habitats. Theodore Mosquin and Cecile Suchal, eds. Ottawa: Canadian Nature Federation and World Wildlife Fund, 1976.

Canadian Endangered Species. Darryl Stewart. Toronto: Gage, 1974.

Endangered Spaces: The Future for Canada's Wilderness. Monte Hummel, ed. Toronto: Key Porter, 1989.

Extinction. Ann and Paul Ehrlich. New York: Ballantine, 1981.

Extinction is Forever—Threatened and Endangered Species of Plants in the Americas and their Endangered Habitats. G. T. Prance and T. S. Elias, eds. Bronx: New York Botanical Garden, 1977.

Fragile Ecosystems. E. Farnsworth and F. Golley, eds. New York: Springer-Verlag, 1973.

The IUCN Plant Red Data Book. Gren Lucas and Hugh Synge. Morges, Switzerland: International Union for Conservation of Nature, 1978.

Noah's Choice: True Stories of Extinction and Survival. David Day. London: Viking, 1990.

The Official World Wildlife Fund Guide to Endangered Species of North America. David W. Lowe. Washington: Beacham, 1990.

Ontario Birds at Risk: Status and Conservation Needs. Madeline J. W. Austen, Michael D. Cadman and Ross D. James. Toronto: Federation of Ontario Naturalists and Long Point Bird Observatory, 1994.

On The Brink: Endangered Species in Canada. J. A. Burnett, C. T. Dauphine, Jr., S. H. McCrindle and T. Mosquin. Saskatoon: Western Producer Prairie Books, 1989.

Our Vanishing Landscape. Eric Sloane. New York: W. Funk, 1955.

Plant Extinction: A Global Crisis. Dr. Harold Koopowitz and Hilary Kaye. Washington: Stone Wall Press, 1983.

Plants in Danger: What Do We Know? Stephen D. Davs et al. Gland, Switzerland: International Union for Conservation of Nature and Natural Resources, 1986.

Rare Vascular Plants in Canada: Our Natural Heritage. George W. Argus and Kathleen M. Pryer. Ottawa: Canadian Museum of Nature, 1990.

Rare Vascular Plants in the Canadian Arctic. Cheryl McJannet, George Argus, Sylvia Edlund and Jacques Cayonette. Ottawa: Canadian Museum of Nature, 1993.

The Rare Vascular Plants of Ontario. G. W. Argus and D. J. White. Ottawa: National Museums of Canada, 1977.

Rare Wild Flowers of North America. Leonard Wiley. Portland, Oregon: Wiley, 1969.

Rare Wildflowers of Ontario. James Pringle and Barbara McKean. Hamilton: Royal Botanical Garden, 1992.

The Sinking Ark. Norman Myers. Oxford: Pergamon Press, 1979.

The Vanishing Lichens: Their History, Biology and Importance. David Richardson. Vancouver: David and Charles, 1975.

Wetlands: Habitat in Peril. David J. Hawke. Erin, Ontario: Boston Mills, 1992.

Wetlands in Danger. Patrick Dugan, ed. London: Mitchell Beazley, 1993.

Where Have All the Birds Gone? John Terborgh. Princeton, New Jersey: Princeton University Press, 1989.

Where Have All the Wildflowers Gone: A Region-by-Region Guide to Threatened and Endangered U.S. Wildflowers. Robert H. Mohlenbrock. New York: Macmillan, 1983.

Wildlife Crisis. Prince Philip and James Fisher. London: Hamish Hamilton, 1970.

Community Gardens

The Allotment: Its Landscape and Culture. David Crouch and Colin Ward. London: Faber and Faber, 1988.

The Community Garden Book. Larry Sommers. Burlington, Vermont: National Gardening Association, n.d.

The Complete Book of Community Gardening. Jamie Jobb. New York: William Morrow, 1979.

The Growing City: A Guide to Urban Community Gardening in Toronto. Toronto: Ontario Public Interest Research Group, 1986.

A Handbook of Community Gardening. Susan Naimark and Boston Urban Gardeners. New York: Charles Scribner's Sons, 1982.

To Dwell is to Garden: A History of Boston's Community Gardens. Sam Bass Warner Jr. Boston: Northeastern University Press, 1987.

Design

Design with Nature. Ian L. McHarg. Garden City, New York: Doubleday, 1969.

Energy Efficient Site Design, Gary O. Robinette. New York: Van Nostrand Reinhold, 1983.

A Gentle Plea for Chaos. Mirabel Osler. New York: Simon and Schuster, 1989.

Groundwork: A Gardener's Ecology. Roger B. Swain. Boston: Houghton Mifflin, 1994.

The Harrowsmith Landscaping Handbook. Jennifer Bennett, ed. Camden East: Camden House, 1985.

Home Landscape. Garrett Eckbo. New York: McGraw Hill, 1978.

Homeowner's Guide to Landscaping that Saves Energy Dollars. Ruth S. Foster. New York: David McKay Company, 1978.

Landscape For Living. Garrett Eckbo. New York: Architectural Record with Duell, Sloan, and Pearce, 1950.

Landscape Planning for Energy Conservation. Gary O. Robinette, ed. Retson, Virginia: Environmental Design Press for American Society of Landscape Architects Foundation, 1977.

Landscaping with Nature: Using Nature's Designs to Plan Your Yard. Jeff Cox. Emmaus, Pennsylvania: Rodale, 1991.

Native Plants: Their Culture and Landscape Use in Eastern United States and Contiguous Canada: A Bibliography. Barbara Emerson. Chapel Hill, North Carolina: North Carolina Botanical Garden, 1991.

The Natural Garden. Ken Druse. New York: Clarkson N. Potter, 1989.

The Natural Garden Book: A Holistic Approach to Gardening. Peter Harper. New York: Simon and Schuster, 1994.

Natural Gardens: Gardening with Native Plants. Jack Kramer. New York: Charles Scribner's Sons, 1973.

The Natural Habitat Garden. Ken Druse with Margaret Roach. New York: Clarkson N. Potter, 1994.

Natural Landscaping. Dean M. Gottehrer. New York: Dutton, 1978.

Natural Landscaping: Designing with Native Plant Communities. John Diekelmann and Robert Schuster. New York: McGraw Hill, 1982.

Natural Landscaping: An Energy Saving Alternative. Carlin T. Kindilien. Lyme, Connecticut: Weathervane, 1977.

Nature's Design: A Practical Guide to Natural Landscaping. Carol A. Smyser and editors of Rodale Press. Emmaus, Pennsylvania: Rodale, 1982.

Nature's Guide to Successful Gardening and Landscaping. William Flemer III. New York: Thomas Y. Crowell, 1972.

Requiem for a Lawnmower (and Other Essays on Easy Gardening With Native Plants). Sally Wasowski. Dallas: Taylor, 1992.

Rock Gardening: A Guide to Growing Alpines and Other Wildflowers in the American Garden. H. Lincoln Foster. Boston: Houghton Mifflin, 1968.

Rodale's Illustrated Encyclopedia of Perennials. Ellen Phillips and C. Colston Burrell. Emmaus, Pennsylvania: Rodale, 1993.

Seasons of Promise: Wild Plants in Winter, Northeastern United States. June Carver Roberts. Athens, Ohio: Ohio University Press, 1993.

Shade and Color with Water-Conserving Plants. James E. Walters and Balbir Backuhaus. Portland: Timber Press, 1992.

Taylor's Guide to Water-Saving Gardening. Norman Taylor. Boston: Houghton Mifflin, 1990.

The Tree-House Effect: The Impact of Trees and White Surfaces on Residential Energy Use in Four Canadian Cities. Hashem Akbari and Haider Taha. Ottawa: Friends of the Earth, 1991.

Water-Conserving Gardens and Landscapes. John M. O'Keefe. Pownal, Vermont: Storey, 1992.

Waterwise Gardening. Fran Feldman and Cornelia Fogle, et al., eds. Menlo Park, California: Lane, 1990.

Working With Nature: A Practical Guide. John W. Brainerd. New York: Oxford University Press, 1973.

The Xeriscape Flower Gardener. Jim Knopf. Boulder: Johnson Books, 1991.

Xeriscape Gardening: Water Conservation for the American Landscape. Connie Ellefson, Thomas Stephens and Doug Welsh. New York: Macmillan, 1992.

Garden Maintenance

The Complete Handbook of Pruning. Brian Halliwell. Vancouver: Cavendish, 1992.

Ecological Gardening: Your Path to a Healthy Garden. Marjorie Harris. Toronto: Random House, 1991.

A Gardener's Guide to Better Soil. Gene Logsdon. Emmaus, Pennsylvania: Rodale, 1975.

The Mulch Book. Stu Campbell. Pownal, Vermont: Storey, 1991.

The Nature and Properties of Soils. Nyle C. Brady. New York: Macmillan, 1990.

Pruning Simplified. Lewis Hill. Emmaus, Pennsylvania: Rodale, 1979.

The Real Dirt: The Complete Guide to Backyard, Balcony and Apartment Composting. Mark Cullen and Lorraine Johnson. Toronto: Penguin, 1992.

Rodale's Garden, Insect, Disease and Weed Identification Guide. Miranda Smith and Anna Carr. Emmaus, Pennsylvania: Rodale, 1988.

The Soul of Soil: A Guide to Ecological Soil Management. Grace Gershuny and Joseph Smillie. Johnsbury, Vermont: Gaia Services, 1986.

Start with the Soil. Grace Gershuny. Emmaus, Pennsylvania: Rodale, 1993.

Lawns

Beautiful Easy Lawns and Landscapes. Laurence Sombke. Old Saybrook, Connecticut: Globe Pequot, 1994.

Building a Healthy Lawn. Stuart Franklin. Pownal, Vermont: Storey, 1988.

The Chemical-Free Lawn: The Newest Varieties and Techniques to Grow Lush, Hardy Grass. Warren Schultz. Emmaus, Pennsylvania: Rodale, 1989.

How to Get Your Lawn and Garden Off Drugs. Carole Rubin. Ottawa: Friends of the Earth, 1989.

Keeping Eden: A History of Gardening In America. Massachusetts Horticultural Society. Boston: Bulfinch, 1992.

The Lawn: A History of an American Obsession. Virginia Scott Jenkins. Washington: Smithsonian Institution Press, 1994.

Redesigning the American Lawn: A Search for Environmental Harmony. F. Herbert Bormann, Diana Balmori and Gordon T. Geballe. New Haven: Yale University Press, 1993.

Turfgrass Insects of the United States and Canada. Haruo Tashiro. Ithaca: Comstock, 1987.

The Wild Lawn Handbook: Alternatives to the Traditional Front Lawn. Stevie Daniels. New York: Macmillan, 1995.

Meadow and Prairie Gardens

A Guide to Natural Woodland and Prairie Gardening. Robert S. Dorney et al. Waterloo: Ecoplans, 1978.

Meadows and Meadow Gardening. Ellen M. Meyers, ed. Framingham, Massachusetts: New England Wild Flower Society, 1990.

The Prairie Garden: 70 Native Plants You Can Grow in Town or Country. J. Robert Smith and Beatrice S. Smith. Madison: University of Wisconsin Press, 1980.

Prairies Restoration for the Beginner. Robert Ahrenhoerster and Trelen Wilson. North Lake, Wisconsin: Prairie Seed Source, 1981.

Wildflower Meadow Book: A Gardener's Guide. Laura C. Martin. Charlotte, North Carolina: East Wood, 1986.

Native Plant Gardening

Bluebells and Bittersweet: Gardening with Native American Plants. Bebe Miles. New York: Van Nostrand Reinhold, 1969.

Ferns: Wild Things Make a Comeback in the Garden. C. Colston Burrell. Brooklyn: Brooklyn Botanic Garden, 1994.

Ferns for American Gardens. John Mickel. New York: Macmillan, 1994.

The Gardener's Guide to Plant Conservation. Nina T. Marshall. Washington: World Wildlife Fund and the Garden Club of America, 1993.

Garden in the Woods Cultivation Guide. William E. Brumback and David L. Longland. Framingham, Massachusetts: New England Wild Flower Society, 1986.

Gardening with Native Plants: A Comprehensive Bibliography, with Annotation. Mary M. Walker. Framingham, Massachusetts: New England Wildflower Society, 1994.

Gardening with Native Wild Flowers. Samuel B. Jones, Jr. and Leonard E. Foote. Portland: Timber Press, 1990.

Gardening with Wild Flowers. Frances Tenenbaum. New York: Charles Scribner's Sons, 1973.

Gardening with Wildflowers and Native Plants. Claire E. Sawyers, ed. Brooklyn: Brooklyn Botanic Garden, 1990.

A Garden of Wildflowers: 101 Native Species and How to Grow Them. Henry W. Art. Pownal, Vermont: Storey, 1986.

Going Native. Janet Marinelli, ed. Brooklyn: Brooklyn Botanic Garden, 1994.

Growing Wildflowers: A Gardener's Guide. Maria Sperka. New York: Charles Scribner's Sons, 1973.

Handbook of Wild Flower Cultivation. Kathryn S. Taylor and Stephen F. Hamblin. New York: Collier, 1976.

Home Guide to Trees, Shrubs and Wild Flowers. William Grimm. Harrisburg, Pennsylvania: Stackpole, 1970.

How to Grow Wildflowers and Wild Shrubs and Trees in Your Own Garden. Hal Bruce. New York: Van Nostrand Reinhold, 1976.

Landscaping with Wildflowers: An Environmental Approach to Gardening. Jim Wilson. Boston: Houghton Mifflin, 1992.

Landscaping with Wildflowers and Native Plants. William H. W. Wilson. San Francisco: Ortho, 1984.

The New Wildflowers and How to Grow Them. Edwin F. Steffek. Portland: Timber Press, 1983.

Pioneering with Wildflowers. George D. Aiken. Englewood Cliffs, New Jersey: Prentice-Hall, 1968.

Taylor's Guide to Natural Gardening. Roger Holmes, ed. Boston: Houghton Mifflin, 1993.

The Wildflower Gardener's Guide: Northeast, Mid-Atlantic, Great Lakes, and Eastern Canada Edition. Henry W. Art. Pownal, Vermont: Storey, 1987.

Wildflower Handbook. National Wildflower Research Centre Staff. Stillwater, Minnesota: Voyageur, 1992.

Wildflower Perennials For Your Garden. Bebe Miles. New York: Hawthorn, 1976.

Wildflowers: How to Identify Flowers in the Wild and How to Grow Them in Your Garden. Rick Imes. Emmaus, Pennsylvania: Rodale, 1992.

Wildflowers in Your Garden: A Gardener's Guide. Viki Ferreniea. New York: Random House, 1993.

Wildflowers on the Windowsill: A Guide to Growing Wild Plants Indoors. Susan T. Hitchcock. New York: Crown, 1984.

The Wild Garden. Judith Berrisford. London: Faber and Faber, 1966.

The Wild Garden: Making Natural Gardens Using Wild and Native Plants. Violet Stevenson. New York: Penguin, 1985.

The Wild Gardener: On Flowers and Foliage for the Natural Border. Peter Loewer. Harrisburg, Pennsylvania: Stackpole, 1991.

The Wild Gardener in the Wild Landscape. Warren G. Kenfield. New York: Hafner, 1970.

Wild Wealth. Paul Bigelow Sears, Marion Rombauer Becker, Frances Jones Poetker and Janice Rebert Forberg. New York: Bobbs-Merrill, 1971.

Pest and Disease Control

Basic Guide to Pesticides—Their Characteristics and Hazards. Shirley A. Briggs and Rachel Carson Council. Bristol, Pennsylvania: Taylor and Francis, 1992.

Common-Sense Pest Control. William Olkowski, Sheila Daar and Helga Olkowski. Newton, Connecticut: Taunton, 1991.

The Encyclopedia of Natural Insect and Disease Control. Roger B. Yepsen, Jr., ed. Emmaus, Pennsylvania: Rodale, 1984.

Outwitting Squirrels. Bill Adler, Jr. Chicago: Chicago Review Press, 1988.

Rodale's Color Handbook of Garden Insects. Anna Carr. Emmaus, Pennsylvania: Rodale, 1979.

Rodale's Successful Organic Gardening: Controlling Pests and Disease. Patricia S. Michalak and Linda Gilkeson. Emmaus, Pennsylvania: Rodale, 1994.

Tiny Game Hunting: Environmentally Healthy Ways to Trap and Kill the Pests in Your House and Garden. Hilary Dole Klein. Toronto: Bantam, 1991.

Propagation

Collecting, Processing, and Germinating Seeds of Wildland Plants. James A. Young and Cheryl G. Young. Portland: Timber Press, 1986.

The Complete Book of Plant Propagation. Graham Clarke and Alan Toogood. London: Ward Lock, 1992.

Directory to Resources on Wildflower Propagation. Gene A. Sullivan and Richard H. Daley. St. Louis: Missouri Botanical Garden, 1981. (Available from National Council of State Garden Clubs, Inc., 4401 Magnolia Avenue, St. Louis, Missouri 63110-3492.)

Garden in the Woods Cultivation Guide. William E. Brumbrack and David L. Longland. Framingham, Massachusetts: New England Wild Flower Society, 1986.

Growing and Propagating Wild Flowers. Harry R. Phillips. Chapel Hill, North Carolina: University of North Carolina Press, 1985.

Growing Native Woody Plants from Seed. Henry Kock. Guelph: The Arboretum, University of Guelph, 1992.

Natural Habitat Restoration Program: Seed Collection Report. G. Waldron. Essex Region Conservation Authority, 1993.

The New Seed-Starters Handbook. Nancy Bubel. Emmaus, Pennsylvania: Rodale, 1988.

North American Native Terrestrial Orchid Propagation and Production. North American Orchid Conference. Chadd's Ford, Pennsylvania: Brandywine Conservancy, 1989.

Notes on the Propagation of Prairie Plants. R. Schulenberg. Lisle, Illinois: Morton Arboretum, 1972.

Plant Propagation Made Easy. Alan Toogood. London: J. M. Dent, 1993.

Pods: Wildflowers and Weeds in their Final Beauty. Jane Embertson. New York: Scribner's, 1979.

Prairie Propagation Handbook. Harold Rock. Hales Corners, Wisconsin: Wehr Nature Center, 1974.

Propagation of Wild Flowers. Will C. Curtis, revised by William E. Brumback. Framingham, Massachusetts: New England Wild Flower Society, 1986.

The Reference Manual of Woody Plant Propagation. Michael Dirr. Athens, Georgia: Varsity, 1987.

The Root Book: A Concise Guide to Planting and Growing Wildflowers and Hardy Ferns. Norma Phillips. 1984. (6700 Splithand Road, Grand Rapids, Michigan 55744.)

Saving Seeds: The Gardener's Guide to Growing and Storing Vegetable and Flower Seeds. Marc Rogers. Pownal, Vermont: Storey, 1990.

Seed Identification Manual. Alexander Martin and William Barkley. Berkeley: University of California Press, 1961.

Seeds and Fruits of Plants of Eastern Canada and Northeastern United States. F. H. Montgomery. Toronto: University of Toronto Press, 1976.

Seeds of Woody Plants in North America. James A. Young and Cheryl G. Young. Portland: Dioscorides Press, 1992.

Water Gardens

The Complete Book of the Water Garden. Philip Swindells and David Mason. Woodstock, New York: Overlook, 1990.

Garden Pools, Fountains and Waterfalls. Staff of *Sunset* magazine. Menlo Park, California: Ortho, 1988.

Ponds and Water Gardens. Bill Heritage. London: Cassell, 1994.

The Water Garden. A. Paul and Y. Rees. New York: Viking, 1986.

The Water Garden. Frances Perry. New York: Van Nostrand Reinhold, 1981.

The Water Garden. George Plumptre. London: Thames and Hudson, 1993.

Water Gardening. Ken Druse. New York: Prentice Hall, 1993.

Water Gardening: Pools, Fountains, and Plants. Jack Kramer. New York: Scribner's, 1971.

Water Gardens: A Harrowsmith Gardener's Guide. David Archibald and Mary Patton, eds. Camden East: Camden House, 1990.

Water in the Garden. James Allison. Boston: Bulfinch, 1991.

Waterlilies and Other Aquatic Plants. Frances Perry. New York: Henry Holt, 1989.

Waterscaping. Judy Glattstein. Pownal, Vermont: Storey, 1994.

Weeds

All About Weeds. Edwin Rollin Spencer. New York: Dover, 1974.

Common Weeds of Canada. Gerald A. Mulligan. Toronto: NC Press, 1987.

Edible and Useful Wild Plants of the United States and Canada. Charles Francis Saunders. New York: Dover, 1976.

Edible Garden Weeds of Canada. Adam Szczawinski and Nancy Turner. Ottawa: National Museum of Natural Sciences, 1978.

A Field Guide to Edible Wild Plants of Eastern and Central North America. Lee Allen Peterson. Boston: Houghton Mifflin, 1977.

Friendly Weeds. Jeff Hill. Mount Vernon, New York: The Peter Pauper Press, 1976.

How to Enjoy Your Weeds. Audrey Wynne Hatfield. New York: Collier, 1973.

Just Weeds: History, Myths and Uses. Pamela Jones. Shelburne, Vermont: Chapters, 1994.

My Weeds. Sara Stein. New York: Harper and Row, 1988.

Ontario Weeds. J. F. Alex. Toronto: Ontario Ministry of Agriculture and Food, 1992.

Roadside Plants and Flowers: A Traveler's Guide to the Midwest and Great Lakes Area. Marian S. Edsall. Madison: University of Wisconsin Press, 1985.

Some Useful Wild Plants. Dan Jason, Nancy Jason et al. Vancouver: Talonbooks, 1972.

Stalking the Wild Asparagus. Euell Gibbons. New York: David McKay, 1962.

Using Wild and Wayside Plants. Nelson Coon. New York: Dover, 1980.

Weeds: Guardians of the Soil. Joseph A. Cocannouer. New York: Devin-Adair, 1950.

Weeds in Winter. Lauren Brown. New York: Norton, 1976.

Weeds of Canada. Clarence Frankton. Toronto: NC Press, 1987.

Weeds of Canada and the Northeastern United States. F. H. Montgomery. Toronto: Ryerson, 1964.

What Good is a Weed? Robert H. Wright. New York: Lothrop, Lee and Shepard, 1972.

Wildflowers and Weeds. Booth Courtenay and James H. Zimmerman. Toronto: Van Nostrand Reinhold, 1971.

Wildly Successful Plants: A Handbook of North American Weeds. Lawrence J. Crockett. New York: Collier, 1977.

Wild Plants in the City. Nancy M. Page and Richard E. Weaver, Jr. New York: Quadrangle, 1975.

Wildlife Attraction

The Bat House Builders' Handbook. Merlin Tuttle et al. Texas: Bat Conservation International, 1993.

Beyond the Bird Feeder. John V. Dennis. New York: Knopf, 1981.

Birdhousing. Peri Wolfman and Charles Gold. New York: Clarkson Potter, 1993.

The Butterfly Book: An Easy Guide to Butterfly Gardening, Identification and Behavior. Donald and Lillian Stokes and Ernest Williams. Boston: Little, Brown, 1991.

The Butterfly Garden. Jerry Sedenko. New York: Running Heads Press, 1991.

The Butterfly Gardener. Miriam Rothschild and Clive Farrell. London: Michael Joseph, 1983.

Butterfly Gardening: Creating Summer Magic in Your Garden. L. Gunnarson and F. Haselsteiner, eds. San Francisco: The Xerces Society/Smithsonian Institution, Sierra Club, 1990.

A Complete Guide to Bird Feeding. John. V. Dennis. New York: Knopf, 1986.

The Expert's Guide to Backyard Birdfeeding. Bill Adler, Jr. and Heidi Hughes. New York: Crown, 1990.

Feeding the Birds. Jan Mahnken. Pownal, Vermont: Storey, 1983.

Feeding Wild Birds in Winter. Clive Dobson. Scarborough: Firefly, 1984.

Garden Birds: How to Attract Birds to Your Garden. Noble Proctor. Emmaus, Pennsylvania: Rodale, 1986.

Gardening With Wildlife. National Wildlife Federation. Washington, 1974.

A Guide to Feeding Winter Birds in Ontario. Bob Waldon. Vancouver: Whitecap, 1991.

How to Attract Birds. M. McKinley. San Francisco: Ortho, 1983.

How to Attract, House and Feed Birds. Walter E. Schutz. New York: Bruce, 1970.

How to Build Birdhouses and Bird Feeders. Donald R. Brann. New York: Briarcliff Manor, 1967.

The Hummingbird Garden. Mathew Tekulsky. New York: Crown, 1990.

Hummingbirds and their Flowers. Karen A. Grant and Verne Grant. New York: Columbia University Press, 1968.

Landscaping for Birds. S. A. Briggs, ed. Washington: Audubon Naturalists Society, 1973.

Landscaping for Wildlife. Carol L. Henderson. Saint Paul, Minnesota: Department of Natural Resources, 1987.

Songbirds in Your Garden. John K. Terres. New York: T. Y. Cromwell, 1961.

Trees, Shrubs and Vines for Attracting Birds: A Manual for the Northeast. Richard M. Degraaf and Gretchin M. Witman. Amherst: University of Massachusetts Press, 1979.

The Wildlife Gardener. John V. Dennis. New York: Knopf, 1985.

Wildlife in Your Garden. Gene Logsdon. Emmaus, Pennsylvania: Rodale, 1983.

Wings in the Meadow. Jo Brewer. Boston: Houghton Mifflin, 1967.

Woodland and Shade Gardens

Arboriculture: Care of Trees, Shrubs and Vines in the Landscape. Richard W. Harris. Englewood Cliffs, New Jersey: Prentice-Hall, 1983.

The Complete Shade Gardener. George Schenk. Boston: Houghton Mifflin, 1984.

A Gardener's Guide to Better Soil. Gene Logsdon. Emmaus, Pennsylvania: Rodale, 1975.

Growing and Propagating Showy Native Woody Plants. Richard E. Bir. Chapel Hill, North Carolina: University of North Carolina Press, 1992.

Growing Woodland Plants. Clarence and Eleanor G. Birdseye. New York: Dover, 1972.

Grow Native Shrubs in Your Garden. F. M. Mooberry and Jane H. Scott. Chadd's Ford, Pennsylvania: Brandywine Conservancy, 1980.

A Guide to Natural Woodland and Prairie Gardening. Robert S. Dorney et al. Waterloo: Ecoplans, 1978.

Native Trees, Shrubs, and Vines for Urban and Rural America: A Planting Design Manual for Environmental Designers. Gary L. Hightshoe. New York: Van Nostrand Reinhold, 1988.

The Natural Garden. Ken Druse. New York: Clarkson N. Potter, 1989.

The Natural Shade Garden. Ken Druse. New York: Clarkson N. Potter, 1992.

Nut Growing Ontario Style. The Society of Ontario Nut Growers. Niagara-on-the-Lake, 1993. (Available from R.R. 3, Niagara-on-the-Lake, Ontario L0S 1J0.)

Plant a Tree: Choosing, Planting and Maintaining this Precious Resource. Michael A. Weiner. New York: Wiley, 1992.

Plants for Shade and Woodland. Allen Patterson. Markham: Fitzhenry and Whiteside, 1987.

Rodale's Successful Organic Gardening: Improving the Soil. Erin Hynes. Emmaus, Pennsylvania: Rodale, 1994.

Shade Gardens: A Harrowsmith Gardener's Guide. Brenda Cole, ed. Camden East: Camden House, 1993.

The Sunday Times Book of Woodland and Wildflower Gardening. Graham Rose. North Pomfret, Vermont: David and Charles, 1988.

Taylor's Guide to Shade Gardening. Frances Tenenbaum, ed. Boston: Houghton Mifflin, 1994.

Tree Maintenance. Pascal P. Pirone. New York: Oxford University Press, 1988.

The Woodland Garden: A Practical Guide. Raymond Foster. London: Ward Lock, 1980.

Carolinian Canada

Conserving Carolinian Canada. Gary M. Allen, Paul F. J. Eagles and Steven D. Price, eds. Waterloo: University of Waterloo Press, 1990.

Critical Unprotected Natural Areas on the Carolinian Life Zone of Canada. P. F. J. Eagles and T. J. Beechey. Toronto: Nature Conservancy of Canada, Ontario Heritage Foundation and World Wildlife Fund, 1985.

A Life Zone Approach to School Yard Naturalization: The Carolinian Life Zone. Steven Aboud and Henry Kock. Guelph: University of Guelph Arboretum, 1994.

Plants of Carolinian Canada. Larry Lamb and Gail Rhynard. Don Mills: Federation of Ontario Naturalists, 1994.

Tree Planting in the Carolinian Life Zone in Canada. Doug van Hemessen. Sault Ste. Marie: Tree Plan Canada, 1994.

Native Plants

The Audubon Society Field Guide to North American Wildflowers. William A. Niering and Nancy C. Olmstead. New York: Knopf, 1979.

Beauty and the Beasts: The Hidden World of Wildflowers. Michael W. P. Runtz. Erin, Ontario: Boston Mills, 1994.

The Biology of Aquatic Vascular Plants. Cyril D. Sculthorpe. London: Edward Arnold, 1967.

Biology of Plants. Peter H. Raven and Helena Curtis. New York: Worth Publishing, 1981.

Cacti of the United States and Canada. Lyman Benson. Stanford: Stanford University Press, 1982.

Canadian Wildflowers. Mary Ferguson and Richard Saunders. Toronto: Van Nostrand Reinhold, 1976.

Canadian Wildflowers. Catherine Parr Traill. Toronto: Coles, 1972.

Canadian Wildflowers Through the Seasons. Mary Ferguson and Richard M. Saunders. Toronto: Key Porter, 1989.

A Checklist of the Flora of Ontario: Vascular Plants. J. K. Morton and Joan M. Venn. Waterloo: University of Waterloo, Biology Department, 1990.

Checklist of the Mosses of Ontario. Robert R. Ireland and Roy F. Cain. Ottawa: National Museum of Natural Sciences, 1975.

Common Wild Flowers of the Northeastern United States. Carol H. Woodward and Harold William Rickett. Woodbury, New York: Barron's, 1979.

Familiar Flowers of North America: Eastern Region. Richard Spellenberg. New York: Knopf, 1986.

The Fern Guide: Northeastern and Midland United States and Adjacent Canada. Edgar T. Wherry. Garden City, New York: Doubleday, 1961.

Ferns and Fern Allies of Canada. W. J. Cody and Donald M. Britton. Ottawa: Agriculture Canada, 1989.

Ferns of the Northeastern United States. Farida Wiley. New York: Dover, 1973.

Field Guide to Northeastern Ferns. Eugene C. Ogden. Albany: New York State Museum, 1981.

Field Guide to the Common Forest Plants in Northwestern Ontario. K. A. Baldwin and R. A. Sims. Thunder Bay: Ontario Ministry of Natural Resources, 1989.

A Field Guide to the Ferns. Boughton Cobb. Boston: Houghton Mifflin, 1963.

A Field Guide to the Orchids of North America. J. G. Williams and A. E. Williams. New York: Universe Books, 1983.

Field Guide to the Peat Mosses of Boreal North America. Cyrus B. McQueen. Hanover, New Hampshire: University Press of New England, 1990.

A Field Guide to Wildflowers of Northeastern and Northcentral North America. Roger Tory Peterson and Margaret McKenny. Boston: Houghton Mifflin, 1968.

A Field Manual of the Ferns and Fern Allies of the United States and Canada. David D. Lellinger. Washington: Smithsonian Institution Press, 1985.

The Flora of Canada. H. J. Scoggan. Ottawa: National Museums of Canada, 1978.

The Flora of Manitoulin Island. J. K. Morton and J. M. Venn. Waterloo: University of Waterloo Press, 1984.

Flora of North America North of Mexico. Dr. Nancy Morin, ed. New York: Oxford University Press, 1993.

Flowers of the Wild: Ontario and the Great Lakes Region. Zile Zichmanis and James Hodgins. Toronto: Oxford University Press, 1982.

Forest Flora of Canada. G. C. Cunningham. Ottawa: Department of Northern Affairs, 1972.

The Geography of the Flowering Plants. Ronald Good. London: Longman, 1974.

Goldenrods of Ontario. John C. Semple and Gordon S. Ringius. Waterloo: University of Waterloo, Biology Department, 1992.

A Graphic Guide to Ontario Mosses. R. Muma. Toronto: Toronto Field Naturalists, 1985.

Grasses: An Identification Guide. Lauren Brown. Boston: Houghton Mifflin, 1979.

Grasses of Ontario. W. G. Dore and J. McNeill. Ottawa: Agriculture Canada, 1980.

Gray's Manual of Botany. Asa Gray, edited by M. L. Fernald. New York: America Book Co., 1950.

A Guide to the Literature on the Herbaceous Vascular Flora of Ontario. James L. Hodgins. Toronto: Botany Press, 1978.

How Flowers Work: A Guide to Plant Biology. Bob Gibbons. Poole, England: Blandford Press, 1984.

How to Identify Plants. Harold D. Harrington. Chicago: Swallow Press, 1957.

How to Know the Ferns and Fern Allies. John T. Mickel. Dubuque, Iowa: William C. Brown, 1979.

How to Know the Grasses. Richard W. Pohl. Dubuque, Iowa: William C. Brown, 1978.

An Illustrated Flora of the Northern United States and Canada. Lord Nathaniel Britton and Honorable Addison Brown. New York: Dover, 1970.

Illustrated Guide to Some Hornworts, Liverworts and Mosses of Eastern Canada. R. Ireland et al. Ottawa: Canadian Museum of Nature, 1987.

Introduction to Lower Plants. F. E. Round. New York: Plenum, 1969.

Introduction to Plant Ecology. Maurice Ashby. London: Macmillan, 1969.

Introduction to Plant Geography. Nicholas Polunin. New York: McGraw-Hill, 1960.

Introductory Plant Biology. Kingsley R. Stern. Dubuque, Iowa: William C. Brown, 1988.

Lichen Handbook: A Guide to the Lichens of Eastern North America. Mason E. Hale. Washington: Smithsonian Institution, 1961.

The Life of Plants. E. J. H. Corner. Chicago: University of Chicago Press, 1981.

Manual of Vascular Plants of Northeastern United States and Adjacent Canada. Henry A. Gleason and Arthur Cronquist. Princeton: Van Nostrand, 1963.

Mosses of Eastern North America. Howard A. Crum and Lewis E. Anderson. New York: Columbia University Press, 1981.

Mosses of the Great Lakes Forest. H. E. Crum. Ann Arbor: University of Michigan Press, 1983.

Mushrooms of North America. Roger Phillips. Boston: Little, Brown, 1991.

Native Orchids of North America North of Mexico. Donovan S. Correll. Stanford, California: Stanford University Press, 1978.

The Native Orchids of the United States and Canada Excluding Florida. Carlyle A. Luer. New York: New York Botanical Garden, 1975.

Native Wild Plants of Eastern Canada and the Adjacent Northeastern United States. Frederick H. Montgomery. Toronto: Ryerson, 1969.

The Natural Geography of Plants. Henry A. Gleason and Arthur Cronquist. New York: Columbia University Press, 1964.

The New Britton and Brown Illustrated Flora of the Northeastern U.S. and Adjacent Canada. H. A. Gleason. New York: Hafner, 1952.

Newcomb's Wildflower Guide. Lawrence Newcomb. Boston: Little, Brown, 1977.

Nonflowering Plants. F. S. Shuttlesworth and Herbert Zim. New York: Golden, 1967.

Orchids of Ontario. R. E. Whiting and P. M. Catling. Ottawa: CanaColl Foundation, 1986.

Orchids of the Western Great Lakes Region. Frederick W. Case, Jr. Bloomfield Hills, Michigan: Cranbrook Institute of Science, 1987.

The Oxford Book of Flowerless Plants. Frank H. Brightman. Oxford: Oxford University Press, 1966.

Plant Communities of the Leslie Street Spit. Verna Higgins et al. Toronto: Friends of the Spit and Botany Conservation Group, University of Toronto, 1992. (Available from P.O. Box 467, Station J, Toronto, Ontario M4T 4Z2.)

Plant Families: How to Know Them. Harry Jaques. Dubuque, Iowa: William C. Brown, 1963.

Plants of Quetico and the Ontario Shield. Shan Walshe. Toronto: University of Toronto Press, 1980.

Plants Without Leaves: Lichens, Fungi, Mosses, Liverworts. Rose E. Hutchins. New York: Dodd Mead, 1966.

Poison Ivy, Poison Oak, Poison Sumac, and Their Relatives. Edward Frankel. Pacific Grove, California: Boxwood, 1991.

Poisonous Plants of the USA and Canada. John M. Kingsbury. Englewood Cliffs, New Jersey: Prentice Hall, 1964.

Suburban Wildflowers: An Introduction to the Common Wildflowers of Your Back Yard and Local Park. Richard Headstrom. Englewood Cliffs, New Jersey: Prentice-Hall, 1984.

A Synonymized Checklist of the Vascular Flora of the United States, Canada, and Greenland. John T. Kartesz. Portland: Timber Press, 1994.

Trilliums of Ontario. James S. Pringle. Hamilton: Royal Botanical Gardens, 1984.

Vascular Plant Families: An Introduction to the Families of Vascular Plants Native to North America. James P. Smith. Eureka, California: Mad River Press, 1977.

Wild Flora of the Northeast. Anita and Spider Barbour. New York: Overlook, 1991.

The Wildflower Book, East of the Rockies. Donald and Lillian Stokes. Boston: Little, Brown, 1992.

Wildflower Folklore. Laura C. Martin. Charlotte, North Carolina: East Woods, 1984.

Wildflowers Across America. Lady Bird Johnson and Carlton B. Lees. New York: Abbeville, 1988.

Wildflowers and Weeds. Booth Courtenay and James H. Zimmerman. Toronto: Van Nostrand Reinhold, 1971.

Wildflowers in Color. Arthur Stuka. New York: HarperCollins, 1994.

Wildflowers of Canada. Tim Fitzharris. Toronto: Oxford University Press, 1986.

Wildflowers of Canada. W. Reynolds. Toronto: Discovery, 1987.

Wildflowers of Eastern America. John Edward Klimas. New York: Knopf, 1974.

Wildflowers of North America: A Guide to Field Identification. Frank D. Venning. New York: Golden, 1984.

Wildflowers of the Great Lakes Region. Roberta L. Simonds and Henrietta H. Tweedie. Chicago: Chicago Review Press, 1978.

Wildflowers of the North. Ruby Bryan. Cobalt, Ontario: Highway Book Shop, 1978.

Wildflowers . . . and the Stories Behind Their Names. Phyllis S. Busch. New York: Scribner's, 1977.

Wild Violets of North America. Viola Brainerd Baird. Berkeley: University of California Press, 1942.

Meadow and Prairie Plants

Prairie Grasses. J. Looman. Ottawa: Agriculture Canada, 1982.

Prairie Plants and their Environment. John E. Weaver. Lincoln, Nebraska: University of Nebraska Press, 1968.

Prairie Wildflowers: An Illustrated Manual of Species Suitable for Cultivation and Grassland Restoration. R. Currah, A. Smreciu and M. Van Dyk. Edmonton: Friends of the Devonian Botanic Garden, University of Alberta, 1983.

North American Range Plants. James S. Stubbendieck, Stephan L. Hatch and Charles H. Butterfield. Lincoln, Nebraska: University of Nebraska Press, 1992.

Wildflowers of the Northern Great Plains. F. R. Vance, J. R. Jowsey and J. S. McLean. Minneapolis: University of Minnesota Press, 1984.

Wildflowers of the Tallgrass Prairie. Sylvan T. Runkel and Dean M. Roosa. Ames, Iowa: Iowa State University Press, 1989.

Trees and Shrubs

The Biography of a Tree. James P. Jackson. Middle Village, New York: Jonathan David, 1979.

Checklist of Ornamental Trees for Canada. Trevor J. Cole. Ottawa: Agriculture Canada, 1979.

The Complete Trees of North America: Field Guide and Natural History. Thomas S. Elias. New York: Van Nostrand Reinhold, 1980.

Diseases of Trees and Shrubs. Wayne A. Sinclair, Howard H. Lyon and Warren T. Johnson. Ithaca: Comstock, 1987.

A Field Guide to Trees and Shrubs. George A. Petrides. Boston: Houghton Mifflin, 1972.

The Forest Trees of Ontario. J. H. White. Toronto: Department of Lands and Forests, 1968.

Identification Guide to the Trees of Canada. Jean Lauriault. Markham: Fitzhenry and Whiteside, 1990.

Native and Cultivated Conifers of Northeastern North America: A Guide. Edward A. Cope. Ithaca: Comstock, 1986.

Native Trees of Canada. R. C. Hosie. Markham: Fitzhenry and Whiteside, 1990.

The Natural History of Trees of Eastern and Central North America. Donald Culross Peattie. Boston: Houghton Mifflin, 1991.

The Pocket Guide to Trees. Keith Rushforth. New York: Simon and Schuster, 1981.

Recognizing Native Shrubs. William Grimm. Harrisburg, Pennsylvania: Stackpole, 1966.

The Shrub Identification Book. George W. Symonds. New York: Barrows, 1963.

Shrubs of Ontario. James H. Soper and Margaret L. Heimburger. Toronto: Royal Ontario Museum, 1982.

The Sweet Maple: Life, Lore and Recipes from the Sugarbush. James Lawrence and Rux Martin. Shelburne, Vermont: Chapters, 1993.

Taylor's Guide to Trees. Boston: Houghton Mifflin, 1988.

Trees: An Introduction to Trees and Forest Ecology for the Amateur Naturalist. Lawrence C. Walker. Toronto: Prentice-Hall, 1984.

Trees of North America: A Field Guide to the Major Native and Introduced Species. Christian Frank Brockman. New York: Golden, 1968.

Trees, Shrubs and Flowers to Know in Ontario. Paul M. Catling and Sheila M. McKay. Toronto: J. M. Dent, 1979.

Natural History

'And Some Brought Flowers': Plants in a New World. Mary Alice Downie and Mary Hamilton. Toronto: University of Toronto Press, 1980.

The Backyard and Beyond: A Guide for Discovering the Outdoors. Edward Duensing and A. B. Millmoss. Golden, Colorado: Fulcrum, 1992.

Canada: A Natural History. John A. Livingston and Tim Fitzharris. Markham: Viking, 1988.

The Early Horticulturists. Ronald Webber. Newton Abbot, England: David and Charles, 1968.

The Evolution of Canada's Flora. Roy L. Talyor and R. A. Ludwig, eds. Toronto: University of Toronto Press, 1966.

Gentle Conquest: The Botanical Discovery of North America. James L. Reveal. Washington: Starwood Publishing, 1992.

The Golden Age of Plant Hunters. Kenneth Lemmon. London: Phoenix House, 1968.

The Great Lakes. Robert Thomas Allen. Toronto: Natural Science of Canada, 1970.

Green Immigrants: The Plants that Transformed America. Claire Shaver Haughton. New York: Harcourt Brace Jovanovich, 1978.

Guide to the Natural History of the Niagara Region. J. C. Lewis, ed. St. Catharines: Cam Lewis, 1991.

Hedgemaids and Fairy Candles: Lives and Lore of North American Wildflowers. Jack Sanders. Camden, Maine: Ragged Mountain Press, 1993.

History of Horticulture in America to 1860. Ulysses P. Hedrick. New York: Oxford University Press, 1950.

John Clayton, Pioneer of American Botany. Edmund Berkeley and Dorothy S. Berkeley. Chapel Hill: University of North Carolina Press, 1963.

Legacy: The Natural History of Ontario. John B. Theberge, ed. Toronto: McClelland and Stewart, 1989.

The Life and Travels of John Bartram: From Lake Ontario to the River St. John. Edmund Berkeley and Dorothy S. Berkeley. Tallahassee: University Presses of Florida, 1982.

A Little Wilderness: The Natural History of Toronto. Bill Ivy. Toronto: Oxford University Press, 1983.

Marked by the Wild. Bruce Litteljohn and Jon Pearce. Toronto: McClelland and Stewart, 1973.

Makers of North American Botany. Harry B. Humphrey. New York: Ronald Press, 1961.

The Natural Heritage of Southern Ontario's Settled Landscapes. John L. Riley and Pat Mohr. Aurora, Ontario: Ontario Ministry of Natural Resources, 1994.

The Natural History of Canada. R. D. Lawrence. Toronto: Key Porter, 1988.

The Natural History of the Toronto Region. J. H. Faull, ed. Toronto: Canadian Institute, 1913.

The Natural History of Wild Shrubs and Vines: Eastern and Central North American. Donald W. Stokes. New York: Harper and Row, 1981.

A Naturalist in the Great Lakes Region. Elliot Rowland Downing. Chicago: University of Chicago Press, 1922.

A Naturalist's Guide to Ontario. W. W. Judd and J. W. Speirs, eds. Toronto: University of Toronto Press, 1964.

Nature, Mother of Invention: The Engineering of Plant Life. Felix Paturi. London: Thames and Hudson, 1976.

The Nature Observer's Handbook: Learning to Appreciate Our Natural World. John W. Brainerd. Chester, Connecticut: Globe Pequot, 1986.

Ontario Prehistory: An Eleven-Thousand-Year Archaeological Outline. J. V. Wright. Ottawa: National Museum of Man, 1972.

The Origin of Cultivated Plants. Franz Schwanitz. Cambridge, Massachusetts: Harvard University Press, 1967.

Our Green Planet: The Story of Plant Life on Earth. David Moore, ed. New York: Cambridge University Press, 1982.

The Physiography of Southern Ontario. L. J. Chapman and D. F. Putnam. Toronto: University of Toronto Press, 1951.

The Plant Hunters: Being a History of the Horticultural Pioneers, Their Quests and Their Discoveries From the Renaissance to the Twentieth Century. Alice M. Coats. New York: McGraw-Hill, 1970.

Plants and Civilization. Herbert G. Baker. Belmont, California: Wadsworth, 1965.

Plants, Man and Life. Edgar Anderson. Boston: Little, Brown, 1952.

Regional Landscapes of the United States and Canada. Stephen S. Birdsale and John W. Florin. New York: Wiley, 1978.

Rhetoric and Roses: A History of Canadian Gardening. Edwinna von Baeyer. Markham: Fitzhenry and Whiteside, 1984.

Studies of Plant Life in Canada. Catherine Parr Traill. Toronto: William Briggs, 1906.

Touring the Giant's Rib: A Guide to the Niagara Escarpment. Lorina and Gary Stephens. Erin, Ontario: Boston Mills Press, 1993.

The Tradescants, Their Plants, Gardens and Museum, 1570–1662. M. Allan. London: Michael Joseph, 1964.

Up North: A Guide to Ontario's Wilderness From Blackflies to The Northern Lights. Doug Bennet and Tim Tiner. Markham: Reed Books, 1993.

Wildlife and Wildlife Habitat

American Wildlife and Plants: A Guide to Wildlife Food Habits. Alexander C. Martin. New York: Dover, 1961.

America's Neighbourhood Bats. Merlin D. Tuttle. Austin, Texas: University of Texas Press, 1988.

Atlas of the Breeding Birds of Ontario. Michael D. Cadman, Paul F. J. Eagles and Frederick M. Helleiner. Waterloo: University of Waterloo Press, 1987.

Atlas of the Mammals of Ontario. Jon Dobbyn. Don Mills: Federation of Ontario Naturalists, 1994.

The Audubon Society Field Guide to North American Birds, Eastern Region. John Bull and John Farrand. New York: Knopf, 1977.

The Audubon Society Field Guide to North American Butterflies. Robert Michael Pyle. New York: Knopf, 1981.

The Audubon Society Field Guide to North American Insects and Spiders. Lorus J. Milne and Margery Milne. New York: Knopf, 1980.

Audubon Society Handbook for Butterfly Watchers. Robert M. Pyl. New York: Scribner's, 1984.

The Backyard Naturalist. Craig Tufts. Washington: National Wildlife Federation, 1988.

Bats. Brock M. Fenton. New York: Facts on File, 1992.

Bats: A Natural History. John E. Hill and James D. Smith. London: British Museum, 1984.

Bees of the World. Christopher O'Toole and Anthony Raw. New York: Facts on File, 1991.

Birds of Ontario. J. Murray Spiers. Toronto: Natural Heritage/Natural History, 1985.

The Birdwatcher's Companion. Christopher W. Leahy. New York: Hill and Wang, 1982.

Butterflies: Their World, Their Life Cycle, Their Behavior. Thomas C. Emmel. New York: Knopf, 1975.

Canadian Songbirds and Their Ways. J. Rising and T. Rising. Montreal: Tundra Books, 1982.

Canadian Wildlife and Man. Anne Innis Dagg. Toronto: McClelland and Stewart, 1974.

City Critters: How to Live with Urban Wildlife. David M. Bird. Montreal: Eden, 1986.

Easy Identification Guide to North American Snakes. H. Simon. New York: Dodd, Mead and Co., 1979.

Familiar Amphibians and Reptiles of Ontario. Bob Johnson. Toronto: Natural Heritage/Natural History, 1989.

A Field Guide to Eastern Butterflies. Paul A. Opler. Boston: Houghton Mifflin, 1992.

A Field Guide to the Birds: A Completely New Guide to All the Birds of Eastern and Central North America. Roger Tory Peterson. Boston: Houghton Mifflin, 1980.

A Field Guide to the Birds' Nests. Hal Harrison. Boston: Houghton Mifflin, 1975.

A Guide to Amphibians and Reptiles. Thomas F. Tyning. Boston: Little, Brown, 1990.

The Habitat Guide to Birding. Thomas P. McElroy. New York: Knopf, 1974.

The Hummingbirds of North America. Paul A. Johnsgard. Washington: Smithsonian Institution Press, 1983.

Insects That Feed on Trees and Shrubs. Howard H. Lyon and Warren T. Johnson. Ithaca: Comstock, 1988.

Introduction to Canadian Amphibians and Reptiles. Francis R. Cook. Ottawa: National Museum of Natural Sciences, 1984.

Ladybirds. Michael Majerus. London: Harper-Collins, 1994.

Landscape Approaches to Wildlife and Ecosystem Management. G. Brent Ingram and Michael R. Moss, eds. Montreal: Polyscience Publications, 1992.

The Lovely and the Wild. Louise deKiriline Lawrence. Toronto: Natural Heritage/History, 1987.

The Mammals of Canada. Alexander W. F. Banfield. Toronto: University of Toronto Press, 1974.

The Mammals of Eastern Canada. Randolph Peterson. Toronto: Oxford University Press, 1966.

The Milkweed and Its World of Animals. Ada Graham and Frank Graham. Garden City, New York: Doubleday, 1976.

The Nature of Birds. Adrian Forsyth. Camden East: Camden House, 1988.

The Ontario Butterfly Atlas. Anthony M. Holmes, Ronald R. Tasker, Quimby Hess and Alan J. Hanks. Toronto: The Toronto Entomologists' Association, 1991. (Available from TEA, 34 Seaton Drive, Aurora, Ontario L4G 2K1.)

Reptiles and Amphibians of North America. Alan E. Leviton. New York: Doubleday, 1971.

Reptiles of North America: A Guide to Field Identification. Hobart M. Smith and Edmund D. Brodie, Jr. New York: Golden, 1982.

Song and Garden Birds of North America. Alexander Wetmore. Washington: National Geographic Society, 1964.

Suburban Wildlife: An Introduction to the Common Animals of Your Back Yard and Local Park. Richard Headstrom. Englewood Cliffs, New Jersey: Prentice-Hall, 1984.

Turtles of Canada. Barbara Froom. Toronto: McClelland and Stewart, 1976.

The Urban Naturalist. Steven D. Garber. New York: Wiley, 1987.

Urban Wildlife Habitats: A Landscape Perspective. Lowell W. Adams. Minneapolis: University of Minnesota Press, 1994.

Wildlife-Habitat Relationships. Michael L. Morrison. Madison: University of Wisconsin Press, 1992.

The Year of the Turtle: A Natural History. David M. Carroll. Charlotte, Vermont: Camden House, 1991.

MAGAZINES

Biodiversity Network News, The Nature Conservancy, 1815 North Lynn Street, Arlington, Virginia 22209.

Biological Conservation, Elsevier Science Publishing, 655 Avenue of the Americas, New York, New York 10010-5107.

Bird Conservation International, Cambridge University Press, 40 West 20th Street, New York, New York 10011-4211.

Birdscope, Cornell Laboratory of Ornithology, 159 Sapsucker Woods Road, Ithaca, New York 14850.

Birds of the Wild, 299 Main Street North, Markham, Ontario L3P 1Y9.

Boston Urban Gardeners Newsletter, Boston Urban Gardeners, 46 Chesnut Avenue, Jamaica Plain, Massachusetts 02130.

Butterfly Gardeners' Quarterly, P.O. Box 30931, Seattle, Washington 98103.

The Canadian Field-Naturalist, Ottawa Field-Naturalists' Club, P.O. Box 35069, Westgate P.O., Ottawa, Ontario K1Z 1A2.

Canadian Gardening, 130 Spy Court, Markham, Ontario L3R 5H6.

Canadian Journal of Botany, National Research Council, Ottawa, Ontario K1A 0R6.

The Canadian Journal of Herbalism, Ontario Herbalists' Association, 11 Winthrop Place, Stoney Creek, Ontario L8G 3M3.

Canadian Plant Conservation Program Newsletter, Devonian Botanic Garden, University of Alberta, Edmonton, Alberta T6G 2E1.

Common Sense Pest Control Quarterly, Biointegral Resource Center, P.O. Box 7414, Berkeley, California 94707-0414.

Community Gardening Review, American Community Gardening Association, 325 Walnut Street, Philadelphia, Pennsylvania 19106.

Conservation Biology: The Journal of the Society for Conservation Biology, Blackwell Scientific Publications, 238 Main Street, Suite 501, Cambridge, Massachusetts 02142.

Diversity, Genetic Resources Communications Systems, 4905 Del Ray Avenue, Suite 401, Bethesda, Maryland 20814-2527.

FLAP Newsletter, 1 Guelph Road, Erin, Ontario N0B 1T0.

Global Biodiversity, Canadian Centre for Biodiversity, Canadian Museum of Nature, P.O. Box 3443, Station D, Ottawa, Ontario K1P 6P4.

Green-Up Times, Bronx Green-up Program, The New York Botanical Garden, Room 317, Watson Building, Bronx, New York 10458.

Grow T.O.Gether Community Gardeners' Newsletter, Grow T.O.Gether Community Gardeners, 238 Queen Street West, Toronto, Ontario M5V 1Z7.

Harrowsmith Country Life, 25 Sheppard Avenue West, Suite 100, North York, Ontario M2N 6S7.

National Wildlife, National Wildlife Federation, 8925 Leesburg Pike, Vienna, Virginia 22184.

Natural Areas Journal, Natural Areas Association, 108 Fox Street, Mukwonago, Wisconsin 53149.

Nature Canada, Canadian Nature Federation, 1 Nicholas Street, Suite 520, Ottawa, Ontario K1N 7B7.

Nature Conservancy, Nature Conservancy, 1815 North Lynn Street, Arlington, Virginia 22209.

Ontario Conservation News, Conservation Council of Ontario, 489 College Street, Toronto, Ontario M6G 1A5.

Organic Gardening, 33 Minor Street East, Emmaus, Pennsylvania, 18098.

The Outdoor Classroom, Evergreen Foundation, 355 Adelaide Street West, Suite 500, Toronto, Ontario M5V 1S2.

Plant and Garden, Gardenvale Publishing Co., 1 Pacifique, Ste-Anne-de-Bellevue, Quebec H9X 1C5.

Purple Martin Update, Purple Martin Conservation Association, Edinboro University of Pennsylvania, Edinboro, Pennsylvania 16444.

Recycling Railway Corridors, Rails-to-Trails, Heritage Canada, Box 1358, Station B, Ottawa, Ontario K1P 5R4.

Restoration and Management Notes, Journal of the Society for Ecological Restoration, Journals Division, University of Wisconsin Press, 114 North Murray Street, Madison, Wisconsin, 53715.

Restoration Ecology: The Official Journal of the Society for Ecological Restoration, Blackwell Scientific Publications, 238 Main Street, Cambridge, Massachusetts, 02142.

Seasons, Federation of Ontario Naturalists, 355 Lesmill Road, Don Mills, Ontario M3B 2W8.

Toronto Field Naturalist, Toronto Field Naturalists, 20 College Street, Suite 11, Toronto, Ontario M5G 1K2.

Toronto Gardens, 1560 Bayview Avenue, Suite 302A, Toronto, Ontario M4G 3B8.

Tree Talk, Tree Plan Canada, 1219 Queen Street East, Sault Ste. Marie, Ontario P6A 5M7.

Urban Forest Forum, American Forestry Association, 1516 P Street N.W., Washington, D.C. 20005.

VitisVine, Green Guerillas, 625 Broadway, 2nd Floor, New York, New York, 10012-2611.

Water Garden Network Newsletter, 480 William Street, Stratford, Ontario N5A 4Y8.

Welcome Home! News of the Grand River Bioregion, 104 Surrey Street East, Suite B, Guelph, Ontario N1H 3P9.

Wild Earth, Cenozoic Society, Box 492, Canton, New York 13617-1035.

Wilderness, The Wilderness Society, 900–17th Street N.W., Washington, D.C. 20006-2596.

Wildflower, Canadian Wildflower Society, 4981 Highway 7 East, Unit 12A, Suite 228, Markham, Ontario L3R 1N1.

Wild Flower Notes, New England Wildflower Society, 180 Hemenway Road, Framingham, Massachusetts, 01701-2699.

NATIVE PLANT SOURCES

Note: If you want to buy native plants that are raised from seed indigenous to your area, query the nursery staff, as many carry plants that are imported from the United States rather than propagated from indigenous genetic stock. Otter Valley Native Plants is one exception—all their stock is raised from locally collected seed.

Aimers, 81 Temperance Street, Aurora, Ontario L4G 2R1.

Annable Wholesale Nursery, 5201 Highway 7 East, Unionville, Ontario L3R 1N3.

Blueberry Hill, R.R. 1, Maynooth, Ontario K0L 2S0.

Brickman's Botanical Gardens, R.R. 1, Sebringville, Ontario N0K 1X0.

Campberry Farm, R.R. 1, Niagara-on-the-Lake, Ontario L0S 1J0.

Canadian Wildflower Society Seed Exchange, 4981 Highway 7 East, Unit 12A, Suite 228, Markham, Ontario L3R 1N1.

Chalk Lake Greenhouses, R.R. 4, Uxbridge, Ontario L0C 1K0.

Clargreen Gardens, 814 Southdown Road, Mississauga, Ontario L5J 2Y4.

Connon Nurseries, 383 Dundas Street East, Waterdown, Ontario L0R 2H0.

Country Squires Gardens, 2601 Derry Road West, R.R. 3, Campbellville, Ontario L0P 1B0.

Dominion Seed House, 115 Guelph Street, Georgetown, Ontario L7G 4A2.

Frank Schenk Nurseries, Belfountain, Ontario L0N 1B0.

Garden Import, P.O. Box 760, Thornhill, Ontario L3T 4A5.

Gardens North, 34 Helena Street, Ottawa, Ontario K1Y 3M8.

Golden Bough Tree Farm, Marlbank, Ontario K0K 2L0.

Grand River Conservation Authority, Box 729, 400 Clyde Road, Cambridge, Ontario N1R 5W6.

Greenbelt Farm, R.R. 5, Mitchell, Ontario N0K 1N0.

Groen's Nursery, 1512 Brock Road, R.R. 2, Dundas, Ontario L9H 5E4.

Hawkswood Gardens, R.R. 1, Elmira, Ontario N3S 2Z1.

Hortico Inc., 723 Robson Road, R.R. 1, Waterdown, Ontario L0R 2H1.

Humber Nurseries, R.R. 1, Brampton, Ontario L6T 3H7.

Keith Somers Trees Ltd., 10 Tillson Avenue, Tillsonburg, Ontario N4G 2Z6.

The Lily Pool, 3324 Pollock Road, Keswick, Ontario L4P 3E9.

Little Otter Tree Farm, R.R. 6, Tillsonburg, Ontario N4G 4G9.

Merlin's Hollow, 181 Centre Street, Aurora, Ontario L4G 1K3.

Metro Toronto Region Conservation Authority, 5 Shoreham Drive, Downsview, Ontario M3N 1S4.

Moore Water Gardens, Box 340, Port Stanley, Ontario N0L 2A0.

Mulligan Seeds, 1600 Apeldoorn Avenue, Ottawa, Ontario K2C 1V5.

Northern Star Plants and Herbs, Box 2262, Station A, London, Ontario N6A 4E3.

Oneida Settlement, Oneida Tree Nursery Project, R.R. 2, Southwold, Ontario N0L 2G0.

Oslach Nurseries, R.R. 1, Simcoe, Ontario N3Y 4J9.

Otter Valley Native Plants, Box 31, R.R. 1, Eden, Ontario N0J 1H0.

Pterophylla, R.R. 1, Walsingham, Ontario N0E 1X0.

Picov's Greenhouses/Water Garden Centre and Fisheries, 380 Kingston Road East, Ajax, Ontario L1S 4S7.

Plantspace, R.R. 5, Rockwood, Ontario N0B 2K0.

Redleaf Nursery, R.R. 1, Hornby, Ontario L0P 1E0.

Reimer Waterscapes, Box 34, Tillsonburg, Ontario N4G 4H3.

Sheridan Nurseries, 606 Southdown Road, Mississauga, Ontario L5J 2Y4 (and five other locations).

Simple Gifts Farm Greenhouse, R.R. 1, Oak Leaf Road, Athens, Ontario K0E 1B0.

Stirling Perennials, R.R. 1, Morpeth, Ontario N0P 1X0.

Stokes Seeds Ltd., Box 10, St. Catharines, Ontario L2R 6R6.

Sweet Grass Gardens, Six Nations of the Grand River, R. R. 6, Hagersville, Ontario N0A 1H0.

T-D Enterprises, R.R. 1, Waterford, Ontario N0E 1Y0.

Vineland Nurseries, Box 98, Vineland Station, Ontario L0R 2E0.

Water Arts, 4158A Dundas Street West, Etobicoke, Ontario M8X 1X3.

Whitehorse Perennials, R.R. 2, Almonte, Ontario K0A 1A0.

William Dam Seeds Ltd., P.O. Box 8400, Dundas, Ontario L9H 6M1.

Woodland Nurseries, 2151 Camilla Road, Mississaugua, Ontario L5A 2K1.

The following publications may also be helpful.

Canadian Plant Source Book. Anne and Peter Ashley. (Available from 93 Fentiman Avenue, Ottawa, Ontario K1S 0T7.)

The National Wildflower Research Center's Wildflower Handbook: A Resource for Native Plant Landscapes. Elizabeth S. Anderson and Annie Paulson Gillespie, eds. Stillwater, Minnesota: Voyageur Press, 1992. (Available from P.O. Box 338, Stillwater, MN 55082.)

The Ontario Gardener's Resource Guide. Wendy Thomas. Vancouver: Whitecap, 1993.

Sources of Native Seeds and Plants. Soil and Water Conservation Society, 7515 N.E. Ankeny Road, Ankeny, Indiana 50021-9764. 1994.

Sources of Propagated Native Plants and Wild Flowers. 1993. New England Wild Flower Society, Garden in the Woods, 180 Hemenway Road, Framingham, Massachusetts 01701-2699.

ORGANIZATIONS

American Backyard Bird Society, P.O. Box 10046, Rockville, Maryland 20849.

American Community Gardening Association, 325 Walnut Street, Philadelphia, Pennsylvania 19106.

Amphibian Interest Group, Metro Toronto Zoo, P.O. Box 280, West Hill, Ontario M1E 4R5.

Aquatic Conservation Network, 540 Roosevelt Avenue, Ottawa, Ontario K2A 1Z8.

Bat Check, Box 1243, Kingston, Ontario K7L 4Y8.

Bat Conservation International, Inc., P.O. Box 162603, Austin, Texas 78716.

Bio-Integral Resource Center, P.O. Box 7414, Berkeley, California 94707.

Canadian Botanical Association, Institut Botanique, Université de Montreal, 4101 rue Sherbrooke est, Montreal, Quebec H1X 2B2.

Canadian Council on Ecological Areas, c/o Canadian Wildlife Service, Environment Canada, Ottawa, Ontario K1A 0H3.

Canadian Lakes Loon Survey, Long Point Bird Observatory, Box 160, Port Rowan, Ontario N0E 1M0.

Canadian Nature Federation, 1 Nicholas Street, Suite 520, Ottawa, Ontario K1N 7B7.

Canadian Organic Growers, P.O. Box 6408, Station J, Ottawa, Ontario K2A 3Y6.

Canadian Parks and Wilderness Society, 160 Bloor Street East, Suite 1335, Toronto, Ontario M4W 1B9.

Canadian Plant Conservation Program, c/o Devonian Botanic Garden, University of Alberta, Edmonton, Alberta T6G 2E1.

Canadian Rails to Greenways Network, Frost Centre, Trent University, Peterborough, Ontario K9J 7PJ.

Canadian Wildflower Society, 4981 Highway 7 East, Unit 12A, Suite 228, Markham, Ontario L3R 1N1.

Canadian Wildlife Federation, 2740 Queensview Drive, Ottawa, Ontario K2B 1A2.

Carolinian Canada Project, c/o World Wildlife Fund, 90 Eglinton Avenue East, Suite 504, Toronto, Ontario M4P 2Z7.

Center for Plant Conservation, P.O. Box 299, St. Louis, Missouri 63166.

Centre for Endangered Reptiles, P.O. Box 1450, Picton, Ontario K0K 2T0.

Civic Garden Centre, 777 Lawrence Avenue East, North York, Ontario M3C 1P2.

Conservation Council of Ontario, 489 College Street, Toronto, Ontario M6G 1A5.

Conservation Foundation of Greater Toronto, 5 Shoreham Drive, Downsview, Ontario M3N 1S4.

Conservation International—Canada, 174 Spadina Avenue, Suite 508, Toronto, Ontario M5T 2C2.

Cornell Lab of Ornithology, 159 Sapsucker Woods Road, Ithaca, New York 14850-1999.

Eastern Native Plant Alliance, P.O. Box 6101, McLean, Virginia 22106.

Ecological Landscaping Association, P.O. Box 572, Groton, Massachusetts 01450.

Elm Research Institute, P.O. Box 805, Harrisville, New Hampshire 03450.

The Evergreen Foundation, 355 Adelaide Street West, Suite 500, Toronto, Ontario M5V 1S2.

Fatal Light Awareness Program, 1 Guelph Road, Erin, Ontario N0B 1T0.

Federation of Ontario Naturalists, 355 Lesmill Road, Don Mills, Ontario M3B 2W8.

Field Botanists of Ontario, R.R. 1, Acton, Ontario L7J 2L7.

Friends of Bats, Metro Toronto Zoo, P.O. Box 280, West Hill, Ontario M1E 4R5.

Friends of the Earth, 251 Laurier Avenue West, Suite 701, Ottawa, Ontario K1P 5J6.

Green Guerillas, 625 Broadway, 2nd Floor, New York, New York 10012-2611.

Grow T.O.Gether Community Gardeners, 238 Queen Street West, Toronto, Ontario M5V 1Z7.

Habitat Conservation Branch, Canadian Wildlife Service, Environment Canada, Ottawa, Ontario K1A 0H3.

Heritage Resources Centre, Faculty of Environmental Studies, University of Waterloo, Waterloo, Ontario N2L 3G1.

Home Habitat Society, P.O. Box 412, Taneytown, Maryland 21787.

Landscape Ontario Horticultural Trade Association, 1293 Matheson Blvd. East, Mississauga, Ontario L4W 1R1.

National Community Tree Foundation, 220 Laurier Avenue West, Suite 1550, Ottawa, Ontario K1P 5Z9.

National Institute for Urban Wildlife, 1091 Trotting Ridge Way, Columbia, Maryland 21044.

National Wildflower Research Centre, 2600 FM 973 North, Austin, Texas 78725-4201.

National Wildlife Federation, 1400–16th Street N.W., Washington, D.C. 20036-2266.

National Xeriscape Council, P.O. Box 767936, Roswell, Georgia 30076.

Natural Habitat Restoration Program, c/o Essex Region Conservation Authority, 360 Fairview Avenue West, Essex, Ontario N8M 1Y6.

Natural Heritage Information Centre, P.O. Box 7000, Peterborough, Ontario K9J 8M5.

Natural Heritage League, 10 Adelaide Street East, Toronto, Ontario M5C 1T3.

New England Wildflower Society, Garden in the Woods, 180 Hemenway Road, Framingham, Massachusetts 01701-2699.

North American Bluebird Society, Box 6295, Silver Spring, Maryland 20906-0295.

North American Butterfly Association, 39 Highland Avenue, Chappaqua, New York 10514.

North American Wetlands Conservation Council, 1750 Courtwood Crescent, Suite 200, Ottawa, Ontario K2C 2B5.

Ontario Association of Landscape Architects, 75 The Donway West, Suite 302, Don Mills, Ontario M3C 2E9.

Ontario Eastern Bluebird Society, 165 Green Valley Drive, Suite 2, Kitchener, Ontario N2D 1K3.

Ontario Nest Records Scheme, Dr. George K. Peck, Department of Ornithology, Royal Ontario Museum, 100 Queen's Park Crescent, Toronto, Ontario M5S 2C6.

Ontario Parks Association, 1185 Eglinton Avenue East, Suite 406, North York, Ontario M3C 3C6.

Ontario Shade Tree Council, 75 The Donway West, North York, Ontario M3C 2H9.

Ontario Society for Environmental Management, 136 Winges Road, Unit 15, Woodbridge, Ontario L4L 6C4.

The Ontario Trails Council, c/o The Frost Centre for Canadian Heritage and Development Studies, Trent University, Peterborough, Ontario K9V 7B8.

Ontario Wildlife Rehabilitation and Education Network, Box 428, Vineland, Ontario L0R 2C0.

Pest Diagnostic and Advisory Clinic, Graham Hall, Room B14, University of Guelph, Guelph, Ontario N1G 2W1.

Pesticide Action League, 31 Ballyronan Road, Don Mills, Ontario M3B 1V2.

Professional Lawn Care Association of America, 1000 Johnsons Ferry Road N.E., Suite C-135, Marietta, Georgia 30068-2112.

Project Feederwatch, Long Point Bird Observatory, P.O. Box 160, Port Rowan, Ontario N0E 1M0.

Purple Martin Conservation Association, Edinboro University of Pennsylvania, Edinboro, Pennsylvania 16444.

Rails to Greenways Network, c/o Canadian Parks/ Recreation Association, 1600 James Naismith Drive, Gloucester, Ontario K1B 5N4.

Roadside Heritage Trees Society, R.R. 6, Guelph, Ontario N1H 6J3.

Safe Soil Network, 14 Sackville Place, Toronto, Ontario M4X 1A4.

Sierra Club of Canada, 1 Nicholas Street, Suite 620, Ottawa, Ontario K1N 7B7.

Sierra Club of Eastern Canada, 517 College Street, Suite 303, Toronto, Ontario M6G 4A2.

Society for Ecological Restoration, Ontario Chapter, c/o Ecological Outlook Consulting, 270 Main Street, P.O. Box 93, Schomberg, Ontario L0G 1T0.

Society for the Study of Amphibians and Reptiles, P.O. Box 626, Hays, Kansas 67601.

Toronto Entomologists' Association, 34 Seaton Drive, Aurora, Ontario L4G 2K1.

Toronto Field Naturalists, 20 College Street, Suite 11, Toronto, Ontario M5G 1K2.

TRAFFIC, 1250 - 24th Street N.W., Washington, D.C. 20037.

Water Garden Network, 480 William Street, Stratford, Ontario N5A 4Y8.

The Weed Science Society of America, 1508 University W., Champaign, Illinois 61821-3133.

Western Hemisphere Shorebird Reserve Network, P.O. Box 936, Manomet, Massachusetts 02345.

Wetlands for the Americas, 7 Hinton Avenue North, Suite 200, Ottawa, Ontario K1Y 4P1.

Wildlands League, 160 Bloor Street East, Suite 1335, Toronto, Ontario M4W 1B9.

Woodland Forestry, 331 Linsmore Crescent, Toronto, Ontario M4J 4M1.

World Wildlife Fund, 90 Eglinton Avenue East, Suite 504, Toronto, Ontario M4P 2Z7.

The Xerces Society, 10 Southwest Ash Street, Portland, Oregon 97204.

INDEX

Sedge, Pennsylvania (*Carex pensylvanica*), 113;
    plantain-leaved (*C. plantaginea*), 113
Seed exchanges, 83
Seed starting, 42, 83–88, 89
    and collection, 84, 85
    and dormancy, 87–88
    and scarification, 85–88
    and stratification, 87–88, 89
    and trees, 46, 85, 87–88
    See also Propagation
Shade gardening, 35–47, 73–74, 79
Shading Our Cities, 36, 46, 47
Shrubs, 40, 67, 77
Sideoats grama (*Bouteloua curtipendula*), 113
Silphium laciniatum. *See* Compass plant
Silphium perfoliatum. *See* Cup plant
Sisyrinchium montanum. *See* Blue-eyed grass
Skardon, James A., 128
Skunk cabbage (*Symplocarpus foetidus*), 110
Smyser, Carol A., 75, 80, 116
Snyder, Gary, 17
"Social Change and the Prairie Movement," 53
Soil, 37, 38, 45, 57, 70–72
    drainage, 72, 73
    nutrients, 72
    pH, 38–39, 71–72, 96
    types, 71
Solidago canadensis. *See* Goldenrod, Canada
Solomon's seal (*Polygonatum biflorum*), 106
Songbird decline, 137
Sorghastrum nutans. *See* Indian grass
Sperka, Maria, 87, 102, 104
Spiderwort (*Tradescantia virginiana*), 101
Spring beauty (*Claytonia virginica*), 106
Spring ephemerals, 36, 85, 96
Stein, Sara, 8, 22, 66, 122, 134, 135
Stolzenburg, William, 138
Strawberry, wild (*Fragaria virginiana*), 108
Stylophorum diphyllum. *See* Poppy, wood
Subarctic Forest Region, 13
Sunflower (*Helianthus annuus*), 101; woodland
    (*H. divaricatus*), 108
"Survey of the Prairies and Savannas of Southern
    Ontario, A," 49

Swamps, 68
Symplocarpus foetidus. *See* Skunk cabbage
*Symposium on Trees and Forests in an Urbanizing
    Environment, A*, 77

Tall-grass prairie. *See* Prairie habitat
Tenenbaum, Frances, 73, 100
Thalictrum dioicum. *See* Early meadow-rue
Tree-House Effect, The, 77
Tiarella cordifolia. *See* Foamflower
Toads, 62, 65, 68
Toothwort, cut-leaved (*Dentaria laciniata*), 103
Tradescantia virginiana. *See* Spiderwort
Trees, 38, 45–47, 67
    and bird attraction, 136–37
    choices, 40–41, 76–77
    and city conditions, 45
    and climate change, 36, 46
    planting, 35, 36, 45–46
    pollution tolerance of, 38, 76–77
Trillium, white (*Trillium grandiflorum*), xviii–xix,
    29–30, 108
Turtle Talk, 17, 18
Twinleaf (*Jeffersonia diphylla*), 106

University of Guelph Arboretum, 42
Uvularia grandiflora. *See* Bellwort

Vernonia gigantea. *See* Ironweed
Veronicastrum virginicum. *See* Culver's root
Vines, 112
Violet, Canada (*Viola canadensis*), 103
Virginia Native Plant Society, 91
von Baeyer, Edwinna, xvii, 143

Walpole Island First Nation, 48–49
Walpole Island Heritage Centre, 49
Wasowski, Sally, 139
Water gardening. *See* Pond habitat
Waterleaf, broad-leaved (*Hydrophyllum canadense*),
    102
Waterlily (*Nymphaea odorata*), 66, 111
Weed Control Act, 122
Weeds, xvii, 9, 12, 22, 54, 57, 70, 117–23, 128, 129,
    130

ABOUT THE AUTHOR

Photo: Andrew Leyerle

Lorraine Johnson is a freelance writer and editor living in Toronto. A director of the Canadian Wildflower Society, she has been growing native plants for many years in her tiny urban plot. Her other works include *The Real Dirt: The Complete Guide to Backyard, Balcony and Apartment Composting*, co-authored with Mark Cullen; and *Green Future: How to Make a World of Difference.*